SACRED WATERS

By the same authors

Mysterious Britain
Mazes and Labyrinths of the World
The Secret Country
A Guide to Ancient Sites in Britain
Alien Animals
Bigfoot Casebook
Earth Rites
The Evidence for Bigfoot and Other Man-Beasts

SACRED WATERS

Holy Wells and Water Lore
in Britain and Ireland

Janet and Colin Bord

GRANADA
London Toronto Sydney New York

Granada Publishing Limited
8 Grafton Street, London W1X 3LA

Published by Granada Publishing 1985

British Library Cataloguing in Publication Data

Bord, Janet
  Sacred waters.
  1. Folklore—Great Britain 2. Water—
  Folklore
  I. Title   II. Bord, Colin
  398'.364   GR141

ISBN 0-246-12036-3

Printed in Great Britain at the
University Press, Cambridge

Contents

Introductory Note and Acknowledgements

As our subtitle 'Holy Wells and Water Lore in Britain and Ireland' suggests, this book is not concerned solely with holy wells, but includes all types of ancient wells and springs, whether or not they have been adopted by the Christian Church. Indeed, as we shall show, many of the wells, including the 'holy wells', still reveal traces of pre-Christian water worship. Since so often the history of a given well has not been recorded, it is difficult to separate the wells into their true categories, and any anonymous well may be a now-forgotten 'holy well'. Therefore we have tended to use the term 'holy well' widely to describe all kinds of ancient wells and springs. Indeed the coverage of this book extends to inland water sources of all kinds, since we have found evidence to show that water in general was considered 'sacred', ie 'worthy of, or regarded with, reverence, awe, or respect'. It is also worth noting that despite the name 'holy well', most are not wells at all, but springs which flow into an artificially constructed stone basin. The names 'spring', 'well' and 'fountain' were virtually interchangeable.

Wherever possible we locate each well in its county. When the county boundaries were rearranged in the 1970s, some counties became impossibly large, so for Wales and Scotland we have used the old, smaller, counties. In England the new counties are sometimes smaller than the old, so we have adopted the new names. This method was chosen so as to narrow down the area in which any well is located, and does not indicate a preference for either the new or old boundaries.

Most people whom we have approached for information on holy wells have been very willing to help, and we should like to thank them all, especially Geoffrey Berry, Christopher Fletcher, Jeremy Harte, Andy Roberts, Margaret Stutley, Mark Valentine, Anthony Weir, the many clergymen and local historians who put us right regarding their local wells, our local librarians at Newtown, Powys, for obtaining obscure reference material, and the countrywide librarians and archivists who directed us to sources of information and old photographs. Many of the recent photographs are our own, but we should also like to thank our other sources for photographs reproduced on the following pages: J. W. Allen, 173; Bath Museums Service, 67;

Geoffrey Berry, 15, 29, 38, 97, 107, 126, 155 (both), 157, 168, 169 (both), 192 (top); British Library, 93; Hamish Brown, 10, 192 (bottom), 195, 196 (both); City of Glasgow District Council – Mitchell Library, 130; Mary Evans Picture Library, 28, 102; Fortean Picture Library, 73, 84; Gloucestershire Record Office, 30, 158; *Lancashire Life*, 164; Lothian Regional Council, 194; National Museum of Ireland, 2, 23, 31, 55, 58, 70, 72; School of Scottish Studies, University of Edinburgh, 64; Anthony Shiels, 200; Ulster Folk and Transport Museum, 62, 201, 206 (bottom); Anthony Weir, 50, 205, 206 (top); Ann and John Welton, 146, 202. Photographs not in this list were taken by ourselves.

Most of the photographs show the wells as they appear now, but in the case of older photographs we have included the known or probable date in the caption.

1. The Pre-Christian Evidence for Water Cults

As we approach the year 2000 it is just possible in the ravaged land of Britain to find traces of a once important cult – the water cult – which may have originated 5000 years ago, when early men first began to make an impression on the face of the land. Today water is available in our homes and no one needs to visit those places where it wells from the earth. People have lost their sense of awe towards water, and an ever-constant clean supply is taken for granted and considered to be everyone's right. Only when there is a drought or disruption of the mains supply do they realise how dependent they are upon water and that it is essential for our crops, our animals, and every human life on the planet.

This link between humans, life, water and the earth was instinctively known by those people who lived before Water Boards came into being, and it was expressed through reverence of the life-giving water, shown at those places where the water was released from the body of the earth – springs and wells – and also at lakes and rivers. It took many forms, including the performing of rituals and the leaving of gifts. Once a source of water became sacred, it was venerated from each generation to the next, often to the bewilderment of recent observers, as shown by this quotation from Dr J. Hill Burton, a nineteenth-century traveller.

The unnoticeable smallness of many of these consecrated wells makes their very reminiscence and still semi-sacred character all the more remarkable. The stranger in Ireland, or the Highlands of Scotland, hears rumours of a distinguished well, miles on miles off. He thinks he will find an ancient edifice over it, or some other conspicuous adjunct. Nothing of the kind. He has been lured all that distance, over rock and bog, to see a tiny spring bubbling out of the rock, such as he may see hundreds of in a tolerable walk any day. Yet, if he search in old topographical authorities, he will find that the little well has ever been an important feature of the district; that century after century it has been unforgotten; and, with diligence he may perhaps trace it to some incident in the life of the saint, dead more than 1200 years ago, whose name it bears.[1]

Modern amenities, including piped water in almost every home, have meant that after hundreds, even thousands of years attitudes towards water have changed, and wells once considered holy are now

St Coleman's Well,
somewhere in
County Clare
(photo *c.* 1910)

left to decay, forgotten and unwanted. The waters' healing role has
been taken over by the National Health Service, and in our technolo-
gical society the springs and holy wells are considered to have nothing
to offer us. This attitude is mistaken, since every act which distances
humanity from its natural heritage is detrimental to physical and
spiritual health. And yet there is a small resurgence of interest in and
concern for holy wells. Some which were derelict have recently been
restored. Concern and care for the sources of sacred water are among
the many actions which show that humanity is slowly awakening to its
environmental responsibilities. Perhaps within the human psyche lies
an urge to correct any imbalance of attitude which develops and this
begins to assert itself when men's actions reach a level which threatens
self-destruction.

So far we have only spoken of Britain, but of course water worship
was equally important and widespread elsewhere in the world. Water
symbols have been found on many goddess and other figurines from
south-eastern Europe, dating from the period 6000–4000 BC, this
probably being the earliest evidence for water cults so far discovered.
Researchers have found examples of water worship in most of the
major civilisations of the world, including ancient Egypt, classical
Greece, Troy, Babylon and ancient Rome; and there is ample evidence
of water worship continuing until the recent past, and perhaps even
being practised in the present, among many groups of people, such as
the Australian Aborigines, the American Indians, and by some African
peoples. The Indian folklorist R. P. Masani, working in the early years
of this century, discovered active water worship among his fellow
countrymen, his interest in the subject having been aroused when in

his capacity as Municipal Secretary of Bombay he received several protests against requisitions for the closure of wells because of the threat of malaria. The well-owners cited traditions concerning the sanctity of the water, and told stories of spirits living in the wells. Also in India are the sacred step-wells, some of them magnificent architectural structures, dating from the seventh century AD and earlier, where the subterranean waters are worshipped.

Although in this book we shall concentrate on studying the water cults as they existed in Britain, this brief list of examples of water worship worldwide demonstrates that the British cults are not isolated but represent only one facet of a universal veneration of water.

The earliest evidence for water cults in Britain is suggestive rather than clear-cut. In his book *The Stone Circles of the British Isles*, Aubrey Burl points out that 'Where an avenue of stones is associated with a stone circle it almost invariably leads from a source of water, indicating the importance of water in the ceremonies that took place in the rings.' At Stanton Drew in Avon, a stone avenue ran from one of three stone circles towards the nearby River Chew. In Wiltshire, a long avenue links Stonehenge to the River Avon, and both the avenues at Avebury are close to water, the Kennet Avenue leading towards the River Kennet, and the Beckhampton Avenue (now demolished) crossing a stream. Avebury dates from the middle of the third millennium BC, the avenues being completed around 2300 BC. Stone circles generally were in use from around 2500 BC (mid-Neolithic) to 1000 BC (late Bronze Age), and over 900 of them are known in the British Isles. It would be an interesting exercise (but beyond the scope of this book) to examine the sites of all the circles to determine what proportion are located near water, and whether such locations are restricted to circles with avenues.

It is not yet known why the stone circles were constructed, though there is some evidence that their purpose was astronomical. Nor is it known why early populations should have wanted to make precise astronomical observations, though many suggestions have been made. The most that we can conclude is that stone circles had multiple uses, one of them likely to have involved water in some ritual way. The archaeologist Colin Burgess has suggested that a water cult developed in the Bronze Age, as a result of the climatic deterioration which took place towards the end of the Bronze Age. The stone circles could only have been successfully used for astronomical observations during a period of fine, clear, dry, weather, and when the climate changed, visibility problems caused their abandonment and the development of a new water-based religion. He cites in support of this idea the many finds of metalwork in lakes and rivers, which we shall shortly describe more fully. However, Burgess's idea that the water cult was brought about by climatic change is not wholly convincing, especially in view of the fact that the siting of certain stone circles near water-courses presumably took place long before the climate began to deteriorate. It may be that the nature of the water worship changed as the climate changed.

It certainly seems to have taken several forms. As well as stone circles and avenues sited near water, there is strong evidence for the veneration of gods associated with water and with the underworld in the form of ritual pits, shafts or wells, of which over a hundred have been excavated in Britain. The earliest pits, such as at Windmill Hill causewayed camp in Wiltshire, date back to the Neolithic period. The very deep shaft or well found at Wilsford, also in Wiltshire, in the early 1960s was dated to 1600 BC, the middle of the Bronze Age. It was found in a burial mound only about two miles from Stonehenge, and on excavation proved to be over 100 feet deep. In it was found pottery, wooden objects such as a hod, a bowl and parts of buckets, rope, and amber beads. Digging this shaft must have been a major task and it was clearly of great significance to its makers. Another Bronze Age shaft at Swanwick in Hampshire, 24 feet deep and 14 feet in diameter, had a five-foot post or stake at the bottom, and there were traces of flesh or blood. Also found were clay loomweights, and in other pits have been found human and animal bones, Roman tiles, charred wood, coins, pieces of statues, pebbles and, at Ashill in Norfolk, hazel nuts and leaves were found beneath such things as pottery, toad bones, bucket staves, a wickerwork basket, an iron knife and urns. In Celtic lore the hazel is clearly associated with wells and water. The spring of Segais in the Land of Promise was traditionally the source of the Rivers Boyne and Shannon, the spring also being the source of all knowledge. Hazel trees grew around it, and their nuts fell into the water, producing bubbles of inspiration, or being eaten by the salmon of knowledge.

The custom of throwing gifts or offerings into wells continued into Roman times, objects having been found in a number of Roman wells in Britain. The tradition has in fact never ceased. All kinds of objects were left as offerings by pilgrims visiting holy wells in medieval times, and right through the centuries until today, when people still throw coins into 'wishing wells'. The custom of throwing objects into lakes also survived into the nineteenth century in Scotland, when people were still throwing offerings of food into the Dowloch at Penport (Dumfries), but in earlier times much larger and more valuable offerings were thrown into lakes and rivers. Beautiful examples of Celtic craftsmanship, such as shields and lunulae (crescent-shaped gold ornaments), have been found in the Rivers Thames, Witham, Trent, Bann, Shannon and others, too often to have been carelessly lost. Hoards of metalwork found in lakes or buried in once water-covered areas attest strongly to the existence of water cults. In Shropshire draining operations uncovered a small hoard (spearheads and sword fragments) near Bishop's Castle, and another at Clungunford (animal bones, spearheads, sword fragments and other objects). Such finds have been repeated countrywide, but one of the most spectacular hoards came from Llyn Cerrig Bach on Anglesey. One hundred and forty-four objects were found, during a period beginning in 1943, when the RAF station at Valley was about to be built. In preparation of the ground, peat was to be spread over the sand, and the peat was being taken from nearby bogs. As the peat was being spread, metal objects and bones were found, and so a thorough search was made. There may well be more Iron Age metalwork lying deeper in the bog, and buried under the runways, both sites now inaccessible. Weapons (swords, spears, daggers, scabbards and shields), chariot fittings and harness constitute the bulk of the material discovered, with also some ox, sheep, pig, horse and dog bones (no human remains), the remains of two well-used bronze cauldrons, a broken trumpet, iron bars (perhaps currency bars) and two iron gang-chains used to link captives by the neck. These chains have been dated to the first century AD, which is probably the period when the whole hoard was deposited in the lake. This may have happened in AD 61, when the Romans were advancing on Anglesey, the last stronghold of the Druids who were a powerful Celtic priesthood. They may have desperately invoked the aid of the gods by means of this huge ritual offering – but in vain.

There is considerable additional evidence to show the importance of water in the Celtic religion, which was generally performed in an outdoor setting. The sacred groves were the temples of the Celts, and the rivers, streams, pools and springs were the focus of deity worship. In France there is direct evidence of river worship, with a temple located at the source of the River Seine, which was sacred to the goddess Sequana, and the name of the River Marne being derived from Matrona, 'Divine Mother'. The Matronae were the Gaulish mother-goddesses. In Britain no remains of Celtic temples at river sources have been found, though there is the Roman temple at Lydney close to the Severn estuary. However, there are numerous examples of river names which contain or were derived from Celtic deity names. Dee is from Dēvā, 'the goddess', 'the holy one', an alternative Welsh name being Aerfen, 'the goddess of war'. The Clyde comes from Clōta, the 'Divine Washer'. (Scottish tales of a hag washing the bloody

Afon Braint,
Anglesey

clothes of those shortly to die, called 'The Washer at the Ford', may be
a memory of this goddess.) Brigantia/Brigit is remembered in the river
names Braint (Anglesey) and Brent (Middlesex). The River Severn is
also the Sabrina or, in Welsh, Hafren, a princess drowned in the river,
whose name is also Sabrann, the old name of the River Lee in Cork.
The ancient name of the Thames, Tămēsa or Tămēsis, is feminine and
probably denotes a river divinity. The Irish rivers Boyne and Shannon
contain the goddess names Bóinn and Sinainn, and the Yorkshire
Wharfe may derive from Verbeia. Several Welsh rivers named Alun
may recall the goddess Alaunae, and the tidal wave on the Trent,
locally known as the Eager, was thought of as a living being, his name
that of the Scandinavian god Ægir. Lakes may also have names
suggestive of ancient veneration. The obsolete Worcestershire place-
name Tyesmere may mean 'a lake sacred to Tiw' (an important Saxon
god of battle, after whom Tuesday is named). In the parish of
Llanerfyl (Montgomery) there is a pool called Llyn Gwyddior, 'pool of
the grove sacred to the deity', or 'the lake of the grove of Ior/God'.
Some non-Celtic deities have crept into this list, but that only reaffirms
the widespread nature of water worship in earlier days.

In the absence of building remains (any temples which the Celts
built were probably simple and of materials which soon decayed), the
only tangible proof of Celtic water worship is in the form of wooden
figure carvings which have survived in some exceptional circumstances. Nearly 200 come from the sanctuary at the source of the River
Seine, and several have also been found in Britain, usually in peat
bogs. It is not clear whether the figures represent deities or are meant
to symbolise the donor of a votive offering. A passage written by the

Roman poet Lucan (AD 39–65) describing a Celtic forest sanctuary shows that water and wooden carvings were closely associated: 'And there were many dark springs running there, and grim-faced figures of gods uncouthly hewn by the axe from the untrimmed tree-trunk, rotted to whiteness.'

A most important aspect of Celtic religion was the head cult. There is strong evidence showing a close association of this cult with sacred springs and pools, some of it having survived even to the present day, albeit in fragmentary form and lacking the power of the original Celtic stimulus. The Celts were head-hunters, but they were not simply collecting battle trophies. To the Celts the head was the most important part of the body, symbolising the divine power, and they venerated the head as the source of all the attributes they most admired, such as fertility, healing, prophecy and wisdom. Heads of important enemies were carried home and displayed on stakes. The most highly prized heads were even preserved in cedar oil and kept in wooden boxes so that they could be admired by visitors. The Celts also used the head as decoration, or more likely as a protective device. Faces appear widely on Celtic artefacts such as dagger hilts, shields and other metalwork, and on coins; while the tradition of carving stone heads has survived into the twentieth century.

In Celtic lore the most familiar legend involving the head cult concerns the Welsh god Bran whose decapitated head was a companion to Bran's colleagues for many years, performing valuable services such as keeping away invaders, prophesying the future, and supplying all the men's needs. The Celtic traditions became so deep-seated that many of them were perpetuated down the centuries, surviving almost to the present day, and this is certainly true of the head cult and its water associations. The Roman historian Livy (59 BC–AD 17) described how Celtic warriors decorated skulls with gold and used them as cups for offerings to the gods, a custom continued in the use of skulls to drink the water at certain holy wells until recent times. The most famous of these was St Teilo's Well at Llandeilo Llwydarth near Maenclochog (Pembroke), where the water was renowned for its ability to cure whooping cough and other ills, but only if drunk out of the remains of St Teilo's skull. (St Teilo was bishop of Llandaff Cathedral, and died in 566; the skull at the well is of course unlikely to have been his, although there are legends to account for its presence there.) The skull was kept by the Melchior family who lived at the nearby farm, and a member of that family born in the house had to lift the water from the well in the skull and hand it to the patient, if the ritual was to be effective. There were stories telling how people had visited the well and drunk the water but had not been cured. On learning later that they should have drunk from the skull, they had returned and performed the ritual correctly, being cured as a result. However, folklorist Jonathan Ceredig Davies, author of *Folk-Lore of West and Mid-Wales*, who tried the cure when staying in the area at the turn of the century, wrote that he did not get rid of his cold, adding: 'perhaps my faith was not strong enough'. D. Parry-Jones, who visited the well many years after Davies, reported in his *Welsh Legends and Fairy Lore* that the last surviving member of the Melchior family had sold the skull for £50 to someone who claimed to be acting on behalf of a museum, and its whereabouts are no longer known. Before then, however, the well had ceased to be visited, and now it no longer exists.

Penglog Teilo is the longest surviving Welsh skull used for healing purposes, though there were others. Water was drunk from a human skull at Ffynnon* Llandyfaen (Carmarthen), and around the fourteenth to sixteenth centuries the skull of a Welsh nobleman, Gruffydd ap Adda ap Dafydd, killed at Dolgellau, was used in the same way, to cure whooping cough and other ailments. Skulls were also kept as relics in medieval Wales, some ancient ones encased in silver being destroyed by Bishop Barlow at St David's because of their pagan connections. Francis Jones, whose book *The Holy Wells of Wales* is undoubtedly the finest on the subject of holy wells yet written, suggests that water was drunk from human skulls in order to acquire the desirable qualities of the skull's original owner, and also the custom indicated a head cult involving kings, heroes and ancestors. Drinking from skulls at holy wells seems to have been most widespread in Wales. Although we have also found references to it from Scotland and Ireland, so far we have located none in England, though possibly the petrified human skull found in a petrifying spring at Warkton (Northampton) was used in a similar way.

The Celtic head cult is remembered in other well lore, perhaps most obviously in the legends which tell how a well came into existence at the place where a severed head fell. The best-known instance of this, with the well still flourishing, is the story of St Winefride, found in two twelfth-century chronicles. She lived around AD 700 in North Wales, the daughter of a Welsh chieftain and niece of St Beuno. One day while at home alone, she was visited by Prince Caradoc who was thirsty after hunting and requested a drink. Winefride's beauty overwhelmed him and the girl fled in terror at his advances. He pursued her, and as she reached the church the enraged Caradoc

---

* *Ffynnon* is the Welsh for 'well'; in Gaelic Scotland *Tobar* is the word used, as also in Ireland.

struck off her head with his sword. Where the head fell, water began to flow from the ground. St Beuno came from the church with his congregation and cursed Caradoc, who died on the spot. St Beuno replaced Winefride's severed head on her neck, breathed into her nostrils and prayed for her life. She revived and was healed, the only reminder of the near-fatal events being a thin white line on her throat – plus of course the holy well, which became famous for its miraculous cures, and is visited to the present day. It is located at the town of Holywell in Flint, and as one of the most important surviving holy wells will be featured again in this book. Other wells also reputedly sprang up where severed heads fell, or the bodies of murder victims lay, and this theme will be featured in more detail in Chapter 6, which describes the folklore of holy well formation.

The washing of severed heads occurs in both legend and custom. St Decuman, who lived as a hermit in the West Country, was brutally murdered by decapitation. Decuman arose and carried his head to a nearby well, where he washed it; and the well thereafter was known as St Decuman's Well. At Marnoch in Banff, it was customary for many years, as part of the practice of Christianity, to wash the skull of St Marnoch, who was said to have been buried there around 650. The water in which the skull was washed was used to heal the sick. As there was also a St Marnoch's Well near the church, it may originally have been the custom to use water from the well, or to wash the skull directly in the well.

In Scotland there are several wells called the Well of the Head (Tobar a' Chinn) or Well of the Heads (Tobar nan Ceann), especially on the Isle of Skye. The head connection is explained by a murder story, which varies with each well but includes a decapitated head or heads being placed or washed in the well. On the Scottish mainland the best-known Well of the Heads is at Loch Oich near Invergarry (Inverness). This well reputedly took its name from an event in the 1660s when seven men were beheaded in revenge for their having murdered two young MacDonalds. The heads were washed at the spring as they were being taken for presentation to MacDonald of Glengarry. A monument erected at the well in 1812 shows a hand holding a dirk and seven heads, and the inscription, carved in English, Gaelic, French and Latin, reads:

As a memorial of the ample and summary vengeance which, in the swift course of feudal justice, inflicted by the order of Lord McDonell and Aross, overtook the perpetrators of the foul murder of the Keppoch Family, a branch of the powerful and illustrious clan of which his lordship was the chief. This monument is erected by Colonel McDonell of Glengarry, XVII Mac-Mhic-Alaister, his successor and representative, in the year of Our Lord

1812. The heads of the Seven Murderers were presented at the feet of the noble Chief in Glengarry Castle after having been washed in this spring; and ever since that event, which took place in the sixteenth century, it has been known by the name of *Tobar-nan-Ceann* or the Well of the Heads.

It is not clear how far truth has been overlaid by legend. The murders certainly occurred, for the seven headless bodies were much later dug out of the mound where they were said to have been buried. If the heads were indeed washed in the well, as tradition relates, this is a striking continuation of Celtic practice in two respects: the taking of heads as evidence of success over enemies, and the association of such heads with water.

As a less violent reminder of the close link between heads and water, heads or faces were carved in stone. At Oswald's Well in Oswestry (Shropshire) there was at one time a stone carved to show the saint's head, and it was believed that the actual head was buried behind it.

The monument erected above the Well of the Heads at Loch Oich, Inverness

The stone head at St Beuno's Well, Tremeirchion, Flint, which acts as an overflow to the large pool behind the wall

Font in Germoe church, Cornwall, of probable Norman date

Some of the rituals performed at the well focused on the stone head. At other wells, the water flowed through the mouth of a stone head. Stones carved with three or four heads or faces have also been discovered, with a hollow or cup on top of the stone as if it were intended to act as a shrine or, in the Christian tradition, as a font. This may echo the earlier Celtic use of actual skulls for this purpose. On later Christian fonts heads were sometimes carved, which again may be a memory of the earlier close link between heads and water.

Although the head cult was strongest among the Celtic peoples, it did not originate with them. The head seems always to have exercised a fascination. In Bavaria, Mesolithic (Middle Stone Age, 10,000–4000 BC) skulls were found which had been taken from the bodies after death, decorated and arranged in groups. Closer in time to the Celts, chalk cylinders found in a child's grave in Yorkshire, dating from around the eighteenth century BC, were decorated with designs suggestive of faces; and a pebble carved as a head was found in a fifteenth-century BC Bronze Age cairn in Cumbria. Skulls with holes bored in them have also been found at prehistoric sites in Britain.

Nor, as we have already suggested, did the head cult die out as the Celts became less powerful. Its intensity may have waned, but it continued in various forms as part of the Christian religion, and it was also active during the Roman era, at which time there was apparently an overlap of imported Roman and native Celtic practices. The term 'Romano-British' is used to describe the sites, artefacts and practices of the native peoples who were subjected to Roman rule, a good example being the well dedicated to the Celtic goddess Coventina and located at Carrawburgh beside a Roman fort on Hadrian's Wall. When excavated in 1876, the well was found to contain a great variety of objects including small bronze heads and a human skull. Clearly the head cult was still followed, as at other Romano-British sites where skulls were found in wells.

The Romans themselves considered water an important aspect of their religious practices, as evidenced by the frequency with which their temples were located at wells or close to a water source. Some were beside rivers, for example the Bourton Grounds temple (Buckingham) beside the River Twin, Chedworth and Wycomb (Gloucester) both beside the River Coln, Frilford (Berkshire) beside the River Ock, Harlow (Essex) beside the River Stort, Colchester (Essex) beside a stream and with a well outside, Pagans Hill (Avon) overlooking the River Chew, and Nettleton (Wiltshire) above a stream. Others had springs, wells or paved ponds close by. Where temples were merely close to a water source, it is unclear what degree of importance water had in the rituals performed there. But where the water source was actually within the temple itself, it was clearly the focal point of the religious practices. The major sites of Roman water worship in Britain known to us today are: Coventina's Well at Carrawburgh (Northumberland), the temple of Nodens at Lydney (Gloucester), the temple of Sulis Minerva and Roman baths at Bath (Avon), a temple at Springhead (Kent), the Roman bath and St Anne's Well at Buxton (Derby) with associated temple, and an enclosed well-shrine at Housesteads (Northumberland).

Coventina's Well at Carrawburgh was discovered by lead prospectors in 1876. It lay close to the Roman fort of Brocolitia, and the well itself was seven feet deep, with an area of over fifty square feet. It was enclosed by thick walls which may not have been roofed. Inside the well were found many items: twenty-four altars, some dedicated to Coventina; inscribed slabs, one carrying a design with three nymphs and another the goddess herself; a stone head, bronze heads, and a human skull; bronze models of a horse, a terrier and a hand; bells, rings, brooches, pottery, glass, pins and many odds and ends; and around 14,000 coins. The skull, as we have already seen, may indicate the practice or at least memory of the head cult, as may the model heads. The presence of pins in the well suggests that fertility was one attribute assigned to the goddess, whose overall function was healing.

The Temple of
Mithras at
Carrawburgh,
Northumberland

The altars and slabs are most likely to have been placed in the well for safe-keeping when danger threatened, and the coins may have been the temple treasury, though some were probably offerings. Although the nearby Temple of Mithras was destroyed in the fourth century, the dates on the coins show that the well was in use into the fifth century. In 1960 a second well was discovered only a few hundred yards away, so in this small area were located three shrines: two wells and the Mithraeum, where a small goddess figure was found. Five Mithraea have been found in Britain, a sophisticated temple in London and four rougher military temples at Caernarfon, Carrawburgh, Housesteads and Rudchester. They were either built close to streams or actually over springs. The significance of water in the cult of Mithras, a god of Persian and Zoroastrian origin, is not clear.

Apart from the Mithraeum, there was also at Housesteads (a Roman fort on Hadrian's Wall) a slab-lined well 4 feet six inches deep, wherein was found pottery, a few coins, pins and beads. That the well was surrounded by walls, together with the presence of two altars, indicates that it was a shrine, and a large building nearby may have been used by worshippers at the well. This may also have been the arrangement at Buxton, where the Roman bath at the later-named St Anne's Well was close to what may have been a temple of Arnemetia, the Celtic goddess to whom the waters were dedicated. The Roman name for Buxton was Aquae Arnemetiae, the waters of Arnemetia. Before it was altered in 1709, the well was lined with Roman lead and surrounded by Roman bricks.

At Springhead, a 25-acre site was found to contain six or seven temples, a public bakery, a mill, shops and other buildings. The name describes the location: there were eight natural springs at the site. That an important religious centre was located here surely cannot be coincidental. One of the temples is unique in Britain. Covering an area

of twenty-nine feet by nineteen feet, it had flint walls three feet thick –
but it had no door and could not be entered. Inside was a clay area
covered with thousands of pottery sherds, and some incense cups. It is
likely to have been a sacred pool, into which votive offerings were
thrown. Another temple, only two feet away, probably housed a
healing god, and the pool is thought to have been associated with this.

Quite definitely a healing centre was the temple of Nodens and
adjoining buildings at Lydney, located on prehistoric earthworks by
the River Severn. The god Nodens was concerned with healing,
hunting and the sea, and he may originally have been an Irish deity,
perhaps the same as Nuada. The name Lydney is probably derived
from the god's name. The healing centre was constructed in the late
fourth century and consisted of a temple sixty feet by eighty feet, a
square courtyard house, a suite of baths and a long, narrow building
containing cubicles. In these the patients may have slept in the hope of
being visited by the god. A wall enclosed the buildings, and beyond
was a water tank which supplied the baths and guesthouse. Excavations have produced many objects from the site (which is now
unfortunately overgrown), including over 8000 coins, nine dogs in
stone or bronze, a bronze arm, pins and bracelets. The pins indicate a
fertility aspect to the healing cult, while the dogs are further confirma-
tion that healing was practised at Lydney. Representations of dogs
have often been found at sites of healing cults involving water. At
Lydney, a bronze dog was found at the bottom of a funnel in the
temple, probably placed there as an offering to the god in the
underworld.

The hot spring at Bath (Aquae Sulis) was presided over by the native
goddess Sulis who from Roman times was linked with the classical
Roman goddess Minerva, and was then known as Sulis Minerva. Her
temple was close to the baths complex, which was a healing centre,
Sulis Minerva being most often invoked in her healing aspect, though
other deities were also invoked here. Objects found include fine
carvings of the goddess and altars dedicated to her, a priest's
tombstone and reliefs depicting other deities.

These major sites, and numerous minor ones (for example, an altar
inscribed on two sides 'Nymphis et Fontibus' was found near Abbot's
Well in Chester) show that the veneration of water and its powers was
carried on from prehistoric times into the Roman era. The Romans
often introduced their favourite foreign deities into Britain as well as
taking native deities into their pantheon. Even after the Roman
influence had departed, the wells were not abandoned, but the belief in
their healing powers persisted. Indeed, during the following centuries
the water cult spread until there were thousands of sacred wells

throughout Britain, each with its pilgrims who could attest to its potency.

It is impossible to discover when individual wells were first identified as sacred places. The finding of a spring close to an ancient or sacred site may have sanctified it in the eyes of the local people, since water welling up from the earth at a sacred site would naturally be considered to possess great potency. Or a well at an ancient site may be itself ancient, having its origins with the people who first erected the standing stones, dug the earthworks, or constructed whatever kind of site it was. There are certainly a large number of holy wells located in close proximity to ancient sites of all kinds. Francis Jones mentions 62 examples of wells associated with megaliths, and 14 of wells near tumuli, and this is in Wales alone, and does not take into account those sites where no trace of the well or the ancient site survives, in written or physical form. A few examples of surviving (at least until very recently) ancient sites and wells throughout Britain and Ireland will further demonstrate how strong is the link between them.

Beginning with circles and standing stones: in Keith parish (Banff) two stone circles had wells close to them, one being known as Tobir-Chalaich, Old Wife's Well (ie Cailleach, or hag, a distant memory of pagan goddesses). At Tullybelton (Perth) (Tulach Bealltuinn, Beltane Hill) on Beltane morning (1 May) it was the custom to

Clach na b-Annait, a standing stone only about 300 feet from Tobar na n-Annait, a holy well at Torrin, South Skye

visit the well, drink some water, walk round it nine times and then round the nearby standing stones. Many other wells were actively linked to their neighbouring stones by a ritual of this kind. A stone beside Grew's Well near Dunkeld (Perth) would protect the pilgrim against rheumatism, if he leaned backwards over it. From Scotland to Wales, where a stone was involved in a ritual at the healing well of Coed y Ffynnon at Penmachno (Caernarfon). The stone was called Carreg y Ddefod (Stone of the Rite). A link is suggested in two Carmarthen parishes, Llanpumsaint and Llanegwad. Both had wells called Ffynnon Newydd, and stones called Carreg Ffynnon Newydd. Ffynnon Fron Las in Trelech parish (Carmarthen), a healing well with a high reputation, had a circle of stones round it, the special nature of which is suggested in a local belief that a strange old man living nearby kept idols round the well. In Ireland, a pillar stone near St Adamnan's Well at Temple Moyle (Donegal) was visited as part of a healing ritual: first the well was circled, then the diseased part of the body was rubbed against the stone.

Burial sites of all kinds — cromlechs, cairns, barrows, tumuli — sometimes had holy wells nearby. In Scotland the so-called Wells of Dee on Braeriach in the Cairngorms (Aberdeen) are the source of the River Dee, and the mossy bank where they are found is topped by a cairn of white quartz stones. An old rhyme told how a key could be found under a stone in Dryburn Well, Orwell parish (Kinross), and this key would unlock the treasure of Cairnavain, a nearby stone cairn, 'That'll mak a' Scotland rich.' But nineteenth-century treasure seekers failed to find anything. A holy well beside St Paul's Chapel on the Hill of Easterton, Fyvie (Aberdeen), was frequented by mothers with sick children, who after drinking the water were passed under the nearby Shagar (= diseased child) Stone, a dolmen. An elaborate healing ritual used to be performed at Strathfillan (Perth) at a pool in the River Dochart said to have been blessed by St Fillan and known as St Fillan's Well. The patients were first immersed in the pool, where they picked up nine stones from the bottom. They then walked three times round three nearby cairns, adding a stone on each circuit. A late eighteenth-century visitor wrote of the ritual:

If it is for any bodily pain, fractured limb or sore, that they are bathing, they throw upon one of these cairns that part of their clothing which covered the part affected; also, if they have at home any beast that is diseased, they have only to bring some of the meal which it feeds upon and make it into paste with these waters, and afterwards give it to him to eat, which will prove an infallible cure; but they must likewise throw upon the cairn the rope or halter with which he was led. Consequently the cairns are covered with old halters, gloves, shoes, bonnets, nightcaps, rags of all sorts, kilts, petticoats, garters, and smocks. Sometimes they go as far as to throw away their halfpence.

The patients were finally taken to the ruins of St Fillan's chapel, where their treatment was continued overnight.

Examples of holy wells close to ancient sites in England are not numerous, probably because there are far more such sites in the upland areas of Scotland, Wales and Ireland. However, one well known to us is St Sativola's which is close to the barrow at Wick (Avon). The saint is also known as St Sidwell, and the field is called Barrow Sidwells. Local women used to take their children to the well in cases of skin or eye disease. Tumuli at Charlton Horethorne (Somerset) also had a spring close by.

In Wales there were cromlechs close to Ffynnon Newydd, Llangynog (Carmarthen), Ffynnon Beuno at Clynnog (Caernarfon), and Ffynnon Cerrig Hirion in Nevern parish (Pembroke), while a healing well on Cefn Bryn, Gower (Glamorgan), was to be found right beneath the cromlech known as Arthur's Stone, or Maen Ceti. This well, Ffynnon Fair, was said to have been brought into existence by St David, who did not approve of the pagan worship at the stone, and so split it with his sword and commanded a holy well to flow. In County Mayo, Ireland, a stone tomb at Srahwee was itself the 'well', its flooded interior being known as Tobernahaltora (Well of the Altar, *altóir* being a word for dolmen or megalithic tomb).

Wells inside forts or close to earthworks may have served initially as a water supply for the people occupying the site, later being taken over and venerated by the local people. An example is Nine-well in a vitrified fort on Finavon Hill (Angus), which was set above the old kirk dedicated to the Nine Maidens. There are other examples in Scotland, and several in England, including the famous hillfort at South Cadbury (Somerset), believed by some to be King Arthur's Camelot. King Arthur's Well lies in a bank to the north-east, outside the enclosure, while Queen Anne's Well is higher up the hill. In Gloucestershire, Our Lady's Well at Hempsted is near to ancient earthworks, while in the Forest of Dean at English Bicknor, a never-failing spring supplies an ancient well inside an earthwork. At Upper Slaughter, a possible Saxon burgh contains a well 30 feet deep, walled with stone, at the bottom of which were found charcoal, burnt bones, pottery and pins. These deposits may be accidental, but they do sound like votive offerings. Near Buckland (Hampshire) there was a spring near an earthwork, while in Nottinghamshire St Catherine's Well was located near an earthwork called the Queen's Sconce near Newark, the spring flowing where the head of a murdered knight fell, according to the legend. The murderer was stricken with leprosy as a punishment, but this was cured by water from the well! In Cumberland, Collinson's Well is a mineral spring near the earthwork called Collinson's Castle at Hutton-in-the-Forest. Tullaghan Well in County

Sligo is on top of a mountain and is said to have appeared when St Patrick prayed for water after all the other wells had been polluted by a demon he was chasing. An older tale has a Celtic leader being killed and his head thrown into this well. There are three cashels (Iron Age stone forts) on the hill, and these together with the stories suggest that the well is an ancient one.

Perhaps the most interestingly located wells near ancient sites are those where there is also a Christian building close at hand. Such sites visibly indicate a continuity from prehistoric times right through the earliest days of Christianity into medieval times and often even to the present day, especially in Ireland where many of the old rituals are still performed. At St David's in Wales (Pembroke) the ruins of St Non's Chapel (seventh or eighth century) lie within the remains of a stone circle, while close by is St Non's Well. Also in Pembroke is Ffynnon Deilo or Ffynnon yr Ychen, near the ruined church of Llandeilo Llwydarth and famous for its ritual involving St Teilo's skull, described earlier. In the churchyard are two megaliths with Ogham (an early Irish script) and Roman inscriptions. In both these Welsh instances, no rituals incorporating all of the elements now survive. But at Dungiven (Londonderry), the well near the ruins of St Mary's Priory was the focal point of an elaborate ritual involving the church, a stone in the river, and a standing stone, a ritual which persisted into this century and may even be performed today. The pilgrims would bow to the well, walk round it several times repeating a prayer, wash their hands and feet in its water, and tie a rag torn from their clothes to a bush over the well. Next they would walk to the River Roe below the old church and there would wash, and bow to the stone while walking round it repeating the prayers. A ceremony was then performed in the ruined church, and finally they processed round the 10-foot-high stone called Cloch-Patrick which stands on a mound near the church.

That this ritual was performed at a well, a natural rock, an old Christian church and a prehistoric standing stone shows that the people of later ages saw no difference between the holy objects of one period and those of another. To them, once the sanctity of an area was established, this sanctity was transferred to any designated edifice or stone at that site, continuously from one period to the next, this attitude also being prevalent in Scotland where the Highlanders would still one hundred years ago speak of going to the *clachan*, ie the stones, to mean that they were going to church. It was this attitude of mind which the early Christian missionaries took advantage of when they sought to supplant the old religion and replace it with the new.

2. The Effect of Christianity on Water Cults

Christians throughout Europe were intolerant of any other form of worship; they called it pagan (ie irreligious, barbaric and unenlightened) and made strenuous efforts to suppress it, as shown by this canon issued by the Second Council of Arles, held around 452: 'If in the territory of a bishop infidels light torches or venerate trees, fountains, or stones, and he neglects to abolish this usage, he must know that he is guilty of sacrilege.' But such instructions when carried out were not always successful in eradicating the deeply held beliefs and long-established customs of the people, and at the beginning of the seventh century Pope Gregory recognised this in a letter he wrote to Abbot Mellitus concerning the arrival of St Augustine in Britain. Pope Gregory recommended that the temples not be destroyed, but converted for Christian use. The people would then continue to visit their sacred places, but their devotions would be directed at the true God rather than at pagan idols. As we shall see, this is what happened with many of the holy wells, and was very probably an important reason for their continued survival for so long.

However, not all wells were taken over in this way by the Christians, and many people still continued their old practices, resulting in more decrees banning water worship. For example in 960, during the reign of the Saxon king Edgar, a canon exhorted: 'That every priest industriously advance Christianity, and extinguish heathenism, and forbid the worship of fountains.' The Saxon King Cnut was still experiencing similar problems in the early eleventh century:

It is heathen practice if one worships idols, namely if one worships heathen gods and the sun or the moon, fire or flood, wells or stones or any kind of forest trees, or if one practises witchcraft or encompasses death by any means, either by sacrifice or divination, or takes any part in such delusions.

Into the twelfth century, edicts banning water worship were still being issued, but gradually, as the influence of Christianity spread across the land, the old customs were overlaid by Christian observances and the pagan aspect of water worship became hidden behind the Christian façade.

Several methods were used to accomplish this takeover. Since water is used in Christian rites, for baptism and handwashing, the well water was adopted for these purposes. Baptisteries were built at wells, and churches were built close to, or even over, wells. The pagan gods were ousted in favour of Christian saints, many wells being dedicated to saints and thenceforward bearing their names. Missionary saints used the wells to baptise their converts, and sometimes they staged a dramatic show of power to convince the people that Christianity was the superior religion. In sixth-century Scotland, St Columba was converting the Picts to Christianity and was able to use a confrontation with the Druids to his advantage. A certain well was believed to be capable of causing many kinds of infirmity, such as leprosy, and the Druids believed that if St Columba touched the water he would be afflicted. But he blessed the well in Christ's name, drank from it, and washed his hands and feet in it, and was not harmed. The demons departed from the water, and from that time the well was known for its healing power. The well may be St Columba's Well at Invermoriston (Inverness).

Martin Martin, in his *Description of the Western Islands of Scotland*, written *c*. 1695, describes the skilful way in which a well on the island of Eigg was dedicated to a Christian saint, the ritual incorporating pagan elements (sunwise circumambulation and lighting candles) and Christian elements (penance and mass), and the whole process resulting in its conversion into a Christian saint's well.

In the Village on the South Coast of this Isle, there is a Well, call'd St Katherine's Well, the Natives have it in great Esteem, and believe it to be a Catholicon for Diseases. They told me it had been such ever since it was consecrated by one Father Hugh, a Popish Priest, in the following manner: He oblig'd all the Inhabitants to come to this Well, and then imploy'd them to bring together a great heap of Stones at the Head of the Spring, by way of Penance. This being done, he said Mass at the Well, and then consecrated it; he gave each of the Inhabitants a piece of Wax Candle, which they lighted, and all of them made the Dessil, of going round the Well Sunways, the Priest leading them; and from that time it was accounted unlawful to boil any Meat with Water of the Well. The Natives observe St Katherine's Anniversary; all of them come to the Well, and having drunk a Draught of it, they make a Dessil round it Sunways; this is always perform'd on the 15th Day of April.

As reported from Eigg, it was often the case that a saint's or holy person's blessing caused a well thenceforth to have healing powers. Eustachius, Abbot of Flai, blessed the well later known as St Eustace's Well at Withersden (Kent), and it afterwards cured all diseases. Ffynnon Ddyfnog (Denbigh) became a healing well as a result of St Dyfnog doing penance by standing in the cold water of a waterfall, while St Cuthbert's (or Cubert's) Well at Cubert in Cornwall reputedly gained its healing power after it was touched by the relics of the saint, being carried to safety by monks from Durham. Sometimes even lesser people than abbots and saints could thus affect wells. At Dale Abbey in Derbyshire, a hermit dug a well and blessed it, saying it should be a holy well and a cure for all ills. In Shropshire, an old pilgrim passing through Ludlow on his way to St Winifred's Well at Holywell blessed the Boiling Well and commanded it to have healing powers in order that a maid at his lodging place could be cured of her sore eyes.

Allegorical stories of saints battling with giants, monsters and demons may be interpreted as symbolising the Christian's fight against paganism. At Bwlch Rhiwfelen (Denbigh) St Collen fought and killed a cannibal giantess, afterwards washing away the bloodstains in a well later known as Ffynnon Gollen. In Ireland, the tales of saints slaying giant serpents may have the same meaning; alternatively they (or some of them) may refer to early sightings of genuine water monsters. St Barry banished a serpent from a mountain into Lough Lagan (Roscommon), and a holy well sprang up where the saint's knee touched the ground.

All these success stories may leave the impression that the Christians were eventually entirely successful in eradicating every trace of the old forms of worship. But that this was not always so is demonstrated by two instances of pagan survivals. On the Isle of Man holy wells were

St Dyfnog's Well
at Llanrhaeadr,
Denbigh

frequented on 1 August – Lhuanys's Day, which name probably refers to the Celtic god Lugh who was remembered annually in a fire festival on 1 August, Lugnasad. The Christian name for the day is Lammas, but the people of the Isle of Man preferred to use the old name until well into the nineteenth century. In Scotland several aspects of pagan ritual survived at the well on the island in Loch Maree (Ross & Cromarty). The name 'Maree' is said to come from St Maelrubha, an Irish saint who founded a church nearby in 673, but the rituals practised on the island undoubtedly owed more to pagan influences than to Christian practices. A bull was sacrified to 'St Mourie' (also known as the God Mourie) on 25 August, the saint's day, offerings of milk were poured on the ground, and the people worshipped a sacred well and a tree. The tree had coins driven into its bark to a height of eight or nine feet. The well water was said to be a cure for lunacy, the afflicted having to kneel before an altar, drink the well water, and be submerged three times in the loch from a boat sailing sunwise round the island. This would be repeated daily for weeks, and such rituals were still being performed in the mid nineteenth century, though the well is now dry.

The lore of holy wells is rich with stories of saints. The wells were sometimes said to have been actually created by the saints, often in miraculous ways, and examples of these will be given in Chapter 6 which is devoted to the many ways in which wells, and also lakes and pools, reputedly came into being. The saints' involvement with holy wells is sometimes factual, sometimes fictional, and sometimes it is difficult to decide which. Some of the saints were individuals whose lives are reliably documented, while the history of others is uncertain, and some may be pagan deities renamed and given invented life histories. One of the saints whom we know to have existed is St Chad, the patron saint of medicinal springs, who was a seventh-century bishop born in Northumbria. In 669 Chad was consecrated bishop of the Mercians, with his see at Lichfield (Stafford), which is the location of the most famous of the holy wells dedicated to him. At Stowe on the outskirts of Lichfield, Chad built a small church near a well where he baptised his converts. It was reported by the sixteenth-century antiquary Leland that it was Chad's custom to stand naked in the well and pray. He was not long at Lichfield, dying in 672, and one wonders if his rigorous penance may have contributed to this. The well gained in popularity after his death and became known as a healing well, large numbers of pilgrims visiting it during the Middle Ages. In the early eighteenth century the well was recommended as a cure by Sir John Floyer, a physician to Charles II, and as a result it enjoyed some fame as a spa. Today the well is still visited, and at least until the last century was being

St Brigid's Well, Mulhuddart, County Dublin, decorated as a Catholic shrine

decorated with greenery and flowers on Ascension Day.

A popular saint with a more obscure and probably apocryphal history is the Blessed Virgin Mary. Over seventy Scottish wells are dedicated to her, and 76 are found in Wales – usually known as Ffynnon Fair. The folklore of Our Lady tells how she actually visited Wales. She is said to have landed at Llanfair near Harlech (Merioneth), where the church is dedicated to her (Llanfair = Church of St Mary). On her walk inland, she drank at a stream, and left impressions on the rock where she knelt. Beside the rock a healing spring began to flow, though this well is now reportedly neglected and overgrown. The Marian cult was and remains widespread, and here Christianity and paganism are closely and curiously interwoven, Our Lady having supplanted the pagan water goddesses (but perhaps in name only). Where today statues of Our Lady adorn shrines erected by Catholic pilgrims at holy wells, centuries ago the pre-Christian pilgrims were making obeisance to representations of their pagan deities.

We cannot here do justice to the multiplicity of saints' dedications and the stories attached to them. In Wales alone there are 500 holy wells which have saints' or Christian-related names, but some of the saints' stories will be told where relevant elsewhere in this book. The water cult certainly flourished in the hands of the Christians, and at the peak of its popularity there must have been thousands of holy wells regularly visited throughout England, Wales, Scotland and Ireland. We have no exact figures, but some regional researchers have provided estimates. Ruth and Frank Morris list nearly a thousand holy wells on the Scottish mainland alone in their *Scottish Healing Wells*; there are also many on the islands. Francis Jones studied nearly 1200 wells in his research for *The Holy Wells of Wales*, while in Ireland, a country especially rich in holy wells, estimates of at least 3000 have been made. In County Dublin Dr Kevin Danaher found 99 holy wells, though in the Ordnance Survey Office there were references to 118, and there are probably even more. Nobody seems to have attempted to calculate how many holy wells there were in England, though in his 1970 survey of Cornish holy wells the Reverend A. Lane-Davies listed 150 for that county alone. Cornwall is better endowed with holy wells than most other counties, so guessing an average of 50 wells per county, multiplied by 44 counties, gives a very approximate and probably conservative estimate of 2000 holy wells in England. The grand total for Great Britain and Ireland may therefore be in excess of 8000, of which unfortunately only a fraction now survives and can be visited (for some examples, see the Gazetteer at the end of this book).

Although many wells were named for saints, by no means all of them were. Some were named after secular people, for example Mr Goodman's Well (Denbigh), which is clear enough; but in some cases confusion could arise: Ffynnon Bedr in Ruthin parish (Denbigh) was named not after St Peter but after a Mr Peter Jones. Some wells were named for the use they were put to: Ffynnon Ymenin or 'Butter well' denotes a well used by dairy maids in the butter-making process. Some were named after trees, and Ellenwell does not necessarily mean St (H)Elen's Well but could mean 'ellern' (elder-tree) well. Others were named after animals, after topographical features, or after characteristics, eg Boiling Well. Some names are suggestive of pagan connections: Wanswell (Gloucester) may derive from Woden's Well, and there was a Thor's Well at Burnsall (North Yorkshire). Many names are distortions, for example the Cornish Veryan, where there is a restored holy well. The parish was formerly St Simphorian, then the 'saint' was omitted to give Severian, and eventually it became St Veryan. This also demonstrates how pseudo-saints' names can develop. In Scotland Verter Well at Hawick (Roxburgh) was originally Virtue Well, from its reputation as a healing well, and Chapelheron Well at Whithorn (Wigtown) was originally Chapel of Kieran. But despite the many exceptions, it is probably safe to say that at least half the holy well names indicate some Christian connection. In many cases that connection is also still visible, in the form of a church close by, or a ruined baptistery or well chapel.

The Christian missionaries probably often built baptisteries or chapels close to or actually over the holy wells which they used to baptise their converts. When the building was no longer used, superseded by a bigger church serving a parish, the stone was often taken away and re-used in later buildings, with the result that few complete baptisteries or chapels remain. There are, however, some in ruins, and others that are known through documentation, or surviving names such as Ffynnon y Capel in Wales. In some places where the site was considered important, the simple baptistery or chapel was rebuilt in the form of a church. On the Isle of Man, keeills (early Christian cells or oratories) were often sited close to holy wells, though few such sites survive today other than as scanty ruins. One example was Keeill Unjin and its associated well Chibbyr Unjin in the parish of Kirk Malew. Both keeill and well were destroyed in 1899 by the farmer whose land they stood on. He could no longer tolerate the pilgrims who were damaging his property. In Cornwall a chapel has survived in a ruined state beside Madron well, its walls having been recently restored. The building was about 25 feet long and 16 feet wide, with walls two feet thick, and still contains an altar stone. It has stone benches, and in one corner is a hollow which may have been used as a font, the water being supplied, through an inlet in the wall, from the well a short distance away.

There are several surviving chapels in Wales, St Non's chapel near the holy well at St David's (Pembroke) already having been mentioned. Even better preserved are the buildings at Ffynnon Gybi (St Cybi's Well) at Llangybi (Caernarfon). There are two well buildings, a custodian's cottage, and a detached latrine, though all are now ruined. In the smaller well building the well itself flows into a small bath, the water then passing through into a larger adjoining building which also houses a bath surrounded by a ledge, and with steps leading down into the water. It is very difficult to date the buildings, but they are thought to be no older than the twelfth century, though the well would have been used as far back as the sixth century when St Cybi was active in the area. A similar situation exists with regard to Ffynnon Seiriol at Penmon on Anglesey. The existing building round the well is probably mainly of eighteenth-century construction, but the well itself was certainly used by St Seiriol in the sixth century, and the outline of a

St Seiriol's Well, Penmon, Anglesey; in the foreground are the remains of the saint's hut

circular stone hut beside the well is thought to have been his dwelling. Many other wells are covered by stone buildings, but most are small and relatively recent, without positive links to early Christian times.

Elaborate well-chapels were sometimes built in medieval times, and two in North Wales are particularly notable, one being in a sad state of neglect, the other site still flourishing. The latter is at Holywell (Flint), where the chapel was built *c.* 1500, probably replacing an earlier shrine. No one knows why St Winefride's Well should have survived all closure attempts and remained one of Britain's most frequented holy wells near the end of the twentieth century, while the nearby Ffynnon Fair (Our Lady's Well, 2½ miles south-west of St Asaph and 12 miles from Holywell), with its equally large chapel dating from the same time as that at Holywell, should have been abandoned. But its location may have played a part in its fate, because the well is in the isolated valley of the River Elwy, some way from the nearest road or settlement. Today the ruins stand forlornly inside their iron railings, overgrown and totally neglected, traces of the site's former glory being difficult to discern. The Reverend Elias Owen, who diligently studied the holy wells of North Wales at the end of the last century, reports that the holy well was probably originally enclosed in a small baptistery measuring about ten by five feet, which later became the southern transept of the chapel, itself sixty by sixteen feet. If this is the case, then the enlarging of the original small building to a chapel indicates the one-time great popularity of the well, as also does the construction of another well at the west end of the chapel. It is this well, whose elaborately designed bathing cistern still survives, which later became known as St Mary's Well. It had a baptistery adjoining it, but not only baptisms were performed at Ffynnon Fair, also marriages and burials. However, Ffynnon Fair was ruinous by the time naturalist and traveller Thomas Pennant (born in the county) wrote about it, in the late eighteenth century:

Y Ffynnon Fair, Our Ladies Well, a fine spring, inclosed in an angular wall, formerly roofed, and the ruins of a cross shaped chapel, finely overgrown with ivy, exhibit a venerable view, in a deep wooded bottom, not remote from the bridge, and this in days of pilgrimage, the frequent haunt of devotees.

Pennant's description still applies two hundred years later.

At Ffynnon Fair the chapel was clearly built as a result of the well's popularity, but that is not necessarily always the reason for a well's being enclosed within the fabric of a church. There are several known instances of this, and the possible reasons are several: the well provided a water source for baptisms; the site was so revered that it

The remains of St Mary's chapel and holy well (Ffynnon Fair) at Cefn, Denbigh

was a natural place to build a church; or perhaps in some instances the intention was to sanctify the site and completely destroy any lingering traces of paganism, by enclosing the well in a Christian edifice. It is interesting that of the fifteen locations known to us, eleven are at abbeys, minsters or cathedrals. Dunfermline Abbey (Fife) has a well in the nave for use in church services, while in Beverley Minster (Humberside) during restoration of the choir in 1879, two old and worn steps were found which had been used as an approach to a well. Canterbury Cathedral's Well of St Thomas, formerly on the north side of the choir, no longer exists, nor does St Pandonia's Well at Ely Cathedral, and the well in Carlisle Cathedral is under one of the pillars. It is said to have been covered over at the request of a dean who believed that it was in some way adversely affecting the music. Ancient wells have also been found at St Patrick's Cathedral, Dublin, Winchester Cathedral, Wells Cathedral, Exeter Cathedral, and in the crypts of York Minster and Glasgow Cathedral. King Edwin is said to have been baptised in the York Minster well in 627 – it was then covered only by a small wooden chapel. It may be that the site of the future York Minster was determined by this event. The crypt of Glasgow Cathedral was built over the spot where the body of Fergus, an anchorite, was buried, brought there by Mungo (the same person as Kentigern), bishop of the kingdom of Strathclyde. St Mungo probably baptised his converts in the well now in the south-east corner of the crypt.

Two of the churches built over holy wells are in Cumbria – St Patrick's at Aspatria and St Oswald's at Kirkoswald. The latter church stands at the foot of the hill from which the well flows, the water passing under the length of the nave and emerging outside the west wall, where it is used as a drinking well. In Marden church (Hereford

The well under Winchester Cathedral, as depicted *c.* 1770

St Oswald's Well,
Kirkoswald,
Cumbria, set
against the church
wall

& Worcester) the well at the west end marks the place where the murdered St Ethelbert, King of East Anglia until his death in 794, was buried. When his body was removed to Hereford, a well arose in the empty grave. Holybourne church (Hampshire) was sited at the source of the Holy Bourne, the stream which gave the village its name. In the past the water was used to cure eye troubles. Some springs still rise beneath the altar and the west end of the nave.

In many more instances were churches built close to wells, as can still be seen today in the number of wells in churchyards or just beyond. Francis Jones recorded nearly two hundred chapels and churches built close to holy wells in Wales, and the same applies throughout the rest of Britain, one good example still in fine condition being St Withburga's Well at East Dereham (Norfolk), which is in the churchyard, only a few yards from the church wall. Other examples of wells very close to churches can be found in the Gazetteer. Occasionally wells were marked by Christian crosses, as at Calmsden and Condicote in the Gloucestershire Cotswolds, both crosses being thought to date from the fourteenth century. In Gloucester itself, an old cross also stood above the spring which supplied the city and cathedral centuries ago. Situated at the foot of Robinswood Hill, this cross took the form of a horizontal stone slab a foot thick, resting on five supporting slabs.

The erection of a church or chapel close to a holy well would certainly have helped to preserve the well and maintain its popularity. In other cases the well's sanctity was reinforced by visible signs of the saint's former presence there, in the form of saints' 'chairs', 'beds', 'footprints', and so on. The following are a small sample of the many examples throughout Britain and Ireland. By Our Lady's Well at Stow

Fourteenth-century well cross at Condicote, Gloucestershire

(Midlothian) was once a large stone bearing a footprint of the Virgin Mary, while it was St Patrick's knees and left hand which were said to have left the marks once to be seen on a rock in a quarry at Portpatrick (Wigtown), where there was also a St Patrick's Well. St Columba's footprints (though he seems to have had two right feet!) are incised on a rock near the holy well and ancient chapel of Keil in Kintyre (Argyll), but these footprints, and others of a similar nature, may have been carved for use in the inauguration ceremonies of kings. There is another example in the Dark Age fort of Dunadd (Argyll) where there are several rock carvings including a man's foot, a circular basin, and a boar, symbol of the royal house. The footprint is reputedly that of the eighth-century Fergus, the first king of Dalriada, kingdom of the Scots, of which Dunadd was the capital. There are also at least two wells in the fort.

At Madron in Cornwall, people seeking a cure at St Madron's Well would as part of the ritual sleep in the grassy St Madron's Bed; while on the Isle of Man women wishing for offspring would drink the water of St Maughold's Well and sit in the saint's chair close by. St Bridget's knees left their impression in a rock in the stream by St Bridget's Well near Dundalk (Louth), and at St Senan's Well at Dunass (Clare) the pilgrims kneel in the marks left by the saint's knees on a flat rock by the well, as they drink the well water. In Ireland some holy 'wells' are hollows in a flat rock, known as bullauns. Near the ruined church of Killalta a bullaun always full of water was said to show where the saint knelt, and the water was believed to cure warts. St Patrick left his mark on many stones throughout Ireland, including the impression of his bottom on a stone at the old church of Cross Patrick in Killala parish (Mayo). When Dr Patrick Logan recently asked a local man if he was sure St Patrick had visited a certain holy well, the man replied: 'Of course I am sure he came here. How else could he have left the track of his knees in that stone?'

Although the Christian Church was quite successful in taking over holy wells, the water cult was by no means totally absorbed into the Church, and retained a strong existence apart from it. Many wells were dedicated to the saints, but the rituals performed and the hopes expressed often had no religious connections, and were not in any way regulated by a Christian priest. As a result, as Christina Hole so aptly expressed it: 'it may be that the simpler pilgrims were not always very clear as to the precise nature of the spirit to whom their petitions were addressed.' This possibility was intolerable to the 'hard-line' Christians, who were openly dismissive of the simple beliefs and practices of the country people, and over the centuries many attempts were made to deter them from visiting the holy wells. This fifteenth-century example, from the Hereford Diocese Cathedral Registers, typifies the line that was taken by the clergy.

Worship of a Well at Turnaston forbidden.

1410. Robert, to the Dean of Hereford our official and all the clergy in our county and diocese, greeting etc.:

Although it is provided in the divine laws and sacred canons that all who shall adore a stone, spring or other creature of God, incur the charge of idolatry, it has come to our ears, we grieve to say, from the report of many credible witnesses and the common report of the people, that many of our subjects are in large numbers visiting a certain well and stone at Turnaston in our diocese where with genuflections and offerings they, without authority of the Church, wrongfully worship the said stone and well, whereby committing

Bullauns used as holy wells at Boherduff, Loughrea, County Galway (photo 1956)

idolatry; when the water fails they take away with them the mud of the same and treat and keep it as a relic to the grave peril of their souls and a pernicious example to others. Therefore we suspend the use of the said well and stone and under pain of greater excommunication forbid our people to visit the well and stone for purposes of worship. And we depute to each and all of you and firmly enjoin by virtue of holy obedience, to proclaim publicly in your churches and parishes that they are not to visit the place for such purposes. Given at Wormsley Sept. 22 in the Year aforesaid.

(Robert Mascall, Bishop of Hereford, 1404–1417)

The water cult fared badly during the sixteenth-century Reformation, saints' effigies being removed from wells, some well-chapels being demolished, pilgrimages to wells being prohibited, and offenders being chastised. But the cult was too strong, and survived these attacks, despite their continuation through the seventeenth century. The famous St Winefride's Well at Holywell (Flint) was not immune, and was under threat more than once during that century. The Chief Justice of Chester, Sir John Bridgeman, complained about the great numbers of people who visited the well (on 3 November 1629, St Winefride's Day, around 1500 people assembled there). In 1637 an attempt to stop such gatherings was made by closing the town's inns, disfiguring the saint's statue with whitewash, and taking away the iron posts round the well. But the pilgrims continued to come, including

The chapel and bathing pool at St Winefride's Well, Holywell, Flint

King James II and his queen, who visited Holywell on 29 August 1686 in the hope that Winefride could help them produce a son.

The same attitude towards well worship prevailed throughout England and Wales, as well as in Scotland where the pronouncements of the Kirk Sessions provide a good record of the harassment suffered by pilgrims. An Act of 1581 referred to the people's inclination to superstition,

> . . . through which the dregs of idolatry yet remain in divers parts of the realm by using of pilgrimage to some chapels, wells, crosses, and such other monuments of idolatry, as also by observing of the festal days of the Saints sometime named their patrons in setting forth of bon-fires, singing of carols within and about kirks at certain seasons of the year.

During the sixteenth and seventeenth centuries the Kirk Sessions seem to have been continually fining people or causing them to perform a penance, for the 'crime' of visiting a holy well. For example, at the Kirk Sessions of Culross (Fife) on 16 July 1637:

> Jhon Ker and Jhon Duncan, websters, called for going with Hearie Wannan, he distracted in his wittes, to the chapel in Stuthle [possibly Struthill in Muthil parish, Perthshire], in Strathearne, he confessed, because they wer informed that ther he might recover his health. It was judged a great scandall and offence; and therefor ar ordered to mak ther repentance publicklie before the congregation, and to pay *ad pios usus* each of them half a dollar, and to be imprisoned 24 hours. For this cause an Act was made that whosoever in the parishe should presume to goe to such suspect places for to sek their health, or sould accompanie thos that under sickness to use such suspect means, to be banished the parishe.

The authorities in desperation sometimes resorted to physically destroying the wells, or at least attempting to. The Well of the Virgin Mary at Seggat in Auchterless (Aberdeen) was twice filled with stones by order of the Presbytery of Turriff, but on both occasions the local people cleared it again, and after a fight lasting over four years the authorities gave in, deciding not to 'waire anie more paines on it'. The well continued for at least 150 years as a centre of pilgrimage.

In Ireland it was the rowdiness of the gatherings of pilgrims which seems to have most worried the authorities, though the Church also disapproved of the superstitious practices. In 1704 the Irish Parliament passed an Act forbidding large gatherings of this kind, but they, and the drunkenness and fighting, continued. Indeed, the water cult maintained its following everywhere until towards the end of the nineteenth century, though today it is only in Ireland that many holy wells are still visited by pilgrims with serious intentions.

3. The Healing Powers of Holy Wells

> For the itch, the stitch, rheumatic, and the gout,
> If the devil isn't in you, this well will take it out.

The water cult has throughout the world been closely associated with magical and miraculous healing, from ancient civilisations to the present day. In India, for example, when R. P. Masani was collecting material for his *Folklore of Wells* at the beginning of this century, he found the belief in the healing powers of wells and tanks to be still very strong. The waters were thought to be inhabited by deities, such as the *Vâchharo*, the spirit who cursed hydrophobia, and anyone in Gujarat bitten by a rabid dog should attend one of the wells inhabited by this spirit and empty two earthenware cups each filled with milk and one pice (a coin) into the water, to obtain protection against hydrophobia. Many other ailments were treated in similar ways. In Britain and Ireland most holy wells are considered to have some curative function. Francis Jones noted that over two-thirds of the 1200 Welsh wells he studied were reputedly curative, with some having other powers also; 370 wells were exclusively healing wells. Today very few holy wells are visited by people seeking a cure, as compared with previous centuries, but a hundred years ago the belief in their powers was still strong, as J. Russel Walker found when he was in Queen's Park, Edinburgh.

While walking in the Queen's Park about sunset I casually passed St Anthony's Well, and had my attention attracted by the number of people about it, all simply quenching their thirst, some possibly with a dim idea that they would reap some benefit from the draught. Standing a little apart, however, and evidently patiently waiting a favourable moment to present itself for their purpose, was a group of four. Feeling somewhat curious as to their intentions, I quietly kept myself in the background, and by-and-by was rewarded. The crowd departed and the group came forward, consisting of two old women, a younger woman of about thirty, and a pale sickly-looking girl – a child of three or four years old. Producing cups from their pockets, the old women dipped them in the pool, filled them, and drank their contents. A full cup was then presented to the younger woman, and another to the child; then one of the old women produced a long linen bandage, dipped it in the water, wrung it, dipped it in again, and then wound it round the child's head, covering the eyes; the youngest woman, evidently the mother of the child, carefully observing the operation and weeping gently all the time. The other old woman not engaged in this work was carefully filling a clear flat glass bottle with the water, evidently for future use. Then after the principal operators had looked at each other with an earnest and half-solemn sort of look, the party wended its way carefully down the hill.[1]

An example of present-day usage is quoted by Ruth and Frank Morris in their *Scottish Healing Wells*. In 1978 at the well in the centre of the village of Scotlandwell (Kinross) they met a woman, her husband and brother who had travelled 40 miles from Edinburgh to fetch well water. One of the men had cancer and claimed that the water did him good: 'If it was good enough for Robert the Bruce, it's good enough for me,' he declared, referring to the belief that water from this well cured Robert the Bruce of his leprosy.

Although many wells were reputedly efficacious for any ailment, many others were believed to cure only one specific affliction, as sometimes shown by their names, such as Eye Well, Cholic Well or Gout Well. Our research has revealed at least seventy-five separate illnesses which specific holy wells were thought to relieve, eye problems being cured by the greatest number of wells. From this we might deduce that in earlier centuries eye troubles were more frequent than they are today. 'Sore eyes' (perhaps caused by smoky cottage interiors?) are often specifically mentioned, but never problems like short or long sight, which are more prevalent today. We can also assume that treatment with the water of a holy well must have had some effect, otherwise why would people have continued to frequent holy wells for this purpose over many centuries? Was it simply that bathing the eyes in cold water effected a cure? Or could it be more complex, as suggested by Peter B. G. Binnall, who in an article on eye-wells observed that there are more eye-wells in western districts, in areas of Celtic influence, and he set out several theories involving Christian and mythological beliefs, some of them rather fanciful. The one which seems to us to have most relevance is that the source of a river or stream in Welsh is *Llygad*, or 'eye'. Wells may have been seen as 'the eye of the god', and the link between this and the pilgrim's own eye was easily made. There was also a saying that 'you must not look into running water, because you look into God's eye', which helps to give credibility to the 'eye of the god' theory to explain eye-wells.

This belief, plus the value of cold water bathing for sore eyes, could have combined to ensure that so many holy wells retained their reputation as eye-wells. There is evidence that this reputation is of long standing, and extends to other cultures. One suggestive piece of evidence was the discovery at the Roman site of Wroxeter (Shropshire) of forty plaster eyes, with an average size of two inches. There was also one eye made of sheet gold. In these eyes the pupils and tear ducts were emphasized, and the quantity of eyes discovered suggests that there was a shrine, and possibly also a well, at Wroxeter where cures for eye ailments were sought, 1500 to 2000 years ago. There is also a 2000-year link between the Romans and the present day at the Llandrindod Wells Eye Well (Radnor). There was a local tradition that the Romans used this well; and in 1983 some of the well water was sent to Margaret Thatcher, the British prime minister, to help with a speedy cure of her eye troubles.

Another affliction frequently mentioned in connection with healing wells is infertility, male and female. A number of wells reputedly provided a cure for this problem, and an Aberdeenshire man remembered how, when he was a boy (probably around the mid-nineteenth century), he hid himself in the bushes and watched the women's ritual at a holy well which had 'a power o' nature for married women'.

There were four o' them, the three barren women and the auld auld wife, and they came into the hollow wi' many's a look over their shoulders in case they'd been seen. The auld wife went doun on her knees on the flat stone at the side of the spring and directed the women. First they took off their boots, and syne they took off their hose; and syne they rolled up their skirts and their petticoats till their wames [abdomens] were bare. The auld wife gave them the sign to step round her and away they went, one after the other, wi' the sun, round the spring, each one holding up her coats like she was holding herself to the sun. As each one came anent her, the auld wife took up the water in her hands and threw it on their wames. Never a one cried out at the cold o' the water and never a word was spoken. Three times round they went. The auld wife made a sign to them. They dropped their coats to their feet again, syne they opened their dress frae the neck and slipped it off their shoulders so that their paps sprang out. The auld wife gave them another sign. They doun on their knees afore her, across the spring: and she took up the water in her hands again, skirpit on their paps, three times the three. Then the auld wife rose and the three barren women rose. They put on their claes again and drew their shawls about their faces and left the hollow without a word spoken and scattered across the muir for hame.[2]

It seems perfectly reasonable that people would believe in the efficacy of well water as a cure for infertility, since, as Mircea Eliade states, 'water symbolises the whole of potentiality; it is *fons et origo*, the source of all possible existence'. In mythologies worldwide this theme is present, and from ancient traditions of the primeval waters, whence all worlds were born, such rituals as Christian baptism have survived to the present. St John Chrysostom, fourth-century Greek patriarch and archbishop of Constantinople, wrote of baptism: 'It represents death and burial, life and resurrection . . . When we plunge our head into water as into a tomb, the old man is immersed, wholly buried; when we come out of the water, the new man appears at that moment.'

Perhaps the same intention to purify by immersion was behind the practice of dipping or washing children in holy wells to cure their many ailments. Some wells were used for specific juvenile ailments such as whooping cough and rickets, but in most instances the well was reputed to cure the whole range of children's ailments. Immersion was the process most frequently used, as at Chapel Wells in Kirkmaiden parish (Wigtown), three salt water 'wells' on the shore near the ruined St Medan's Chapel. An eye-witness describes how the 'wells' were still being used in the second half of the nineteenth century:

The child was stripped naked, and taken by the spaul – that is, by one of the legs – and plunged headforemost into the big well till completely submerged; it was then pulled out, and the part held on by was dipped in the middle well, and then the whole body was finished by washing the eyes in the smallest one . . . An offering was then left in the old chapel, on a projecting stone inside the cave behind the west door, and the cure was complete.[3]

This must have been a very traumatic experience for the child, somewhat akin to the immersion 'shock treatment' applied to mad people, but the similarity to the baptismal rite is also clear. Less of a shock to the system, but still an experience never forgotten, was the visit paid to a holy well by a child early in the nineteenth century, here recalling the event in 1876:

I remember, as a child, to have been surreptitiously taken, by an Irish nurse, to St John's Well, Aghada, county Cork, on the vigil of the saint's day, to be cured of whooping cough, by drinking three times of the water of the holy well. I shall never forget the strange spectacle of men and women, creeping on their knees, in voluntary devotion, or in obedience to enjoined penance, so many times round the well, which was protected by a grey stone hood, and had a few white thorn trees growing near it, on the spines of which fluttered innumerable shreds of frieze and varied coloured rags, the votive offerings of devotees and patients.[4]

This well obviously cured adults as well as children, and probably a variety of diseases too, as did many healing wells. Ailments most often named (apart from sore eyes, infertility and childhood illnesses, already mentioned) are warts, scrofula/king's evil, leprosy, skin complaints, rheumatic ailments, mental troubles and toothache. Also curable by specified holy wells was the following wide range of problems: tumours, deafness, lameness, jaundice, fever, headache, stomach problems, ague, epilepsy, ruptures, gout, erysipelas, sprains and swellings, consumption, asthma, scurvy, broken bones, dropsy, paralysis, ulcers, sores and abscesses, gravel, hydrophobia, debility, fits, melancholia, cancer, dyspepsia and indigestion, measles, freckles, wounds, piles, coughs, alcoholism, female complaints, bowel complaints, shortness of breath, bruises, colic, lumbago, diarrhoea, nausea, dumbness, gangrene, inflammation, glandular problems, numbness, itch, polypus, pox, dysentery, spasms, weak back and sinews, wens, and bladder stone.

There were also wells whose water was said to promote your appetite, preserve you from disease, make your hair grow, sweeten your blood, provide you with nourishment, ensure your life, and make you beautiful. With some of these we are definitely entering the realms

St Agnes Well, Humphrey Head, near Grange-over-Sands, Cumbria, at the foot of limestone cliffs on the shore of Morecambe Bay. Its water was believed to be beneficial for rheumatism, gout and bilious complaints, and it was bottled and taken to Morecambe for sale as late as the 1930s

of magic. A well by St Kieran's church at Errigal Keerogue (Tyrone) had miraculous powers indeed: while the church was being built, the workmen used an ox to carry the building materials by day, and in the evening it was slaughtered to feed them. Its bones were thrown each evening into the well, and each morning the ox reappeared, fit and ready for the day's work. Also in Ireland, on Aran Island was a well which would give new life to dead fishes immersed in it.

More realistically, a number of wells were reputed to heal sick animals, mainly cattle and horses. St Agnes fountain at Doulting (Somerset) specifically cured the 'quarter-ail' (cattle paralysis), but not if the cattle were stolen. The water of St Walstan's Well at Bawburgh (Norfolk) was particularly valuable for sick animals, as St Walstan was the patron saint of agricultural workers and sick animals. At one time the water could be bought in the streets of Norwich. A saint was also invoked at a well used to cure sick horses, St George's Well at St George near Abergele (Denbigh). The rich would sacrifice one horse at the well, by this means hoping for the saint's blessing on the rest, which sounds like a pagan rather than a Christian procedure. Horses with distemper were sprinkled with the well water and blessed.

In Ireland a lake in County Mayo, rather than a well, was frequented in order to preserve the health of the livestock. That a lake rather than a well should be chosen is not so strange, and later in this chapter we will give other alternatives to wells which perform the same function. Loughharrow was in the centre of a bog in Bohola parish, and how its water was being used on 'Garland Sunday' in the early nineteenth century is described here.

The people it is said swim their horses in the lake on that day to defend them against incidental evils during the year and throw spancels and halters into it which they leave there on the occasion. They are also accustomed to throw butter into it with the intention that their cows may be sufficiently productive of milk and butter during the year. The *clodime* (lump of butter) thrown in at a time does not be more than a quarter of a pound weight. After the crowds have gone away, the poor who have not the necessaries of life otherwise than by obtaining them by alms from liberal or charitable persons, assemble and carry off as much of the butter as they can gather out of the lake. There was formerly a tree at this place around which the people were in the habit of fastening by a noose, cords (*buracha*) that were used in tying cows. The Roman Catholic bishop of the diocese in which the parish containing the old church and lough is situated, got the tree cut down in order to prevent the people from getting on with such ceremonies. The priests have dissuaded the people from getting on with their ceremonies at the lake so far that they are altogether giving them up. The stations are still practised on the patron day, but the people are ceasing from throwing butter into it; or going on with their other practices at it.[5]

Another commentator reported that

To this lake they bring large pieces of butter, and throw them therein to the saint of the lake, praying him to save their cattle that year. Here they have pipers, and fiddlers, and tents of every description in which whiskey is sold, and they dance round the lake and drink whiskey. Here parties, and families, and parishes, come to fight and quarrel; here all manner of debaucheries are committed, and young people are corrupted. In the end they all bring home bottles of the lake water, and shake it among their cattle; and if any person become sick, some of it is spilled into his ears.[6]

This was a large and popular gathering, well attended despite the attempts of the Church to stop it. Patrick Logan reported that butter was still being thrown into the lake as late as 1950, and the practice may continue yet.

As their cattle and horses were so important to the country people, it is not surprising that they should try to ensure the animals' well-being. There are many other places in Ireland where cattle were sprinkled with, and horses were ridden through, holy water. Other livestock such as sheep and pigs were also blessed at holy wells, and there are some references too to mangy dogs: St Anthony's Well in the Forest of Dean (Gloucester) would cure mangy dogs, as well as humans' skin diseases and sore eyes.

A final story about animal healing demonstrates the strength of the people's faith in the power of the wells. One of the holy wells of the Isle of Man, Chibbyr Baltane, was located in a field at Ballalonney farm, owned by Thomas Moore at the beginning of this century. He wrote:

We had a pony and trap when we were younger . . . The pony got sick and very poor in flesh, so we put the pony in the field where the well was, as we thought to die; but to our surprise the poor pony got very fat and fine looking. He had no grass to eat to make him fat, so that it was altogether the water of the well that made him so fat and well.[7]

Perhaps it was also the lazy life which suited this pony, and perhaps some member of the family was secretly feeding him!

At most wells it was not enough simply to drink the water to effect a cure. The patient must also perform the time-honoured rituals customary for that well. Well rituals in general will be discussed in Chapter 4, but here we will briefly describe a few which specifically relate to healing.

Some wells were only active on a certain day of the year, or at a certain time. Baglan Well (Glamorgan) could only be used on the first

Stone steps
leading down into
the water-filled
stone tank at St
Cybi's Well,
Llangybi,
Caernarfon

three Thursdays in May, one of them being Ascension Day, to cure children with rickets, while in Ireland it was believed that the water in the wells dedicated to St John the Baptist boiled up at midnight on 23 June, and that for the first hour on the 24th (the saint's day) any illness could be cured by it. Sunrise and sunset are times frequently mentioned: the water of a well at Symondsbury (Dorset) should be used just as the sun's rays touch it at sunrise. Two wells near Portpatrick (Wigtown), which were said to cure rickets, should be visited only at the change of the moon. Such beliefs carry echoes of pagan practices, but at other wells the influence is definitely Christian: St Maughold's Well (Isle of Man) 'had its full virtue only when visited on the first Sunday of harvest, and then only during the hour the books were open at church' (ie when the priest was saying Mass).

Being at the well at the correct time was not enough; there were special ways in which the water must be used. At some wells bathing was the custom, by total or partial immersion, and stone tanks with steps leading into the water were often built for that purpose. Elsewhere it was sufficient simply to wash the wound or afflicted part, or just to drink the water. At some Welsh wells the water must be drunk from a skull, while in Scotland the water of the Whooping Cough Well at Balquhidder (Perth) should be drunk from a spoon made from the horn of a living cow. This was not an uncommon practice, and maybe it was felt that the life-force of the animal would be absorbed by the patient along with the water. The patient had sometimes to say special words, either a recognisable religious formula or an incantation whose meaning is now indecipherable, such as the words spoken at Ffynnon Fair, Rhaeadr (Radnor):

> Frimpanfroo, frimpanfroo,
> Sali bwli la
> Iri a.

Patients might also have to walk round the well a certain number of times, and perhaps visit other nearby places such as a standing stone or a chapel or church. Sometimes the cure could only be completed by sitting in the saint's chair and trying to sleep there, as at Canna's Well, Llangan (Carmarthen), where the cure for ague and intestinal complaints included sleeping on the stone known as Canna's Chair. Elsewhere the patient had to sleep in the nearby chapel or church, or at a neighbouring farmhouse. At some wells, especially in Scotland, there were special healing stones at or in the wells, small stones which had to be touched as part of the ritual. Sometimes they resembled parts of the human body and were known as the 'ee-stehn' or 'heidstehn', the afflicted part being rubbed with the appropriate stone. A spring in a graveyard beside Loch Torridon (Ross & Cromarty) was said to contain three stones which continually whirled round the well. To obtain a cure, one of the stones was carried in a bucket of water to the patient, who had to touch the stone, which was then returned to the well where it again began to whirl. But when one of the stones was used to cure a goat, it sank to the bottom of the well on its return and remained motionless.

Holy wells often have trees close to them, and sometimes these are vital to the healing process. At Easter Rarichie (Ross & Cromarty) the spring known as Sul na Ba (the cow's eye) originally flowed through a tree trunk, but later moved its position because it was insulted. Also at Easter Rarichie was the Well of the Yew which cured the 'white swelling' so long as the tree stood beside it. When the tree was cut down, the well lost its power. Some healing 'wells' were actually water-filled tree stumps, of which there were several in Ireland.

At the majority of wells it was customary to leave an offering of some kind, usually a pin, a pebble or a piece of clothing fastened to a tree. The patients probably expected that as the cloth rotted, so the illness would fade. A variation of this was practised at the Chink Well at Portrane (Dublin). This was a freshwater well by the shore, which was covered by salt water at high tide. Pilgrims seeking a cure would leave a piece of bread on the edge of the well, and if the tide took the bread, the illness would go along with it. This important aspect of well ritual will be given fuller treatment in the following chapter. Meanwhile, to demonstrate the importance of ritual at healing wells we will describe the complete process which had to be performed at several wells. First to the island of Lewis (Outer Hebrides), where St Ronan's Well near the Butt of Lewis was considered able to cure insanity. The patient must first walk seven times round the nearby ruined Temple of St Molochus (Teampull Mòr or Great Temple). Water was then brought from the well in a special jar which was kept in the hereditary custody of one family. The water was sprinkled on the patient, who then had to lie on the place in the chapel where the altar once stood. If he slept well, his recovery was assured. In rituals such as this we see a strange mixture of pagan and Christian practices. But this cure for madness is mild compared with the procedure at some other wells. In his *Survey of Cornwall* (1602) Richard Carew, the sixteenth/seven-teenth-century Cornish antiquary, describes how St Nun's Well at Altarnon was used as a 'bowssening' well for the cure of madness:

The water running from St Nunne's Well fell into a square and close-walled plot, which might bee filled at what depth they listed. Upon this wall was the franticke person set to stand, his backe towards the poole; and from thence, with a sudden blow in the brest, tumbled headlong into the pond, where a strong fellow, provided for the nonce, tooke him and tossed him and tossed him, up and downe, alongst and athwart the water, until the patient, by forgoing his strength, had somewhat forgot his fury. Then was hee conveyed to the church, and certaine masses sung over him; upon which handling, if his right wits returned, St Nunne had the thanks; but, if there appeared small amendment, he was bowssened againe, and againe, while there remayned in him any hope of life for recovery.

Similar cruelty was practised at other wells, and the description 'kill or cure' seems appropriate. On reflection we are no more successful, or kinder, in our treatment of insanity four hundred years later – electric-shock treatment, drug therapy and incarceration having taken the place of bowssening, but a humane and successful cure still eludes us.

Epilepsy is another baffling affliction which merited a complex ritual at Ffynnon Degla, Llandegla (Denbigh). The patient had to visit the well on a Friday after sunset; wash his hands and feet in the water; walk three times round the well, carrying a cock in a basket and saying the Lord's Prayer three times; prick the cock with a pin and throw the pin into the well; give a groat to the parish clerk at the well; walk three times round Llandegla church, again carrying the cock and repeating the Lord's Prayer; enter the church and put a groat in the Poor Box; lie down under the Communion Table with his head on the Bible and covered by a carpet, until daybreak; blow into the cock's beak to transfer the disease to the bird; place some silver in the Poor Box; leave the cock in the church (if it died there the patient was cured); revisit the well and walk round three times more, saying the Lord's Prayer as before. Francis·Jones comments that 'at Ffynnon Degla we are in the presence of stark paganism'. He also adds that the cock has been associated with epilepsy in other places and at other times, one being sacrificed against the illness in Scotland as recently as this century.

The people who visited holy wells in the hope of a cure clearly believed that the wells had the power to cure, and the long survival of holy wells demonstrates the strength of this belief. Successful cures reinforced the belief, being remembered, retold, and sometimes recorded. The famous St Winefride's Well at Holywell (Flint) has seen many cures. In 1606 Sir Roger Bodenham visited the well and obtained instant relief from a painful disease of the feet, after every known medical remedy had been tried. In the nineteenth century a pamphlet was published entitled 'Authentic Documents relative to the Miraculous Cure of Winefred White, of Wolverhampton, at St Winefred's Well, alias Holy well, in Flintshire, on 28 June, 1805, with Observations thereon', describing how a paralysed servant girl was cured after a pilgrimage to the well. More recent cures are recorded in the Catholic press from time to time, as in 1916 when Scotsman John MacMullan's cure of a chronic spinal disease was reported in the *Catholic Times and Catholic Opinion*. However, not all pilgrims to Holywell have left cured, the unfortunate Sir George Peckham having actually died at the well. According to an account of his life, he had 'continued so long mumbling his paternosters and *Sancta Winifreda ora pro me*, that the cold struck into his body and after his coming forth of that well he never spoke more.'

The number of cures recorded for St Winefride's Well may simply reflect its great popularity over many centuries. Other wells have their notable success stories, sometimes attested to by friends and relations, sometimes by more famous and independent witnesses. In Ireland, a mother's faith in St Brigit was recorded at Burren (Galway) by Lady Gregory at the turn of the century:

I brought my little girl that was not four years old to Saint Brigit's well on the cliffs, where she was ailing and pining away. I brought her as far as the doctors in Gort and they could do nothing for her and then I promised to go to Saint Brigit's well, and from the time I made that promise she got better. And I saw the little fish when I brought her there; and she grew to be as strong a girl as ever went to America. I made a promise to go to the well every year after that, and so I do, of a Garlic Sunday, that is the last Sunday in July. And I brought a bottle of water from it last year and it is as cold as amber yet.[8]

Jesus Well at St Minver (Cornwall) cured a woman of erysipelas in 1867, as she told the authors of *Ancient and Holy Wells of Cornwall*. Orthodox medical treatment having had no effect on her long-standing complaint, she began to bathe the diseased parts regularly in the well, also reciting the 'Litany to the Holy Name of Jesus'. Her affliction disappeared and never returned.

The Reverend Elias Owen, who diligently researched and recorded the holy wells of north and mid Wales at the end of the nineteenth century, noted two cures from the middle of the last century which were related to him by participants. When visiting his brother who was vicar of Llangoed on Anglesey, he was introduced to a gentleman farmer who told them that many years before he had gone to St Seiriol's Well, Penmon, at dead of night to fetch water for a friend who appeared to be dying. On drinking the water, the sick man revived and was soon completely cured, being still hale and hearty forty years later. The Reverend Owen also heard of a cure received at Ffynnon Arthur in the parish of Llanfihangel Ynghwnfa (Montgomery), a well famous for curing bruises. This informant's brother had hurt his leg playing football, and the flesh had wasted away. After two or three years, as a last resort he began to bathe daily in the holy well, and received a complete cure. The Reverend Owen saw the man: 'he was as straight as an arrow, and appeared as strong and healthy as any mountaineer. He firmly believed in the efficacy of the water, and told us all about his wonderful cure.' He explained that he had not tried the well water sooner because 'it had already waned in reputation, and it was considered superstitious to frequent it for health's sake.'

In 1640, an impressive cure at Madron Well (Cornwall) was vouched for by a bishop. The patient was John Trelille, who had been crippled for sixteen years following an accident. When he reached the age of twenty-eight he dreamed that if he bathed in Madron Well or the stream running from it, he would recover his strength. He resolved to make the effort to test his dream, and so, according to one account of the miracle,

. . . thither he crept, and lying before the altar, and praying very fervently that he might regain his health and the strength of his limbs, he washed his whole body in the stream that flowed from the well and ran through the chapel. After which, having slept for one hour and a half in St Maderne's bed, through the extremity of the pain he felt in his nerves and arteries, he began to cry out, and his companions helping him and lifting him up, he perceived his limbs and joints somewhat expanded, and himself become stronger, insomuch that partly with his hands he went more erect than before. Before the following Thursday he got two crutches, resting on which he would make a shift to walk, which before he could not do; and coming to the chapel as before, after having bathed himself, he slept on the same bed, and awakening, found himself much stronger and more upright; and so, leaving one crutch in the chapel he went home with the other. The third Thursday he returned to the chapel, and bathed as before, slept, and when he awoke rose up quite cured; yea, grew so strong that he wrought day-labour among other hired servants; and four years after listed himself as a soldier in the king's army, where he behaved himself with great stoutness both of mind and body; at length in 1644 he was slain at Lyme in Dorsetshire.[9]

Bishop Hall of Exeter visited Madron and saw John Trelille for himself: 'besides the attestation of many hundreds of the neighbours, I saw him able to walk and get his own maintenance. I took strict and impartial examination in my last triennial visitation. I found neither art nor collusion, the cure done, the author an invisible God.'[10]

The few cures we have recorded could be multiplied many times over, many of them experienced by people who had failed to find relief through conventional medical treatment. If a story from Scotland is to be believed, the success of one holy well, St Drostan's at Newdosk (Angus), was so distasteful to the local doctors that they decided to poison the well. When the people heard of their intention, they banded together to attack and kill the doctors!

Nowadays doctors need no longer fear competition from holy wells, since in most quarters the idea that a cure could be obtained merely by drinking some special water would be regarded as superstitious nonsense. Nevertheless, cures continue to happen, and some are recorded in the press. In 1981 we read of a newly discovered well in Dunoon (Argyll) which, it is claimed, has helped rheumatism, arthritis, migraine, and other ailments. In 1982 a press report told of a grandmother who became a 'new woman' after drinking the water of a well near her Sheffield home. In 1974 Mrs Joyce Baddon was crippled with arthritis and a spinal disease, unable to walk and having to wear a special corset and collar. The pain she suffered was only temporarily relieved by drugs. She said:

At first I was sceptical about the water, but I was willing to try anything. I had to climb the stairs on my hands and knees. In the early hours I would lie awake, the pain in my back as fierce as toothache. Specialists told me there was no permanent cure, only relief through drugs and physiotherapy. I was determined not to live a life like that. So I put away the corset and collar they gave me and went to the well. After drinking the water several times a day for two weeks the pain was only half as severe. Gradually it lessened until within three years I was as fit as a fiddle. I no longer take the water regularly, but always keep a reserve at home. Although the water smells horrible, it tastes quite normal.[11]

Her husband added: 'It is hard to believe she is the same woman. Something in the water had a miraculous effect on her. Now she has the energy of a youngster, studies until two am, and is often up and about by seven.' Mrs Baddon plays squash and tennis, as well as going jogging and horseriding. She has started an Open University degree course, and plays bit parts on films and television. The water that wrought Mrs Baddon's miracle cure came from a well under an old millstone between the hamlet of Gunthwaite and the village of Ingbirchworth near Barnsley (South Yorkshire).

There can be little doubt that people do sometimes find cures at healing wells. What brings about the cure is not easy to decide, but there seem to be two possibilities:

1. the water does contain something which acts upon the body; or
2. the patient's own intrinsic healing abilities are stimulated by visiting the well.

If the water really does have a physical effect, the question immediately arises as to how the people who first used the wells knew or discovered which disease or diseases any particular water source would cure. Was this learned over a period of time, by trial and error, or did they somehow know instinctively? The very same problem exists with herbalism: how did the original herbalists know which plant (and which part of the plant) to use to treat any specific ailment? If we accept that ancient, 'uncivilised', people lived much closer to nature than we do in the twentieth century, we may also find it conceivable that their greater sensitivity to the life force in all its manifestations was sufficient for them to select the right plants by instinct. This is not impossible, since animals normally use and avoid plants instinctively. So the same principle might also have been applied to water sources.

However, as we have seen, the use of water from wells and springs has from the earliest times been closely linked with various religious practices, and as a result has acquired all manner of symbolism and ritual, which can hardly avoid influencing the susceptible pilgrim. The well was a holy place, frequented by the pagan deity or Christian saint (often virtually the same so far as the pilgrim or patient was concerned), and the water would naturally therefore have miraculous properties. Thus a patient visiting the well in search of a cure would be in a susceptible frame of mind, and his concentration on the purpose of the visit would be further reinforced by the careful performance of the well's rituals, which as we have shown could be very complex. These are the ideal circumstances for the body's own self-healing powers to be stimulated, and it is hardly surprising that cures were often reported.

By thus explaining how holy wells might operate, we do not intend to 'explain away' or diminish this kind of cure. On the contrary, we believe it has lessons for the present-day doctor and patient. Current research indicates that many of today's illnesses are stress-induced, often coming about as the body's reaction to an unbalanced lifestyle, and experiments have shown that there are ways of stimulating the body to heal itself without involving drastic methods such as surgery or drugs, the latter treatment very often causing other problems even more severe than the original disease. In particular, experiments involving the placebo effect have shown that patients who believe they are taking a highly effective drug, when in fact they are only taking a dummy pill, can often be cured more effectively than those patients taking real drugs. The parallel here with the pilgrim at the holy well, who believes a draught of the water will cure him or her, is obvious. This type of cure was belittled by sceptics, as shown in the following instance, probably dating from the eighteenth century. The final sentence demonstrates that such cures were not necessarily lasting, especially if, as in this case, the patient's faith was in any way damaged, and the conditions which brought about the illness in the first place remained unchanged.

I was myself a witness of the powerful workings of imagination in the populace, when the waters of Glastonbury were at the height of their reputation. The virtues of the spring there were supposed to be supernatural, and to have been discovered by a dream to one Matthew Chancellor. The people did not only expect to be cured of such distempers as were in their nature incurable, but even to recover their lost eyes, and their mutilated limbs. The following story, which scarce exceeds what I observed upon the spot, was told me by a gentleman of character. 'An old woman in the workhouse at Yeovil, who had long been a cripple, and made use of crutches, was strongly inclined to drink of the Glastonbury waters, which she was assured would cure her of her lameness. The master of the workhouse procured her several bottles of water; which had such an effect, that she soon laid aside one crutch, and not long after the other. This was extolled as a miraculous cure; but the man protested to his friends that he had imposed upon her, and fetched the water from an ordinary spring.' I need not inform the reader, that when the force of imagination had spent itself, she relapsed into her former infirmity.[12]

The healing procedure need not be, and indeed was not, confined to holy wells. If the conditions of belief and ritual were present, any water source could be effective. A number of lakes in the north and west were credited with healing powers, such as Loch Sianta in the north of Skye (Inverness); Halie Loch, Loch Heilen and St John's Loch, all near Dunnet (Caithness); Dow or Dhu Loch (Dumfries); St Tredwell's Loch in Papa Westray (Orkney); and the most often mentioned healing loch in Scotland, Loch Monaar/mo Naire/Manaar in Strathnaver (Sutherland), which traditionally gained its power from a white stone possessed by an old woman. When one of the Gordons of Strathnaver tried to steal it, she resisted and he tried to drown her in the loch. She threw in her magic stone, crying 'May it do good to all created things save a Gordon of Strathnaver!'. As he stoned her to death, she cried 'Manaar! Manaar!' (Shame!), hence the loch's name. The beliefs and practices relating to the loch show no difference from those at a holy well. It is especially efficacious on the first Monday of February, May, August and November (Old Style), and pilgrims travelled great distances, even from as far as Orkney and Inverness, seeking a cure, as late as the end of the nineteenth century. The gathering on 12 August 1877 (Lammas, Old Style) is here described by an eye-witness.

The impotent, the halt, the lunatic, and the tender infant were all waiting about midnight for an immersion in Loch Monaar . . . the night was dark, so dark that one could not recognise a friend or foe, but by close contact and speech. About fifty persons all told were present near one spot, and I believe other parts of the loch were similarly occupied, but I cannot vouch for this – only I heard voices which would lead me so to infer. About twelve stripped, and walked into the loch, performing their ablutions about three times. Those who were not able to act for themselves were assisted, some of them being led willingly, others by force, for there were cases of each kind. One young woman, strictly guarded, was an object of great pity. She raved in a distressing manner, repeating religious phrases, some of which were very earnest and pathetic. She prayed her guardians not to immerse her, saying it was not a Communion occasion, asking if they could call this righteousness or faithfulness or if they could compare the loch to the right arm of Christ. These utterances were enough to move any person hearing them. Poor girl! What possible good could immersion do her? . . . I may add that the practice of dipping in the loch is said to have been carried on from time immemorial, and it is alleged that many cures have been effected by it.[13]

In Wales several lakes include the word 'Ffynnon' in their name, showing that they were once thought to have the same powers as holy wells. Llyn Ffynnon Lloer (Caernarfon) was one such, where people gathered to dance at sunrise on May Day. The Irish Loughharrow has already been described. Other holy lakes in Ireland were Loughaneeg (Roscommon) where children wasting away in a decline were bathed, Loughanleagh (Cavan) which cured skin diseases by application of the water and mud poultices, and the sacred lake of Loughadrine (Cork), which cured all manner of diseases. This lake was visited on several days in the year, the pilgrims throwing bread and biscuits into the water as offerings to the holy fishes, and rags were tied on the surrounding bushes. The clergy objected to the pilgrimages and the accompanying revelry, and brought the visits to an end.

Certain pools in streams or rivers were thought to have healing powers, such as, in rural Scotland, river pools under a bridge leading to a churchyard – 'the bridge over which the dead and the living pass'. Water from these pools was used to cure illnesses brought on by the influence of the 'evil eye', being taken to the patient in a wooden ladle into which a piece of silver was dropped. After recitation of a charm, three sips were drunk by the patient, the rest of the water being sprinkled round him and his fireside. This procedure was experienced when he was a child by the folklore writer Donald A. Mackenzie about a hundred years ago. A pool in the stream known as Fillan Water (near Tyndrum, Perth) was used in a healing ritual, the patient going three times round the pool and then being immersed before spending some time bound inside St Fillan's church nearby. If he escaped from his bonds before morning, he would recover.

Some waterfalls also have healing powers, such as Pistyll Brido near Old Colwyn (Denbigh), where the grandfather of the folklorist T. Gwynn Jones remembered holding his sprained ankle under the fall. He also told of other cures sought there. On Skye (Inverness), a

The Wart Well at Dungiven, County Londonderry, in a bullaun and surrounded by rags (photo 1970s)

waterfall at Scorrybreck has below it a rock trough where a girl was said to have been cured of leprosy. She lay in the trough after it was emptied, and stayed there until it filled again. Water in stone containers of many kinds was held to be curative. St Wallach's Bath near Edinglassie (Aberdeen) was a deep rock cavity close by the river, filled from a spring, where children were bathed. On the Isle of Man an unusual rock container was a sarcophagus in the cemetery of St Maughold's church. This was continually filled with water from a spring. The water was 'sweet to the draught, wholesome to the taste, and it healed divers infirmities . . . whosoever drinketh thereof, either receiveth instant health, or instantly he dieth.' A rock basin in the floor of a cave near Campbeltown (Argyll) was kept filled by drops from the cave roof, and was known as St Kieran's font or holy well, as the saint was said to have lived in the cave. A similar basin in a cave near Sanna, Ardnamurchan (Inverness), was frequented by people seeking the water which was reputed to make you happy and strong. In two instances the dripping water was not caught by a basin but by the patient. The Dripping Well at Craigiehowe (Ross & Cromarty) was a cure for deafness. The patient would lie down on the floor of the cave and let the water from the roof drip into first one ear and then the other. The 'dropping cave' in Kirkmaiden parish (Wigtown) was known as Peter's Paps, and sufferers with whooping cough would stand, face upturned, below the drips, letting the water fall into the open mouth.

Where water held in a rock basin was sought for a cure, the basin tended to be fairly small. Sometimes these basins were fed by springs, sometimes they had no visible water supply but remained filled with water nonetheless. In Wales, Ffynnon y Cythraul, the Devil's Well, near Llanfihangel-y-Pennant (Caernarfon), was a rock basin one foot deep, always filled with water but with no apparent water supply. It was used as a cure for weak eyes and warts. Warts were also said to be cured by the water in Irish rock basins, known as bullauns, these being hollows in a stone, often several hollows together in one stone, and usually found near old churches or monasteries. No one knows why they were made, but suggestions include primitive baptismal fonts, mortars for grinding grain, and oil lamps. The Deer Stone at Glenda-lough (Wicklow) should be visited by the patient on Sunday, Tuesday and Thursday in the same week, and each time he or she must go round it seven times on bare knees.

In all the healing waters so far described, the water for the cure has come from a special place. There are also cures to be had from water from no particular source, but the water has been sanctified or rendered curative by having a certain object dipped in it. Special stones were often used for this purpose, and the practice is of great antiquity, not just in Britain. Pebbles known as charm-stones were used in Scotland. These could heal without being immersed in water, but their power could also be transferred to water by immersion. One famous charm stone was the Lee Penny, a dark red, semi-transparent gem set in a silver coin. It was kept at Lee, a house near Lanark, and was believed to have the power to cure most ailments, but especially hydrophobia. When Lady Baird of Saughton Hall had the symptoms of rabies at the beginning of the eighteenth century, she sent for the Lee Penny and drank and bathed in water in which it had been dipped, the result being a cure. Like many other such amulets, it was also used to cure cattle, and phials containing water in which it had been dipped were hung in the cattle byres. Amulets were used in the same way in Ireland, and the Irish also had great faith in water in which shreds of old Irish manuscripts had been soaked. For centuries sacred relics have been immersed in water, as for example a piece of King Oswald's Cross which was used to sanctify water then given to cure human or animal ailments among the Saxons. But the Scots went one better: they used an actual piece of a saint. St Marnan or Marnoch was a seventh-century missionary in Banff, and after his death his head was kept as a sacred relic in the church of Aberchirder. Periodically, so it is said, it was washed and the water taken by the sick.

Undoubtedly the cures were largely caused by suggestion, the same effect described earlier in relation to healing wells. In the case of cattle which could not be aware of the associations of the relics or amulets, it could be that their owners, in the expectation of a cure, were influenced to take greater care of their beasts.

In the seventeenth and eighteenth centuries water had a new lease of life as a healing medium when mineral springs and spas became fashionable. While the holy wells appealed to the simple country folk, the spas were patronised by the gentry. As the demand grew, more and more mineral springs were discovered and developed, some of them experiencing only short-lived fame, others becoming major resorts. The therapeutic waters usually fall into one of three main groups: the saline waters with dissolved salts such as magnesium sulphate, and used for inflammatory and congestive disorders such as dropsy, gout and liver complaints; the chalybeate waters with their reddish colour and iron taste, which contain iron salts and were considered to have tonic and restorative powers, being used to treat anaemia and many other ailments; and the sulphur waters which were used as a bath for skin complaints and rheumatism and arthritis (as hot baths), as well as being drunk.

It is very likely, of course, that the water of the traditional healing wells often had the same therapeutic composition as the water so

St Ann's Well,
Great Malvern,
Hereford &
Worcester, high
up in the Malvern
Hills

enthusiastically sought at the spas. Eighteenth-century antiquarians of a scientific bent interested themselves in the analysis of holy well water in order to find how cures were effected. For example, Dr Borlase wrote of the well of Colurian in Ludgvan parish, in his *Natural History of Cornwall* (1758):

In the morning before the water is stirred there is a skin or film on the surface, of a rainbow colour, shooting to and fro, by which it may be presumed that there is sulphur or naphtha mixed with this water, which rises and settles on the top. In a calm but not very warm morning on 7th August, 1734, before six o'clock, I found the water, both in the enclosed well and without where it ran exposed to the air, almost blood warm, and the common water, which runs nine feet from the chalybeate, as cold as snow . . . by which it is to be concluded that the chalybeate spring derives a sensible heat from the bed of iron, vitriol, and pyrites, which it passes through. Two persons, of which I have sufficient proof, by drinking and washing the part affected, have been cured of king's evil.

In some places the water source was both holy well and spa. This is still clearly shown at Malvern (Hereford & Worcester), which in the eighteenth and nineteenth centuries became a famous and prosperous hydropathic centre. Its surviving grand architecture recalls its heyday; while two of the holy wells which began its reputation can still be visited. The water from the holy well at Little Malvern, and the eye-well close by, was bottled from 1622 onwards as the fame of the wells increased. In the eighteenth century Dr John Wall analysed the water of these and St Ann's Well at Great Malvern not far away and concluded that 'the efficacy of this water seems chiefly to arise from its great purity'. A bath house was built at the Little Malvern holy well in

1757, and accommodation for the many visitors. By 1820 the centre of the water cure had moved to St Ann's Well, and a small bath and pump room extension were added to the well-house. The next sixty years were the boom years for Malvern, but by the end of the century the spa craze was finished. A similar pattern of development and decline took place elsewhere, though a few of the major spas still provide treatment facilities, and at others the surviving buildings are being restored as interest in their history grows.

Spa centres worth visiting include Bath (which was the Roman town of Aquae Sulis; here the Romans built the first baths round the shrine of the goddess about AD 76); Tunbridge Wells (whose chalybeate spring was discovered in 1606); Buxton (another Roman site, Aquae Arnemetiae, though neither of the two Roman baths survives); Cheltenham (whose flagging reputation was boosted in 1788 by a visit from King George III and his family); Leamington Spa (whose impressive Royal Pump Room of 1814 still survives); Harrogate (whose Tewit Well, discovered in 1571, began its fame; by 1900 over 90 mineral springs were known in a small area, and today many spa period buildings survive); Malvern (with two holy wells, many interesting buildings and beautiful scenery); and Llandrindod Wells (another town of grand spa architecture and recent revival of spa buildings). There are many other spas in Britain where springs and wells, and the great buildings that grew up round them, can still be seen, and prospective spa visitors should not begin their travels without a copy of Kathleen Denbigh's *A Hundred British Spas* to guide them.

4. Pilgrimages, Rituals and Gifts

Although many wells could be visited at any time, a considerable proportion were believed to be at their most potent on one special day in the year. The first Sunday in August was popular, or 1 August (Lammas) or 12 August (Lammas Old Style). There is some evidence from the days chosen that the custom of visiting a well on a certain day may be a relic of the ancient water cult. For example, the Christian festival of Lammas (Old English *Hlâf-mæsse*, loaf mass) coincides with the Celtic festival of Lugnasad, a seasonal festival in honour of the god Lugh. Here and elsewhere in the year, the Christians placed their festivals at times already held sacred by the people, and perhaps this was part of their strategy to absorb the old religious practices rather than displace them. So the well-visiting days often coincide with both Christian and pagan festivals. Other popular days were 1 May (the Celtic Beltane, 12 May Old Style) or the first Sunday in May, 1 February (Imbolc) and 1 November (Samhain), though these two winter dates were not so popular as the summer ones; also popular was 24 June (Midsummer and St John the Baptist's Day), and saints' days.

These annual gatherings were very well attended, even though they were often held early in the morning; the time was as important as the

The holy well at Macroom, County Limerick, decorated on the saint's day (photo 1955)

date. One such gathering, representative of many others, was on the first Sunday in May at Craigie Well in Ross & Cromarty's Black Isle, and a nineteenth-century witness wrote:

I arrived about an hour before sunrise, but long before, crowds of lads and lasses from all quarters were fast pouring in. Some, indeed, were there at daybreak who had journeyed more than seven miles. Before the sun made his appearance, the whole scene looked more like a fair than anything else. Acquaintances shook hands in true Highland style, brother met brother, and sister met sister, while laughter and all kinds of country news and gossip were so freely indulged in, that a person could hardly hear what he himself said.[1]

The people also remembered to drink from the well, and they each left a thread or a piece of cloth on the briar beside the well.

At some wells the annual gathering remained popular into the twentieth century, as at Culloden Well (Inverness), a press report here describing the event in 1934.

The practice of visiting Culloden Well on the first Sunday in May, judging by the number of pilgrims who made the journey yesterday, is growing despite declamation and the protests of Highland ministers. It is an age-old custom in the Highlands, and has been described as pagan and superstitious. Buses heavily laden were run from Inverness almost every hour yesterday, and there were motoring parties from all parts of the North. Most of the visitors had a drink from the well and observed the old custom of dropping a coin into the well and silently expressing a wish for good luck in the future. Others placed a piece of cloth on the adjoining trees, also an ancient custom which has given to the spring the name of Cloutie Well. County policemen regulate the traffic, and the money dropped into the well [on this occasion about £24] is distributed among Highland charities.[2]

As the two preceding quotations show, the gatherings often had the atmosphere of a holiday rather than of a religious occasion. The gathering was often the excuse for a fair or wake, and the Reverend J.E. Vize's description, written in 1884, of what used to happen in the parish of Forden (Montgomery) is typical of events elsewhere.

The Sunday well used to be considered a great day in the parish. On the first Sunday after Trinity people used to assemble from the adjoining villages in great numbers at a well in King's wood. The well water was said to be very good in taste, as it is now. The folks used to drink it either pure, or with a little sugar in it. Tables were taken to the place, from which buns, cakes, and other things might be purchased. After due time the people used to go to the 'Cock Inn' for amusements. These were various, and included ball-playing, gambling, dancing, and similar sports. Sometimes men became angry with each other as the beer was consumed. Men stripped themselves to fight each other. One of my informants well remembers seeing fourteen men stand up to fight at one time.[3]

As might be imagined, such goings-on were not generally approved of by the Church, and in at least one instance the fair was stopped. The Reverend J. Wilson describes the fair which used to be held at St Cuthbert's Well in Bromfield parish (Cumbria).

It formerly was the custom for the youth of all the neighbouring villages to assemble at this well early in the afternoon of the second Sunday in May, and there to join in a variety of rural sports. It was the village wake, and took place here, it is possible, when the keeping of wakes and fairs in the churchyard was discontinued. And it differed from the wakes of later times chiefly in this, that no strong drink of any kind was ever seen there, nor anything ever drunk but the beverage furnished by the Naiad of the place. A curate of the parish, about twenty years ago, on the idea that it was a profanation of the Sabbath, saw fit to set his face against it; and having deservedly great influence in the parish, the meetings at Helly-Well have ever since been discontinued.[4]

It seems somewhat unfair that this apparently harmless gathering was stopped, when the men did not even consume alcohol there, in contrast to the wake at Forden, and elsewhere. The Church's dis-approval of the gatherings called patterns or patrons (ie a gathering in honour of the patron saint) at holy wells and other sacred places in Ireland is perhaps more justified, in view of the amount of violence that often occurred. One eye-witness reported that

... it seems more like the celebration of the orgies of Bacchus, than the memory of a pious saint, from the drunken quarrels and obscenities practised on these occasions. So little is there of devotion, or amendment of life or manners, that these places are frequently chosen for the scenes of pitched battles, fought with cudgels, by parties, not only of parishes, but of counties, set in formal array against each other, to revenge some real or supposed injury, and murders are not an unusual result of these meetings.

It is hard to believe that many of those who took part in the fighting had originally gone in a spirit of pilgrimage to a holy well. But very often the two went together, at least in Ireland, and a seriously intended pilgrimage was often followed by boisterous and aggressive behaviour. Dr Patrick Logan, who has made a modern study of Irish pilgrimages, commented: 'Pilgrims in any age are not noted for their piety, the *Canterbury Tales* make that clear, but anyone who has ever gone on a pilgrimage knows it is a memorable and enjoyable experience – something which is part of the nature of man. These days pilgrims may be called tourists.' Some pilgrimages were completely serious, of course. People seeking cures or other favours would make a pilgrimage to a holy well alone or in small groups with no thought of merry-making. Sometimes a large group of people would make a pilgrimage for a special reason, as in 1913 when 300 to 400 people from a religious community undertook a pilgrimage to St Walstan's Well at Bawburgh (Norfolk) to give thanks for the miraculous cure of one of their companions who had had his eyesight restored by the use of water and moss from the well. The pilgrims gathered at a distance from the well in order to remove their shoes and make the final part of the pilgrimage barefoot. After their thanksgiving, most of them drank from the well, and many took away water in bottles.

When a holy well's 'special day' came round, it was quite common for the people to decorate the well with flowers and greenery. We have seen references to this happening in Scotland – St Margaret's Well, Dunfermline (Fife), was decorated every 20 July, the saint's day, until 1649, when the Kirk Sessions stopped the 'holywell annals' at this and other wells – Northumberland, the Lake District, Staffordshire, Cheshire (where the salt springs or brine pits were decorated and blessed), Derbyshire, Shropshire, Worcestershire (at St Richard's Well, Droitwich, another salt-well), Gloucestershire, Hertfordshire, Devon, the Isle of Wight, and Wales. Today the only well-dressing area that most people have heard of is Derbyshire, where the custom still thrives. The colourful scenes and designs painstakingly created from petals and other natural objects are usually on a religious theme, and are worth seeing, especially at the most famous locations such as Tissington, Tideswell, Buxton and Youlgreave. The elaborate well-dressings of today are a relatively recent development, the wells previously being decorated with simple garlands of flowers and green branches. In the Glamorgan and Carmarthen areas of Wales, the people would throw flowers on the grass, stones and bushes around the wells when they went to draw water on Easter Monday. In Diserth parish (Radnor), mistletoe was used to decorate the well on New

A crowd of pilgrims gathers at St Columcille's Well, Rosaveel, County Galway (photo probably late 1940s)

Well-dressing at
Tideswell,
Derbyshire

Year's Day. Apart from the well-known Derbyshire locations, well-dressing is still also practised at Endon and Newborough in Staffordshire, at Bisley in Gloucestershire, and has recently been introduced at Midgley near Halifax in West Yorkshire and at Holywell in Cambridgeshire. It probably also occurs at other places, of which we have not heard.

Another once-popular custom on the well's 'special day' was to mix sugar with the well water before drinking it. This has already been mentioned in relation to Forden (Montgomery) on the Wales/Shropshire border, where this took place at a group of Trinity Wells in the area. Often the young people would meet at these wells to 'plight their troth', drinking the sugared water from the same cup. But the sugared water custom also happened elsewhere in Britain, including the English Midlands and West Yorkshire, where Palm Sunday or Spanish Sunday was the appropriate day. A sweetener (brown sugar, Spanish liquorice, peppermint, or sweets) was broken up and mixed with a little tap water the night before, and then on the Sunday the children, for it was largely a children's custom, would go to the nearest holy well and walk round it the traditional number of times before filling their containers with well water. After vigorous shaking the sweetened water was ready to drink.

We have seen in the previous chapter that visits to holy wells were often accompanied by the performance of rituals, sometimes simple, sometimes very complex. The most complex are recorded from those areas where the well cult has survived the longest – Scotland and, especially, Ireland – and it is possible that similar complex rituals were once performed at English and Welsh holy wells, but were eventually forgotten before being recorded. The rituals were composed of all or several of the following elements: praying at the well, walking sunwise round the well, drinking the water, bathing parts of the body with the water, using any special healing stones at the well, hanging a rag on a tree or bush by the well, dropping a pin or other small object into the water, and perhaps also walking round adjacent trees, stones, and buildings. The following example includes most of these elements, and so it is a complex and lengthy ritual. It is taken from notes made in August 1919 by J. H. Hutton when he visited the holy well and ruined church of St Conal on the island of Inishkeel in Gweebarra Bay, County Donegal.

These pilgrimages take place whenever the spring tides make it possible for pilgrims to cross over the sands dry footed to the island and perform their pilgrimage and return before they are cut off from the mainland by the water.

The pilgrims are principally persons from neighbouring villages on the mainland, but seem to include also a certain number from more distant parts. Their object seems to be generally to obtain relief from some sickness.

The pilgrims take off their shoes and stockings (if they are wearing any) as soon as they have reached the island.

They then walk barefoot to the holy spring, a trickle of water with a strong iron flavour, on the rocks on the north side of the island. Here they first wash their feet in one of the rock pools before approaching the spring, in front of which they kneel and pray, afterwards drinking a little from a limpet shell. The water is also bottled and taken away by some.

After this the pilgrim comes up on to the grass above the rocks and spring, where there are three heaps of stones. Round each of these he walks at least three times, and taking stones from the bottom places them on the top; after walking round a heap of stones he kneels before it to pray.

On leaving the three stone heaps the pilgrim goes east towards a large block of stone also partially covered by the stones contributed by pilgrims, and bearing among others a rounded oval black stone with four parallel white strata in it. Here again he walks round, puts one or more stones on the top and prays. He also takes the oval stone with the white strata, crosses himself with it, passes it round his body, and if he so desires, touches with it any afflicted part of his body.

Next he climbs on the wall into the churchyard and walks three times round a ruined chapel on the north side of it, prays, and then moves down to the chapel of St Conal itself. This chapel has the east, south and west walls still standing. The pilgrim walks round it from the east end, round by the south side and back, round the west end to the east again, bowing or curtseying while passing the doors on the south side, and also in some cases when passing in sight of the altar, while coming up by the ruined north wall. The chapel is circumambulated at least three times, the pilgrim then entering the chapel over the north wall and kneeling in front of the altar.

The altar consists of a stone slab lying on the ground, once apparently raised on other stones beneath it like a dolmen. It has a round hole in the north end and four rounded stones lying on it which are regarded as healing stones. The pilgrim kneels in front of the altar and grinds round one of the healing stones in the round hole. He then takes each healing stone in turn, crosses himself with it, passes it round his waist from left to right, applies it in some cases to any particularly afflicted part of the body (one pilgrim was seen to touch her foot with it), crosses himself with it again and replaces it upon the altar.

The pilgrim then leaves the chapel by the doorway on the south side, kneeling and praying in the doorway before leaving. One old woman – the same that touched her foot with the healing stone – was seen to scrape some grit off a stone of the doorway and apply it to her big toe.

The pilgrims after leaving the chapel of St Conal have completed the observance and return to the shore where they can put on their shoes again. While at the well and the altar they tear off bits of rag, sometimes apparently brought for the purpose, and leave bits sticking in the rocks near the spring and under or near the altar stone. Some drop pence through the round hole in the stone, and some leave rosaries, scapulars, hair-pins, hair-combs and similar articles by or under the altar stone. The object of the pilgrimage seems to be to obtain relief from some specific complaint, but it is said that the water of the holy spring has properties other than curative in that it has the power of driving away rats and similar vermin when sprinkled in the house. The altar seems to be sometimes spoken of as the 'bed' of St Conal.[5]

Some aspects of the ritual are self-explanatory, but the circumambulation is worth examining in some detail, and later we shall also examine the reasons for leaving rags on bushes and dropping gifts into the water. Circumambulation is in fact a fairly common feature of holy well ritual. Usually the pilgrim had to walk three times round, but sometimes it was seven or nine times. Always the direction was sunwise – *deiseil* or *deasil* (and other variations in spelling). In Gaelic *deas* means south and to the right, the Latin for right-hand is *dexter*, and in early Indian texts the word for clockwise circumambulation was *pradaksinā*, which also has similar elements; and all these words derive from the same root meaning 'the right'. Anti-clockwise circumambulation was withershins or widdershins (from the old German meaning 'against course'), and was considered unlucky or even evil. In

St Ciaran's Well, Clonmacnoise, County Offaly, where pilgrims celebrate the saint's day in September, hanging offerings on the whitehorn bush, circling and praying at the well, the stone cross and other places in a four-hour ritual. (photo 1910–30)

the ancient Irish *Book of Ballymote* is an account of a magical well in the garden of the King of Leinster. No one except the king and his cupbearers could approach the well without losing their sight. The queen approached it in order to test its powers, and she walked round it three times withershins, or against the sun. The well sent out a torrent of water and three waves carried the unfortunate queen out to sea. In the Scotland of the early seventeenth century, an old woman living alone in Kirkcudbrightshire was accused of witchcraft and on conviction was rolled downhill in a blazing tar barrel. One of the charges against her was that she walked withershins round a well near her cottage which was used by other people. The well was afterwards known as the Witch's Well. These episodes must surely serve as cautionary tales to anyone tempted to transgress the usual custom of walking *deasil* round a holy well.

The importance of the sunwise circumambulation is emphasised in this account of the ritual at St Tredwell's Loch, a healing lake in Papa Westray (Orkney).

In olden times the diseased and infirm people of the North Isles were wont to flock to this place and get themselves cured by washing in its waters. Many of them walked round the shore two or three times before entering the loch itself to perfect by so doing the expected cure. When a person was engaged in this perambulation nothing would induce him to utter a word, for, if he spoke, the waters of this holy loch would lave his diseased body in vain.[6]

At a few wells the circumambulation and the method of using the water were interlinked, again stressing the importance of both elements of the ritual. Chibbyr Unjin in Malew parish (Isle of Man) was visited by childless women who had to lie full length and take the well water into the mouth, then keep it there while getting up and walking three times round the well. Then the water was spat on to a rag which was hung on a thorn bush. The well was in use up until 1899 when the farmer filled it up with earth to stop the annual midsummer pilgrimage.

The rationale behind *deasil* circumambulation seems to have been simply that the movement echoed that of the sun or, as John C. Irwin explains: 'It reflected the need once universally felt to live in harmony with cosmic forces represented in this case by the sun as ultimate generator of life. To circumambulate clockwise was to identify with the sun's diurnal course, regarded as life-enhancing and bringing luck.' He also explains that withershins circumambulation was identified with the sun's nocturnal course, and signified death and misfortune. These associations are deep-seated and worldwide, and extend into many other areas than holy well rituals. In Scotland it was customary for expectant mothers to go three times sunwise round a church to ensure an easy birth; a wedding party would circumambulate the house three times before entering; and boats would row around sunwise three times before starting their journey. Even pots were stirred with the sun. No doubt these customs are or were also performed in other parts of Britain. Certainly coffins were widely carried sunwise round some feature such as a cairn or a cross. Cards are dealt clockwise, and of course clock hands follow the sun (though this may derive from the shadow direction of the sundial). Finally one last example, from the many that could be given, which demonstrates how important the notion of sunwise ritual was and probably still is, although few people today are consciously aware of it. F. T. Elworthy related how in Somerset, at the turn of the century,

a number of children were brought to be baptised, and, of course, were ranged in a group round the font. The officiating minister, not being accustomed to such a number, or not knowing the custom, began with the child on his right hand, of course following on in order, and going round to the child on his left. This action caused great indignation; parents, who had never before seen the importance of having their children baptised at all, were quite sure that now they had not been done properly, and must be taken to another church, 'to be done over again'. Thus it was held of far greater moment that the parson should proceed from left to right than it was that the children should be baptised or not.[7]

As the centuries passed and religious beliefs changed, in many areas the saints' wells were less esteemed and pilgrims no longer approached them with such feelings of devotion. In this way the many so-called 'wishing wells' came into being. People ceased to offer prayers to the saints, they made a wish instead. But sometimes the associated ritual

survived, as at Walsingham (Norfolk) where the wishing wells are in
two small stone basins. The wish-maker had to place his right knee in
a stone between the wells, dip his bare hands into the water up to the
wrists, make a silent wish, then withdraw his hands and swallow the
water held in them. Such rituals and the leaving of a pin or coin are
relics of the rituals performed when the wishing wells were used as
healing wells, as many of them formerly were. Interestingly, their
change to wishing wells is in one way a reversion to paganism, and
even today people still use wishing wells to make serious wishes. This
is borne out by finds of modern coins in surviving holy wells, and by
occasional press reports of successful wishes, such as that published in
July 1983. Sixty-three-year-old Bernard Halls of East Ham, London,
had requested early retirement but his request had been rejected.
While on a coach trip he threw a 2p coin into a wishing well at
Cheddar Gorge and wished for a change of luck. While the rest of his
party were visiting Stonehenge he checked his pools coupon and found
that he was a winner. The amount was £251,597, and his comment
was: 'I think I'll be retiring all right now.'

Doubtless not all the wishes made at wishing wells were kind ones,
and this fact was acknowledged in that some wells were known as
cursing wells. It was said that curses could be whispered at the Devil's
Wishing Well near Bishop's Lydeard church (Somerset), while at
Ffynnon Gybi near Holyhead (Anglesey) the names of victims of the
curses were written on paper and hidden under the bank of the well.
This well could also be used for healing and divination. There were

The wishing well
in Glen Lyon,
Perth, where you
should drop a
penny in the water
before making
your wish (photo
1965)

other cursing wells in Wales, but the most famous was Ffynnon Elian near Llanelian yn Rhos church (Denbigh), now filled up but not quite forgotten. To be effective, the curse had to be laid through the well's guardian, and a large fee had to be paid. An even larger fee was paid for the removal of a name from the well. In the early 1800s the guardian's income from the well was nearly £300 a year. The victim's name was written in a book and also placed in the well on a piece of slate or parchment. A pin was dropped in the well, and Biblical passages were read by the guardian. The person laying the curse drank some well water, and also had some thrown over him or her, three times, as he/she spoke the details of the curse. Sometimes wax effigies were made and stuck with pins before being placed in the well. To have a curse lifted, the victim had to attend the well, read parts of the Bible and listen to the Psalms being read, and also had to walk three times round the well. The guardian emptied the well and the victim was handed the slate bearing his or her name or initials. On returning home he/she had to continue to read parts of the Bible, and to drink from a bottle of the well water. This may all sound like the height of superstition, and no doubt it was, but it is quite clear that until less than a hundred years ago, some people took it very seriously, and to that extent it can be said to have worked. There are many recorded cases of people believing themselves cursed if their name was placed in the well. One woman at Dolanog (Montgomery) was bedridden for years, only rising again at the death of the enemy who had cursed her. The Reverend Elias Owen met her, and he also recorded the following incredible tale.

Some nine years or so ago [*c.* 1873] I went to officiate at a funeral in Trefeglwys parish [Montgomery]. The house, where the dead was, consisted of two parts, the front was a small hall and the landlord lived there; the behind portion was a farm, and this was occupied by a farmer whose wife was dead, and whom I was going to bury. I went to the hall part of the premises, and was introduced to the old gentleman owner, who was dressed in a suit of black clothes. After the usual religious service which takes place at the house whence a funeral departs, the procession started, and I noticed that the old gentleman started with the rest towards the church. Since he was related to the deceased lady, I expected to see him sit among the relatives in the seat next the chancel in Trefeglwys Church, but he was not there. Being rather surprised at this very unusual behaviour, I made inquiries as to the cause, and I was informed that Mr --- had not left his house for years and years, and, upon further inquiries, I was told that he dared not do so. This answer only aroused my curiosity, and, in answer to other questions, I was told that he had been witched when a young man. What I gleaned about this remarkable event was somewhat as follows. That Mr --- had been put into Ffynnon Elian (Elian's Well) because of some love affair, that he had found himself ailing after he had been cursed, and that he had himself gone to the well to ascertain whether the fair revenger had been there before him; this, he found, had been the case. His name written on a stone was found in the well by the custodian of the well, and so the evil which Mr --- had feared had been accomplished; and now the question was, how is the curse to be counter-acted. This the astute guardian of the well informed him was possible for a consideration, and the fulfilment of a certain condition, and this was, that Mr --- was never upon any account to leave the bounds of his own property, and he was told that, as long as he complied with the terms, the evil curse should not injure him. With these hard terms he had complied, and from early manhood to old age, he had never been known to go beyond the limits of his own small estate. He lived thus exiled for the length of an ordinary man's life. He was social enough when visited, and he would occasionally accompany any stray caller upon him to the boundary of his property, and then return to his voluntary prison. Upon the occasion of the burial mentioned above, the old gentleman accompanied the mourners as long as the procession went through his own property, and then he turned back to the hall.

Since I have left the neighbourhood, Mr --- is dead; he died a bachelor, and, to the end of his life, he never left the bounds of his property. He was taken thence to be laid with the dust of his forefathers in the quiet churchyard of Trefeglwys.

This is a singular instance of the great faith placed, not by the unlearned, for Mr --- was not an uneducated man, but by all parties alike, . . . in charms and curses and witches.[8]

So even as late as the second half of the nineteenth century, the power of the well was still strong. Early in the century great efforts had been made to close the well, but despite its physical destruction the springs remained and were opened up again by the guardian, who at this time was John Evans, known as Jac Ffynnon Elian. Despite two gaol sentences he continued his activities, finally repenting and becoming a devout Christian. Even then the well continued in use, at least up to 1870, but thereafter its reputation was in decline, though many still went in fear of its powers. At the end of the century this threat was still used in the locality: *mi 'th rof yn Ffynnon Elian* – I'll put thee in Elian's Well.

From the late nineteenth century cursing wells can be traced back nearly two thousand years to Roman Bath, where around forty curses have been found inscribed on lead sheets. One discovered in 1880 in the reservoir below the King's Bath reads, in translation: 'May he who carried off Vilbia from me become as liquid as water. (May) she who obscenely devoured her (become) dumb, whether Velvinna, Exsuper-eus, Severinus, Augustalis, Comitianus, Catusminianus, Germanilla (or) Jovina.'

The practice of laying curses was also strong among the Irish peasantry, the ritual often involving rounded stones which were kept for that purpose. They stood together on a raised table or altar, often

One of the Roman
curses found at
Bath

in graveyards or near old churches, sometimes by holy wells. The stones would be turned while the curse was repeated. Associated with cursing stones are swearing stones, such as the Leac Fheichin, St Fechin's Stone, near Lough Corrib (Galway), and close to a spring and a church. Persons suspected of crimes were dared to visit the stone to swear their innocence. They had to turn the stone repeating the correct 'rites and incantations', and if they were speaking the truth, all would be well. But if they were guilty, St Fechin would take certain vengeance.

Some holy wells were also able to identify thieves and other criminals. At two wells in Llanbedrog (Caernarfon) a thief's victim could discover who was the thief by dropping pieces of bread into the water while speaking the names of the suspects. The bread sank when the thief was named.

Other wells were believed to have the ability to predict the future, especially with regard to the prospects for a sick person. Some could predict the likelihood of matrimony, others foretold national events. Some wells would bubble up to indicate the future recovery of a sick person, but if the water remained still, death was imminent. Death was also predicted by the sinking of an item of the patient's clothing thrown into the well. If it floated, he would recover. On the Isle of Lewis (Outer Hebrides), water from St Andrew's Well at Shadar was taken to the patient's home and a small wooden dish was floated on it.

If the dish turned sunways, recovery was predicted; if against the sun, death would result – an echo of the *deasil* circumambulation described earlier. Some wells housed sacred eels and these could predict recovery, for example by coiling around the patient's legs when he stood in the well (at Ffynnon Gybi, Llangybi, Caernarfon). At Ardnacloich well, Ardfern (Argyll), the belief was that 'if the sick dieth [ie will die] a dead worm is found at the bottom of the water or fountain, and if the sick shall recover a quicke [live] worm is found in it', while at St Michael's Well, Kirkmichael (Banff), the movements of a fly were watched for information as to the patient's chances of recovery. A well's wildlife was sometimes believed to have more general prophetic abilities, so long as one could read the signs, as was found by the Reverend Elias Owen:

Several years ago, [ie 1880s] I visited Valle Crucis Abbey, near Llangollen [Denbigh], and there I was told I might ascertain my future history, if an eel that was in the well would condescend to make his appearance. I went there, and immediately the eel came out of his chamber, and moved gracefully through the water; but as I was not an adept in the art of reading his language, I failed to obtain a glimpse of my future life.[9]

Rather more easy was the interpretation of the answers given by a bell hidden deep in a well at Whitnash near Leamington (Warwick). The bell was said to have been dropped into the well when being blessed before installation in the church. People would visit the well at night, drop a stone into the water and ask a question. At daybreak the bell would reply, with one ring for yes, and two for no.

There were many ways of discovering one's romantic fate. St Caradog's Well, Haverfordwest (Pembroke), was visited on Easter Monday morning by women who offered three pins, then watched the water, hoping to see the faces of their future husbands. Some wells indicated a lover's faithfulness or otherwise by the behaviour of blackthorn spines thrown on to the water; or else by the movement of a feather, rag, or handkerchief. The first partner of a newly married couple to drink at Ffynnon Gynon, Llangynwyd (Glamorgan), would be the dominant partner. The same was believed of the well at St Keyne (Cornwall), the story being told in a poem by Robert Southey about a man who hurried to the well after his wedding in order to drink of the water first, so that he would 'be Master for life'. But he was too late:

> I hasten'd as soon as the wedding was done,
> And left my Wife in the porch;
> But, i' faith, she had been wiser than me,
> For she took a bottle to Church.

National events, usually disasters, were foretold in a variety of ways. St Helen's Well, Rushton Spencer (Stafford), would suddenly become dry after flowing continuously for eight to ten years, usually in May when springs are full of water, and the people believed that it foretold some calamity. The well is said to have run dry before the outbreak of Civil War, the beheading of King Charles I, the corn scarcity of 1670, the Popish Plot of 1679, the death of King Edward VII, and the First World War. St Nipperton's Well, Ashill (Somerset), ebbed and flowed to foretell national disasters. Water sources other than holy wells were also believed to be able to foretell major events such as war, famine and pestilence, and there are examples of springs, pools, lakes, rivers, and streams whose changes (becoming dry or overflowing, both contrary to the prevailing weather, or running with blood) were said to have taken place before such events. In Hertfordshire they were called 'woe-waters'.

Accounts of the prophetic abilities of the Drumming Well at Oundle (Northampton) may give us some insight into this supposed prophetic ability. The well was famous at one time for its periodic drumming noise, as described here by a seventeenth-century witness:

When I was a schoolboy at Oundle . . . about the Scots' coming into England, I heard a well in one Dob's yard drum like any drum beating a march. I heard it at a distance: then I went and put my head into the mouth of the well, and heard it distinctly, and nobody in the well. It lasted several days and nights, so as all the country people came to hear it . . . When King Charles II died I went to the Oundle carrier at the Ram Inn, in Smithfield, who told me their well had drummed, and many people came to hear it.[10]

The occasions of the drumming were recorded in the *Northampton Mercury*, where an article published on 11 June 1744 linked the drumming to various national events. For example,

It beat again, June 4, 1701, and usher'd in the Commencement of a glorious War; wherein we humbled the Power of *France*, drove that insolent Nation that Year out of *Guelderland*, and saw our Fleet come Home laden from Vigo with the Spoils of Spain, teaching 'em what it was to provoke the Anger of Britain.

But the Beating, Dec. 7, 1702, of the Drumming Well seem'd to prophecy that the *Bavarian*, who the following Spring declar'd for *France*, should soon be drumm'd out of all his Dominions; which accordingly came to pass after the Battle of *Hochstedt*, previous to which Battle this Martial Well drumm'd again June 4, 1704, and beat a glorious Point of War for ten days together, the largest Space of Time it had ever beat; which accordingly foreshew'd all our Train of Successes 'till 1707.

There is much more in this vein, and a close reading shows that the author has cast around for events, his final statement that ten days of drumming in 1704 predicted 'all our Train of Successes 'till 1707' showing that a precise link between drumming and major events is not always to be found! Of course it was always possible to find some national event that had occurred near the time of the drumming, and minor events could be used when major ones such as the deaths of kings were lacking. But the people's acceptance of the prophetic powers of water, against all common sense, does provide one more example of the awe in which water sources were held.

The pilgrim's final act before leaving a holy well was usually to leave some object in or by the well, and these objects are generally regarded as gifts or offerings. The most popular 'offering' was a pin, usually bent, and a number of wells are actually called Pin Well; Rag Wells also indicate the frequency with which the 'offering' was a rag, tied to a nearby bush or left in a hole by the well. Apart from pins and rags, almost any small item could be and was left: pine cones, corks, coins, keys, bread and cheese, stones and pebbles (often of white quartz), buttons, beads, buckles, pipes, fish hooks, thorn points, religious objects, flowers, and so on. At some places nails were hammered into nearby trees, and visitors to St Thenew's Well in Glasgow used to nail up small 'tin-iron' shapes representing the parts of the body they wished to be cured. Patients thankful for a cure would sometimes leave their crutches at the well; and in a few cases animal sacrifices were made, usually of fowls.

An assortment of offerings at St Sourney's Well, Drumacoo, near Kilcolgan, County Donegal (photo 1966)

The custom of leaving an 'offering' at a holy well was not overlooked by the Church, and some clergy took steps to see that the money was directed their way. Collection boxes were sometimes left at the wells, or the priest involved himself more closely in the activity at the well, as at St Erasmus's Well, Ingestre (Stafford), where a chapel was erected by the well. The priest received a fee from pilgrims to offer prayers for their recovery (the well water was known as a cure for leprosy, itch and scabs). The value of the offerings during the reign of King Henry VII was £6 13s 4d a year. At St Faith's Well, Hexton (Hertford), according to the seventeenth-century lord of the manor, Francis Taverner, the pilgrims gave offerings to the priest and he was able to influence the movement of objects which they threw into the well. If the priest was satisfied with the offering he caused the object to float, which meant that the pilgrim's petition was granted; but if he was dissatisfied the object sank. The most popular wells could produce large sums of money, as at Whitekirk (East Lothian), where so many miracles were performed at Our Lady's Well that in 1309 the monks of Melrose erected a shrine to the Virgin Mary. Over 15,000 pilgrims visited the well in 1413 and their offerings totalled 1422 merks (around £1000).

Any object left at a holy well should not be disturbed, certainly not stolen, for it was believed that the illness suffered by the giver would be transferred to the thief. In view of this, it is surprising to learn that in Balquhidder (Perth) people attending the nearby church would call at the Whooping Cough Well and dip their hands into the water to get a few coins, if they had forgotten to bring any collection. Perhaps they reasoned that as they were passing the money on to the Church, they were not exactly stealing it.

No one is quite sure why objects were left at holy wells, why bent pins were so favoured, and why rags were tied to bushes. There are several possibilities: that all are gifts or offerings to the god or saint connected with the well, left in order that he will look favourably on their request; that the pins were bent in order 'to exorcise the evil spirit supposed to afflict the person who dropped them in' (according to folklorist E. Sidney Hartland, who in 1893 published his thoughts on the significance of pin and rag wells); that a rag was used to rub the diseased part and then hung on a bush, with the idea that the disease would be transferred to the rag, and would gradually leave the patient as the rag rotted; that rags are just another form of offering, whole garments being left originally; that, as E. Sidney Hartland concluded,

. . . the practices of throwing pins into wells, of tying rags on bushes and trees, of driving nails into trees and stocks, and the analogous practices throughout the Old World, are to be interpreted as acts of ceremonial union with the spirit identified with well, with tree, or stock. In course of time, as the real intention of the rite has been forgotten, it has been resorted to (notably in Christian countries) chiefly for the cure of diseases, and the meaning has been overlaid by the idea of the transfer of the disease.

He explained that every object was thought to retain an invisible link with its owner or, in the case of such things as stones, with the person who handled it last, and that by leaving an object at the sacred well the pilgrim would remain 'permanently united with the god' and in receipt of his beneficent influence.

All the holy well rituals have degenerated and continue to degenerate, so that today instead of rags pilgrims leave tissues (which could not be used to dip into the water and wipe the diseased part, then tied to a bush, without immediately disintegrating), or else they leave rags of man-made fibre which will not rot, evidently unaware that it was at one time believed that for the charm to work the rag must rot away. Pilgrims have always followed the accustomed rituals uncomprehendingly, without any knowledge of or curiosity about their significance, and that is why the rituals gradually change in response to changing circumstances. Many of the holy well rituals are hundreds of years old, some may even stem from prehistoric times. Little wonder that they are now somewhat changed from their original form and are so difficult to interpret. As with the healing rituals described in the previous chapter, the significance of the 'offerings' was probably

Crutches and sticks were left by pilgrims at St Columba's Well near the Rock of Doon (also called Doon Well), Kilmacrennan, County Donegal; they have been covered with rags, perhaps because there are no suitable trees near the well

The more usual procedure was to attach the rags to the trees and bushes, as at St Helen's Well, Walton, West Yorkshire (photo 1934)

irrelevant to the pilgrims: what mattered was that the act of following the rituals had a positive effect. The belief held by the pilgrim would be reinforced by the performance of the ritual acts, and he/she would receive a psychological benefit. That this is so, is suggested in a description of the scene at St Bartholomew's Well, Pilstown (Waterford), by a visitor in 1855:

The venerable thorns which overshadow it bore a motley appearance, being covered with red, blue, and green ribbons, and rags, as if torn from the dresses of pilgrims, and tied up as a *finale* to their 'rounds' and prayers. An old crone engaged in going her 'rounds' said, they were tied up by each, to leave all the sickness of the year behind them.[11]

5. Disappearing Wells, Saints' Blood, and Other Water Lore

Many holy wells were located close to churches or other religious sites, and were generally accessible, but sometimes their location was rather remote, presumably because the water source was believed to have some special quality and therefore the people must visit it wherever it was, however inaccessible. A number of Irish holy wells are on the tops of hills and mountains, in mountain passes, and in bogs, and some are found on the seashore, being covered by sea water at high tide. In England and Wales some wells were on parish boundaries, and in such cases the well was probably established first, later used as a suitable boundary marker. In past centuries the custom of 'Beating the Bounds' was widely performed at regular intervals, when a party would perambulate their parish boundary in order that its precise location should not be forgotten. So that the younger generation in particular would remember it, boys were whipped or bumped at boundary stones, and sometimes ducked in holy wells. This happened for example at the hamlet of Holywell in Passenham parish (Northampton), where the parochial boundary was walked every other year and boys dipped in the well which gave the hamlet its name. At Churchstoke (Montgomery) there were twelve wells along the parish boundary. One well in Burton parish (Denbigh) marked the England/Wales boundary, and another near Llanymynech (Montgomery) was aptly named the Three Counties Well as it stood at the meeting point of Shropshire, Denbighshire and Montgomeryshire.

The visual appearance of holy wells also varied considerably, from an insignificant hole in the ground to an impressive complex of buildings. Stone-faced pools with steps to facilitate bathing are often seen, while the most popular healing wells often had stone bath-houses, and perhaps a cottage for the custodian. Simple chapels were sometimes also built. In the early days it is probable that all holy wells were open to the sky, roofed buildings being a relatively recent development, probably not more than five hundred years old. A few holy wells have unexpected buildings at their site, or even, as at Woolston (Shropshire), actually over the well. Here a small half-timbered building was erected in the sixteenth or seventeenth century as the court-house of the manor, and courts were held there until about 1824. This choice of location may not seem so strange once it is recalled that from earliest times gatherings, both formal and festive, from lawmaking to fair days, were held at significant sites marked by mounds, standing stones, oak trees, stone crosses and holy wells. Even the shape of the enclosed pool could vary from the usual rectangle. The Well of the Wine at Glen Elg (Inverness) was three-cornered, Ffynnon Assa in Cwm parish (Flint) was polygonal, according to Thomas Pennant, though the number of sides is not stated, and the stone basin at Ffynnon Fair, Cefn (Denbigh), is definitely octagonal, still being in good repair.

At wells where stone structures were built, a niche can often be seen, usually in a wall above the water, where a statue of the saint would have stood, or an effigy would be carved on the face of a stone, but these have rarely survived. At St Sampson's Well, Golant (Cornwall), the figure of St Sampson can still be seen carved on the wall. The

St Winifred's
Well, Woolston,
Shropshire

The octagonal pool at Ffynnon Fair, Cefn, Denbigh

wooden image of St Fumac at St Fumac's Well, Botriphine (Banff), was washed in the well annually by the custodian, and the water was valued as a cure. The image was also carried in procession round the parish on the saint's day. It was washed away in a flood in the late eighteenth century, and when found at the river mouth it was ordered to be burnt as 'a monument of idolatry' by the minister. At St Anne's Well, Llanmihangel (Glamorgan), the carved figure of the saint was made so that the well water flowed from her breasts; while at Ffynnon Beuno, Tremeirchion (Flint), the overflow from the pool still exits through the mouth of a carved head.

British folklore is rich in tales of underground passages connecting sites of antiquity, most of the passages unlikely to have any basis in reality. Some holy wells are traditionally named as the locations of the openings of underground passages, as with the Lady Well at Thornbury (Hereford & Worcester) from whence a passage was said to lead to Thornbury Camp. In Humberside there was said to be a passage to another Lady Well, at Kilnwick, from Watton Abbey. At Longthorpe holy well near Peterborough (Cambridge), there were three underground chambers, from one of which a passage was said to connect the well with Peterborough Cathedral, but as an early twentieth-century researcher noted,

Of course there never was such a passage; to make one under the intervening water meadows would require very considerable engineering skill and much money, and certainly the builders of this crude hermitage could never have done it. A passage to some near building on higher ground, such as the old Manor House, is thinkable.[1]

The traditional story of a musician volunteering to explore the course of an underground passage, told of several locations throughout Britain, is also told of Culross (Fife), the valiant piper entering the tunnel at the Newgate and playing as he moved forward, his course being tracked above ground from the sound of the music. When he reached the ruined church and the Monk's Well, the music ceased, and the piper was never seen again. However the dog that accompanied him later re-emerged at the Newgate, hairless and near death.

One important aspect of holy well siting, which anyone visiting a number of wells will almost certainly notice, is the frequency with which they are located near trees. This might seem at first to be merely a result of the wells being in rural areas, where there are usually plenty of trees and bushes, but the link is closer than that. Many wells appear to have an especially important tree or bush growing beside them, these often being used for hanging rags on, though this may be only a secondary function. Their principal significance seems to be as a relic of ancient tree worship, which once may have been as important as water worship. (We have already written at length on tree worship in our earlier book *Earth Rites*.) Even when tree worship was no longer actively practised, the beliefs of an earlier age still influenced the

St Anne's Well, Whitstone, Cornwall, with a thorn bush growing close by

people, as shown by this quotation from Martin Martin's *Description of the Western Isles of Scotland* (*c.* 1695): '. . . there is a small coppice near to the Well [at Loch Shiant, Skye], and there is none of the natives dare venture to cut the least branch of it, for fear of some signal judgement to follow.' Likewise in Staffordshire, where at Ilam were St Bertram's tomb, well and ash tree in close proximity. The folklorist F. W. Hackwood reported that 'in olden times the ash was so venerated that the people deemed it extremely unlucky, if not positively dangerous, to break a bough of it.' In Ireland similar beliefs were held, as was reported to Lady Gregory when she was collecting folklore at the turn of the century:

There were ash trees growing around the blessed well at Corker, and one night Deeley, the uncle of Pat Deeley that lives beyond, and two other men went to cut them down, to get the makings of a car-body. And the next day Deeley's lip was drawn down – like this – and water running from it for the rest of his life. I often see him; and as to the two other men, they died soon after.[2]

In the two previous quotations, the holy trees were ash. The other main species found by wells are thorn, mountain ash or rowan, oak, holly, and yew. According to legend, the thorn which overshadowed St Mullen's Well at Listerling (Kilkenny) grew from the saint's staff which he stuck into the ground. Many sacred trees in Ireland have a similar legendary origin. The involvement of trees in the rituals performed at holy wells has already been described in Chapter 3 in regard to healing, and in Chapter 4 concerning rag wells. A variation on the custom of hanging rags and clothing in the trees was the practice of hammering coins into the bark of a tree, as occurred at St Maelrubha's Well on the island in Loch Maree (Ross & Cromarty). So many coins had been added that the tree was covered with them up to a height of eight or nine feet.

Since the water supply to any well is dependent on factors such as topography and rainfall, and can be affected by natural changes or human interference, there will be times when wells cease to flow, temporarily or permanently. When this has happened, reasons are offered by the local people, their vivid imaginations at work as they search for cause and effect. St Trillo's Well at Llandrillo (Merioneth) is said to have stopped flowing because a dead cat or dog was thrown into it, but the well later re-emerged half a mile from its former location. This theme, of real or imagined insult to the well causing it to lose its power, move its location, or cease flowing altogether, is widespread. St Corbet's Well on the Touch Hills (Stirling) was said to preserve for a year anyone who drank from it on the first Sunday in May, before sunrise, and it was visited by great crowds at the height of its popularity. But the drinking of spirits became more popular than the drinking of well water, so St Corbet withdrew the valuable qualities of the water, then eventually the water itself stopped flowing. Tobar an t-Solais (Well of Light) in Mellifont parish (Louth) moved because butchers washed cattle intestines in it. St Maelrubha's Well (Ross & Cromarty) lost its power when a mad dog was pushed into it by a shepherd. Both dog and shepherd died within a week. The mad dog taken by a farmer to drink from the churchyard well at St Edrine (Pembroke) recovered, but the farmer died and the well dried up. However, the grass growing at the base of the church walls took over the role and the power of the well water, and this 'grass of the mad' was eaten in a bread sandwich in order to effect a cure. Other 'insults' which could cause a well to withdraw its favours included: a woman washing her clothes in a well; not following the well ritual (for example, a woman who hoped for a quick cure for the scurvy which afflicted her child immersed it in the Fuaran Allt an Ionnlaid – Well of the Washing Burn – at Clachnaharry (Inverness) instead of drinking the water and praying several times); and immersing animals in wells intended only for the healing of humans. A mineral well at Monzie (Perth) lost its power about 1770 when two trees, the guardians of the well, fell.

Some wells which were filled in simply reappeared elsewhere, or were redug by the persons who filled them in. In Herefordshire one landowner, annoyed at people trespassing to visit the well, filled it in, but obviously felt guilty because when his house was inexplicably flooded he saw this as a punishment from the spirit of the well. He dug a new well in his meadow and the water stopped flowing into his house. The new well, at Little Birch, was called Higgins Well after the landowner. A farmer who closed the wells at Trellech (Monmouth) was told by 'an old little man' who appeared at one of the wells that in punishment for his act, no water would flow on his farm. So the farmer reopened the wells, and his water supply returned. An Irish well was rediscovered by accident around 1800 when a farmer moved a large hollowed-out stone to use as a drinking trough for his cattle. Soon his livestock and his children became ill, and he returned the stone, feeling its removal may have caused the trouble. The ill-health vanished, and the farmer also discovered a well of fresh water at the place where the hollowed stone stood. The well was soon attracting the local people, who held 'patterns' there, until one day a man was killed in a fight. As a result of this, the pilgrims found that their prayers and rituals were to no avail: the well had lost its power. Even the sacred trout no longer appeared, and the well, being obviously cursed, was abandoned.

During the last hundred years or so, increasing numbers of wells have been abandoned, filled in, built over, and in a variety of ways lost for good. The following reasons for the disappearance of wells demonstrate the threat that has faced and still faces these vulnerable antiquities. The draining of agricultural land and other improvements have played a large part in the disappearance of holy wells throughout Britain. When wells are drained, any stonework is usually broken up and may be used as building stone, as occurred at Musselburgh (Midlothian), where after the Reformation the stones from the chapel and shrine of the famous Well of Our Lady of Loretto were used in building the town jail and elsewhere. The arrival of the railways and the resulting disturbance of the surrounding terrain can account for the loss of some wells, such as St Ann's Well at Nottingham which was very popular until the late nineteenth century when, in 1887, it was buried under a railway embankment. This was later removed and a pub built on the site. The water of St Shear's Well at Dumbarton (Dunbarton) was piped across the River Leven in the early eighteenth century, to supply water to the town, but in many places the well water has become unsuitable for drinking. Tarlair Well at Macduff (Banff) suffered an unusual fate – the well-house was destroyed by a mine washed in on the tide during the war. St Patrick's Well at Portpatrick (Wigtown) was also destroyed by explosion, but in 1821 and as a result of quarrying. The rock bearing the alleged impressions of the saint's hands and knees was also destroyed. Other disastrous developments include road construction and the laying of sewers (two wells were lost in Lewisham, London, about 1866, for this reason; also in London, St Chad's Well was lost under King's Cross Station). The destruction continues, and as the ingenuity of mankind continues to devise new enterprises, so the threats to holy wells increase in number and variety. Recently Ffynnon Deg At Caerwys (Flint) has been submerged under permanent floods which are part of a fish farm, though from the shore the aerated spring water can still be seen continually bubbling up.

Some wells acquire fame because of their strange physical properties, such as never freezing or never running dry; in fact these two phenomena are often found together. An example was St Andrew's Well at Kirkandrews-on-Eden (Cumbria), which was 'not affected by the most intense frost or the longest drought'. The recent drought of 1976 was a good test of a spring's ability to keep flowing, and many did so. Such springs must rely on a source of water deep within the

The stoup in the porch of Llanidan old church, Anglesey

earth. Less easily explained is the constant presence of water in stone basins not fed by any water supply. One was at Comrie (Perth), a basin in a large stone supposedly fashioned by St Fillan. It was said to be seldom without water, even in a drought, and was used for washing sore eyes. On Anglesey, a holy water stoup in the porch of the old church at Llanidan always contains water, though there is no apparent source of supply and the church is now derelict.

A few wells are reputedly bottomless, such as Ffynnon Ddol, Llanddulas (Denbigh), but lakes and pools were more often credited with this. The 'Knucker holes' of Sussex were ponds said to be bottomless, 'Knucker' coming from the Anglo-Saxon *nicor*, a water monster, which were presumably thought to live in these pools. Some pools quickly lose the attribute of being bottomless when they dry up, as happened to Dozmary Pool on Bodmin Moor (Cornwall) in 1859.

A number of wells whose water ebbed and flowed have been recorded, this variation in water level said to be caused by a nearby river or by the sea, according to whichever is the closest, though Tobar na bile (Well of the Margin) at Inverliever (Argyll) was believed to ebb and flow with the fortunes of the local lairds. Ffynnon Leinw in Cilcain parish (Flint) was much written about by antiquarians, because of its mysterious ebbing and flowing, which took place twice daily, but contrary to the sea tides (the sea is about seven miles away): the well water would diminish when the tide was in, and increase when it was out. Its water source having been tapped by the Hendre mine, Ffynnon Leinw is now fed by surface water and no longer ebbs and flows, so this well-documented phenomenon cannot be scientifically investigated.

The 'flaming well' at Wigan (Greater Manchester) was probably unique, the explanation for this phenomenon, recorded in 1658 and 1739, being that gas from the coal mines escaped through the same rock fissures as the water, and when the gas was lit, it burned very close to the flowing water, making it seem that the water was on fire. It is recorded that the water got so hot, eggs could be boiled in it.

Strange noises issued from some wells, and we have already described the famous Drumming Well at Oundle (Northampton). There were also drumming wells at Harpham (Humberside), and at Hill Wootton (Warwick), this one heard only in 1642, 1660 and 1669. At Forthampton (Gloucester), the wells were said to make a curious whistling noise sometimes, probably caused by air moving through the rock fissures. Air is also released at 'blowing wells', sometimes in puffs strong enough to blow out a candle.

Such phenomena must have seemed very mysterious and helped to intensify people's awe of wells, as is indeed shown by their tendency to believe that drumming noises were prophetic of major events. But even more mysterious to them must have been the 'petrifying wells' of which the most famous today is the Dropping Well at Knaresborough (North Yorkshire). The water at these wells contains carbonate of lime which, when deposited on plants round a well, or any other objects, hardens them and makes them seem to be made of stone. Most of the petrifying wells have only acquired local fame, and few people realise how widespread they were. In Northamptonshire, for instance, there were hundreds, while others were found in Gloucestershire (Magdalen Well, Tetbury), Montgomeryshire (a spring in Gunley Wood, Forden), Staffordshire (several, for example on Morredge), Somerset (the holy well at Watchet), Norfolk (at Deopham), Suffolk (at Cranmore Green near Long Melford), Bedfordshire (at Barton in the Clay), and in Scotland, a well near Terras Water (Dumfries).

Other wells produced mysterious substances, such as the small bones, the size of sparrows' bones, reportedly sprayed out with the water from the Well in the Wall, in Checkley parish (Staffordshire), in every month except July and August. The Well of Kilbar on Barra (Outer Hebrides) was said to throw out the embryos of cockles, which made their way somehow to the sandy beaches where they grew to full-size cockles, Barra being the only island in the area that has excellent cockles. Another Barra well, near Tangstill, threw out barley grain in July and August in a fertile year. The holy well near Cranfield church (Antrim) contained gypsum crystals, translucent and resembling amber, which were known as Cranfield Pebbles, and it was believed that the owner of one would never drown (if a man) or never suffer a dangerous childbirth (if a woman).

On rare occasions, wells have produced milk, or a milk-like substance. This is said to have happened at St Winefride's Well, Holywell (Flint), for three days after the saint's death, while at St Illtyd's Well on Gower (Glamorgan), in a year unknown, a copious stream of milk was seen to flow by a number of witnesses, who

. . . testified that while they were looking at the milky stream carefully and with astonishment, they also saw among the gravel curds lying about in every direction, and all around the edge of the well a certain fatty substance floating about, such as is collected from milk, so that butter can be made from it.[3]

St Llawddog milked a cow over a well on Bardsey Island, so the well then produced milk instead of water for his visitors. The water of Ffynnon Cegin Arthur, in Llanddeiniolen parish (Caernarfon), had an oily appearance, said to have been caused by animal fat from Arthur's Kitchen. Wells containing oil are often associated with St Catherine and the oil is believed to have healing properties. The best-known of these is St Katherine's Balm Well at Liberton near Edinburgh. The drops of black oil in the water come from a coal seam at the water's source, but the traditional explanation is that the well flowed from a drop of miraculous oil brought from the tomb of St Catherine on Mount Sinai. The oily water was once famous as a cure for skin diseases.

Several wells produced a substance which was described as blood, sometimes that of a saint, as at Canterbury Cathedral where the water of a healing well in the precincts was said to be stained red with the blood of the murdered St Thomas à Becket. One legend claimed that the blood-stained dust from the cathedral was thrown into the well after the murder. Murders are a frequent explanation for red wells. Two Breconshire wells flowed with blood after the beheading of princes, while further north Collen's Well, a small tarn near Llangollen (Denbigh), became red when a giantess was murdered and the murderer used the well to wash the blood from his clothes. Blood Well at Llanyblodwel (Shropshire) was named from a great massacre which took place nearby, some of the bodies being thrown into the well, according to the legend. Other water sources were said to run with blood or turn red as a warning of tragedy, or at the time of the event itself. The river at Bothel (Cumbria) ran with blood in 1649 when

Charles I was executed, as did the stream beside Dilston Hall (Northumberland) when the owner, the Earl of Derwentwater, was beheaded in 1716. St Tredwell's Loch on Papa Westray (Orkney) had a habit of turning red when anything unusual was about to befall a member of the Royal Family, while St Winnin's Well at Kilwinning (Ayr) was said to turn to blood when war threatened. Red marks on pebbles by or in holy wells were 'saint's blood' – the blood of St Winefride at Holywell, St Michael's blood at Rockfield (Monmouth), and the blood of a beheaded Catholic priest at Priest's Well in Darran Wood (Monmouth).

Laneast holy well, Cornwall, formerly used for butter-making (photo 1891)

In all cases it is clear that the reddish appearance of the water gave rise to the colourful legends, and this has happened quite recently, as at Glastonbury (Somerset) where legends are still in development. Chalice Well was originally Chalk Well, or Blood Spring because of its colour. Only recently has the idea taken hold that the Holy Grail is hidden there, and that the water of Chalice Well is mixed with Christ's blood. There are several explanations for the red water which causes such legends. Chalybeate springs containing iron are usually reddish in colour, and can leave rusty-red deposits. There are red algae which in large quantities can give the appearance of blood, and in the case of Collen's Well, the folklorist the Reverend Elias Owen visited it and decided that the reddish colouring came from the peat particles suspended in the water.

In contrast to the strange tales which proliferated at some holy wells, elsewhere the well water had more straightforward domestic uses, being valued because its sacred nature was thought to give it special properties. Among the most prosaic domestic uses were tea-making, beer-brewing, distilling, butter-making, boiling meat and washing clothes. The inhabitants of Berkhamsted (Hertford) believed that the wearers of clothes washed in St John's Well would have good health, but this practice polluted the water, which was reputed to cure diseases like leprosy and scrofula, and to soothe sore eyes. Some washerwomen were fined in 1400, and wardens were appointed to ensure that the well was used only for legitimate purposes. At Painswick (Gloucester) various orders were issued down the centuries to stop people polluting the water, by the washing of clothes and other things, including 'the entrails of swine', in Tibby or St Tabitha's Well. Similar prohibitions are recorded elsewhere, so presumably the practice of washing clothes in holy wells was quite widespread.

The value of water from holy wells was widely appreciated and it was in great demand in some areas, being actually sold on the streets. A penny a quart was the price for water from Pennyquart Well at Croxton (Stafford), but the recorded prices varied greatly, up to a guinea a quart for water from an Oxford well. A Cumbrian landowner who decided to profit from a holy well on his land built a house over it, whereupon the well dried up; when he pulled the house down, the water began to flow again.

Holy well water also had its part to play at the significant times in people's lives. At Carmyle (Lanark) the Marriage Well was visited by marriage parties on the day after the wedding and the couple were toasted in well water. In Warwickshire, holy well water from certain 'caudle wells' was sometimes used in place of old ale in a recipe (old ale, oatmeal, sugar, spices) known as caudle which was given as special nourishment to women after giving birth. As we have already seen, baptismal water was very often obtained from a holy well near the church.

Not only holy water was valued, but pure rain water, dew, and running water also had importance in some areas. Pure rain water was used as a cure for sore eyes, but it must be collected in a clean vessel during June, and could then be stored in a bottle, where it would remain pure for any length of time. In Somerset lore, dew could also be used to 'clear the sight', but in many areas 1 May was the important time to use dew, and young girls would wash their faces in it before sunrise in order to retain their good complexions. On the Isle of Man this ritual was also believed to protect them against witchcraft, and in Cornwall 'May dew' was also used in elaborate healing rituals. Running water was used to seal bargains, lovers standing on opposite banks of a stream and clasping hands across the water. Neither the Devil nor ghosts nor any supernatural beings were able to cross running water, and folklore contains many tales of people escaping such pursuers by crossing a stream.

From prosaic domestic usage of holy well water, we move to some rather more esoteric domestic uses. Holy well water has gained a reputation for achieving some strange results, the link between cause and effect sometimes being unclear. It was at one time customary for Barra (Outer Hebrides) fishermen to drink from St Clair's Well every Sunday, in the hope of getting good herring catches. Perhaps they were putting themselves under the protection of St Columba, who was said to have frequented the well. The fishermen of the Hebrides would also visit certain wells in order to ensure favourable winds for their expeditions. One such well was on the island of Gigha (Argyll). First its covering of stones must be removed, then the well itself cleaned out with a wooden dish or clamshell. Then water was thrown several times in the direction from which the wind was desired, and incantations were spoken. Afterwards the stones must be replaced, or a hurricane would blow. Wells for controlling the weather were also found on the Isle of Man and in Ireland. Tobernacoragh, or the Well of Assistance, on the island of Inishmurray (Sligo), would be drained into the sea in order to calm a tempest. But the visitor to Tobar na Suil on top of the 200-foot mountain Slieve Sneacht (Donegal) must take care not to disturb the mud at the bottom of the well, or during his downward journey rain or snow could fall, or a mist descend.

If the claim that its water could turn milk into cream is true, the well at Crudwell (Wiltshire) must have been valued, while even more sought-after must have been the water from Welsh wells drawn between 11 and 12 pm on New Year's Eve and Easter Eve, for this was believed to turn into wine. A similar belief was held concerning the water in St Mary's Well, Culloden (Inverness), which was believed to turn to wine for a short time on 1 May; while the Silver Well near Otterburn (Northumberland) could reputedly turn objects into precious metal. The 'cream' or 'flower' of the well was valued in many areas. This was the first water drawn from a well in the New Year, and there was sometimes rivalry among young girls wishing to be the first. In the Scottish Highlands they would chant:

> The flower o' the well to our house gaes,
> An' I'll the bonniest lad get.

As well as favourable matrimonial prospects, this water gave good luck and beauty. At the three wells in Wark (Northumberland), the drinker of the 'flower of the well' would have marvellous powers, including the ability to fly through the air at night, and pass through keyholes. In some parts of Scotland the 'cream' of the water was drunk on the first Sunday in May; while in Ireland the first water drawn after midnight on 1 May was called 'the purity of the well' and was kept throughout the year as a charm against witchcraft.

Many wells seem to have been used in this way: to protect against witchcraft, against curses, against the fairies, against diseases, or, as Fitz's Well near Princetown (Devon), to help pixie-led travellers find the right path. A drink of its water would set them on their way. Scottish parents whose baby had been spirited away by the fairies and a changeling left in its place, used to lay the changeling in a stone trough called the Fairies' Cradle, which stood near St Bennet's Spring, near Cromarty (Ross & Cromarty), and their child would then miraculously be restored to them. The Cradle was broken up by the parish minister in the mid-eighteenth century. Also in Scotland, holy well water was sprinkled on oatmeal cakes as they were drying, to protect the baking from any supernatural creatures that might extract the substance from them, as was believed could happen. Sometimes the water was 'silvered' by being poured over a new silver coin and then given to cattle to protect them against the Evil Eye, or to cure cattle injured by it.

Animals have already been mentioned from time to time in connection with holy well lore, which indicates how important they once were in people's everyday lives. Some wells were specifically for healing animals; but other wells paradoxically were 'insulted' if an animal was dipped there or allowed to drink the water. On Harris

(Outer Hebrides) there was a cave which contained two wells, one of which would dry up if a dog drank from it, the other being intended for drinking only by dogs. St John's Well at Harpham (Humberside) had the useful ability of subduing the largest and fiercest animals, a mad bull becoming as quiet as a lamb if brought to the well (though how they induced the mad bull to go to the well is not revealed). While visiting St Michael's Well at Llanfihangel Ynghwnfa (Montgomery), the folklorist the Reverend Elias Owen saw the farmer whose land it was on, who began to complain about the well being neglected by the Church authorities. He also told the Reverend Owen that his cattle refused to drink the holy well water, preferring another source. Whether this was because they were aware of its sanctity, or simply that the water was by then not fit for drinking anyway, we do not know. Certain Welsh lakes were avoided by living creatures. Birds would not fly over Llyn Moel Llyn (Cardigan), and those that tried it fell dead. Llyn Cwm y Llwch (Brecon) was said to be avoided by birds and cattle, who would not drink at it, or even approach it.

A few wells were actually believed to be harmful if their water was drunk. St Chad's Well near Lichfield (Stafford) was said to cause ague if the water was drunk, while anyone swallowing the water of Ffynnon Fach at Llanfihangel Ynghwnfa (Montgomery), intended to be used for bathing weak eyes, would fall down dead. In warning a story was told of a man who disbelieved and drank the water. He died on the spot and was buried by the well, a mound being pointed out as his grave. Illness or death could also befall anyone desecrating a holy well, or sometimes a violent storm would arise, and there are many examples of this in holy well lore. The farmer who filled in Tubber-kileilhe, in Ballyvooney townland (Waterford), contracted a running sore, which did not heal until he had reopened the well. The men who worked to drain a well in Boherboy parish (Cork) had sore eyes and eventually went blind, and a number of people in Ireland who desecrated the sacred trees by holy wells also suffered injury or death. Likewise the removal of a trough at a well, or an inscribed stone, could have unpleasant consequences, and to remove pilgrims' offerings was usually, but not always, punished. A man who took gifts from a cave in Ardnamurchan (Argyll) fell and broke his leg before reaching home, while a piper who stole money from the Gout Well in Minnigaff parish (Kirkcudbright) was soon seized by an attack of gout. However the coins in the Iron Well, a wishing well in Glen Lyon (Perth), were looked on as a free money supply by the local children, with no apparent penalty for their removal.

Sometimes the local belief in retribution was strong, although not supported by experience, as was discovered by the youngsters who

St Cuby's Well, Duloe, Cornwall. When the squire wished to move the stone basin around 1863, he had to agree to provide pensions for the families of any men who died as a result of touching the stone

resolved to find the gold said to lie in a kettle beneath the Kettle Stone at the spring known as Tobar-Fuar-Mòr (the Big Cold Well) at Corgarff (Aberdeen). The gold was presented by people seeking a cure to the well's guardian spirit, who placed it in the kettle for safe-keeping, and death would soon befall anyone who tried to steal it. James Farquharson of Corgarff resolved to find the gold when he was a boy in the early nineteenth century, and armed with picks and spades he and his companions set out. Despite much hard work, they found no gold beneath the stone and were returning home disappointed when they met an old woman who, on hearing what they had been doing, told them they would die within a few weeks. Needless to say, James Farquharson was still alive over fifty years later, when he told his story to the folklorist the Reverend Dr W. Gregor. But the beliefs and stories persist. In the late 1970s a car park was constructed near St Colman's Well near Cranfield church (Antrim) and the well was cleaned out. The workman who found coins in the well was urged by his workmates to put them back, but he didn't. Instead he used the money for a 'binge', and was killed by a car the same night, or so the story goes.

The intentional draining of some lakes could also bring warnings to the desecrators, usually in the form of violent storms. After only four yards of a channel was dug to divert the water of Llyn Moel y Llyn

The well at
Beeston Castle,
Cheshire

(Cardigan), when the farms were suffering from drought around
1800, a tremendous storm blew up and the work was immediately
halted. When boys dug a gulley through a dam at Llyn Cwm Llwch
(Brecon) in order to let the water out, they were confronted by a ghost
of an old woman, or a man in a red coat in another version of the
story, who warned of the dire consequences if they continued.

Similar tales are told of attempts to find treasure supposedly hidden
under water in wells, pools, lakes, streams and rivers. A well at Camlet
Moat by South Mimms Castle (Hertford) holds an iron chest filled
with Sir Geoffrey de Mandeville's treasure. Many attempts have been
made to retrieve it, but each time it can be raised only so far before it
falls back. The treasure in Beeston Castle's 366-foot well (Cheshire)
was 200,000 marks hidden by King Richard II, or the Beeston family
jewels, no one knows for sure, because the treasure has never been
found. All attempts were thwarted by the demons guarding the well,
and some men even died from fright on seeing the demons. In recent
times the well was cleaned out, but neither demons nor treasure were
seen. In Kildonan parish (Sutherland) the treasure guardian took the
form of a two-headed black dog. When a pool was drained to find the
pot of gold, it is said that the dog set up such a hideous howling
nightly at midnight that the culprit was compelled to fill up the loch
again, and he hadn't even found the treasure. The Viking treasure in
Loch Stack (Inverness) is also guarded by a black dog. Callow Pit at
Southwood (Norfolk) contains a chest full of gold which was once
nearly rescued by two men, but at the last minute a black arm emerged
from the water, accompanied by the smell of sulphur, and took back
the chest, the men being able to retain only the ring on the chest lid,
which they afterwards fastened on Southwood church door. The chest
in Wimbell Pond at Acton (Suffolk) is also guarded by a supernatural
being, a small white figure who cries out 'That's mine!' A local laird

emptied a pool under the waterfall at Crawfurdland Bridge near Kilmarnock (Ayr) to get at the gold hidden there, but as his workmen were digging, a voice was heard crying out that the laird's home was in danger. All the men rushed off, and when they returned, having discovered it was a false alarm, they found that the stream had refilled the pool.

Perhaps the treasure so often said to be hidden at water sources is symbolic of the sanctity of the water itself and its importance in people's lives. Perhaps it derives from the gifts of money left in holy wells by centuries of pilgrims, or perhaps from occasional finds of real buried treasure. In 1922 there was such a case, though the 'treasure' does not seem to have amounted to much, on Lewis (Outer Hebrides), where according to tradition an Irish pedlar was murdered for his money in the mid-eighteenth century. The money was hidden in or near a well in the vicinity of Carloway, and thereafter a light was frequently seen by the local people, travelling between the place where the pedlar's body was thought to be buried and the well, where it vanished. In 1922 three young men who had themselves watched the light, dug in the ground near the well and found a sealskin purse containing Irish pennies dating to the mid-eighteenth century. Since that time the light has not been seen.

We conclude this chapter with an account of some of the more famous people who have been associated with holy wells over the centuries. Saints are not included here, as they feature elsewhere, notably in Chapters 2 and 6. Our first famous personage, heading a rollcall composed largely of royalty, is a king whose actual existence is disputed. Whether he existed or not, King Arthur's name has become linked with many places throughout Britain, including some wells and pools. Chalice Well at Glastonbury (Somerset) is said to be the place where King Arthur's Holy Grail is hidden, and there were Arthur's Wells near Walltown (Northumberland) and at South Cadbury Castle (Somerset), the possible site of King Arthur's Camelot. The name of Arthur's Fountain at Crawford (Lanark) dates back at least as far as 1339, when Fons Arthuri is referred to in a land grant. On Alderley Edge in Cheshire is a wishing well associated with Merlin, the Welsh magician who played a leading role in Arthur's story. On the rock above the well a head is carved, and this inscription:

Drink of this and take thy fill for the water falls by the wizards will

Uther Pendragon, King of Britain and father of Arthur, was said to have healed his wounds, after a battle with the Saxons, at a holy well near St Albans (Hertford).

The wishing well
on Alderley Edge,
Cheshire

Apart from the legend, also current in many other places in Britain, that King Arthur lies sleeping in a cave beside Marchlyn Mawr (Caernarfon), his main watery connection involves the marvellous sword Excalibur, which was a gift from the Lady of the Lake, and at the end of his life was to be thrown into a lake where it would be grasped and taken down by a mysterious hand. There are many contenders for the honour of being the pool where Excalibur lies hidden, including Broomlee Lough (Northumberland), Dozmary Pool and Looe Pool (both in Cornwall), a lake near Bosherston (Pembroke), Llyn Llydaw (Caernarfon), and the mere (as it was then) at Pomparles Bridge near Glastonbury (Somerset).

Our other monarchs definitely existed, but we cannot always be sure that their reported visits to these holy wells actually took place. As an example of this problem, St Columba's baptism of the Pictish King Brude, which would have taken place in the sixth century, was said to have happened at a number of wells such as Fuaran Allt an Ionnlaid (Well of the Washing Burn) near Clachnaharry (Inverness), and the Holed or Font Stone at Abriachan (Inverness). Another early

Scottish king was Macbeth, who died in battle at Lumphanan (Aberdeen) in 1057. He is said to have drunk from Macbeth's Well during the battle; or alternatively after death he was beheaded and his head washed in the well. Alfred, King of Wessex, is said to have prayed for water to refresh his men, during his battles with the Danes in the ninth century, and so were formed the Six Wells at Stourton (Wiltshire). Early in the thirteenth century, wounds on the legs of King John are said to have been healed with water from a well at Goldington (Bedford). The Black Prince (1330–76), eldest son of Edward III, is said to have bathed his leprosy in water from the Black Prince's Well or the Leper's Well at Harbledown (Kent), which he used to visit when travelling through Canterbury *en route* for his victorious battles in the Hundred Years War. During the fifteenth century a well was specially made for Henry VI when he was a fugitive living at Bolton Hall (North Yorkshire). During the Battle of Bosworth (Leicester) in 1485, at which Richard III was defeated by Henry VII, Richard drank at a well which thenceforth became famous as King Richard's Well. In the same year of 1485, St Anne's Well at Brislington (Avon) was visited by Henry VII (and in 1502 by his wife Elizabeth). But it is not likely that this visit was made during his march from Milford Haven through Wales and the Midlands to Bosworth Field, as it would have been off his direct route. However, during that march he is said to have rested at Ffynnon Dudur near the Cardigan/Carmarthen border.

To return to Scotland for a while: Robert Bruce, King of Scotland 1306–29, suffered from leprosy, and at least three wells were repu-

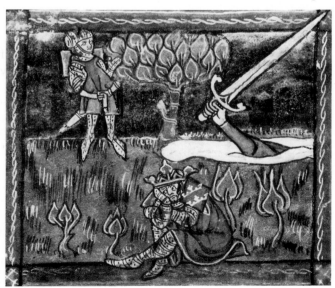

King Arthur, Sir Bedevere, and the sword Excalibur as depicted in a fourteenth-century manuscript

Dozmary Pool on
Bodmin Moor,
Cornwall

tedly used by him in his search for a cure. He is said to have been
responsible for a well at Prestwick (Ayr) which flowed where he stuck
his spear in the sand while resting from his struggles with the English.
He stayed for several days, and his leprosy was reputedly cured. He is
said to have built a leper hospital for those who could not afford
treatment. The well at Scotlandwell (Kinross) also claims to have
cured his leprosy; and he also visited the St Lazarus Well at Muswell
Hill (London), being granted a free pass by the King of England to do
so. During the sixteenth century James V of Scotland frequently visited
the Mineral Spring at Saline (Fife), and he also visited Our Lady of
Loretto Well at Musselburgh (Midlothian) before travelling to France
to fetch his bride. In the same century, Mary Queen of Scots is said to
have rested at the Queen's Well, Tongland parish (Kirkcudbright),
during her flight through the area. It was James VI of Scotland who in
1617 ordered that St Katherine's Balm Well at Liberton (Edinburgh)
should be protected, as described here in 1664 by Matthew Mackaile:

His Majesty King James VI, the first monarch of Great Britain, of blessed
memory, had such a great estimation of this rare Well, that when he returned
from England to visit his ancient kingdom of Scotland in anno 1617, he went
in person to see it, and ordered that it should be built with stones from the
bottom to the top and that a door and a pair of stairs should be made for it,
that men might have the more easy access into its bottom for getting of the
oyl.

In unhappy circumstances, the Marquis of Montrose drank at Fuaran
Allt an Ionnlaid (Well of the Washing Burn) at Clachnaharry (Inverness) in 1650 while on his way to execution in Edinburgh. A century
later, Prince Charles Edward Stuart, 'Bonnie Prince Charlie', stayed
for some weeks in the outer isles, and while on South Uist he drank

from Tobar Creag-an-Fion, to which he gave its name by calling it 'the Well of the Rock of Wine'.

Our English royal visitors continue with Henry VIII, who patronised the Well of Our Lady at Walsingham (Norfolk), walking barefoot the last two miles to the well. He was later responsible for the persecution of some holy wells. Charles I and his queen stayed with their court for several weeks at Wellingborough (Northampton) in 1628 and 1637, so that the queen could take a course of treatment at the Red Well, a chalybeate spa. King Charles is also said to have taken a drink at the King's Well at Ellerton (Shropshire) when staying at Chetwynd Park. Charles II is associated with two wells: the Royal Spring at Longhope (Gloucester), where he stayed at an inn and drank the waters, and Collinson's Well at Hutton-in-the-Forest (Cumbria), where he stopped to quench his thirst while marching south to battle at Worcester. James II and his queen paid a visit to St Winefride's Well at Holywell (Flint) on 29 August 1686 to ask for the blessing of a son (who was duly born in June 1688). George III reigned from 1760 to 1820, and is said to have sent from Windsor for supplies of the water from a holy well at Hook Heath, Woking (Surrey), used to cure weak eyes. The name of Tobar na Clachan Gealaich (Well of the White Stone) at Glen Mark (Angus) was changed to Queen's Well after the visit in September 1861 of Queen Victoria and the Prince Consort, and a 20-foot-high inscribed memorial was erected to commemorate the event.

Other famous names linked to holy wells include Sir Everard Digby, one of the Gunpowder Plotters, who in 1605 visited St Winefride's Well, Holywell (Flint), in a group of pilgrims. The chalybeate spring at Brow (Dumfries) was visited by Robert Burns just before his death in 1796, in a last attempt to regain his health. Our Lady's Well at Whitekirk (East Lothian) was visited by Aeneas Silvius, later Pope Pius II, in 1435 in fulfilment of a vow he made when caught in a storm at sea. Over a hundred years earlier, in 1297, Black Agnes, Countess of Dunbar, had received relief from an injury after drinking from the holy well, and it was she who built a chapel and chantry there in her gratitude.

It is clear that holy wells were not patronised solely by the peasantry, and that members of the upper strata of society were not above visiting them, and often with an apparent belief in their efficacy in bringing about a desired result.

6. The Creation of Wells and Lakes

Although many holy wells are of great antiquity, it is impossible to determine the age of most of them, nor is it possible to determine how they were originally established. Many must have arisen spontaneously as springs, but others were probably wells dug down to reach underground water sources which had been located by water-divining methods. There is little documentary evidence relating to this aspect of holy wells, but there is a report of one well that was located by divination, and that was dug for the use of Henry VI (1421–71) when he was a fugitive in hiding at Bolton Hall (North Yorkshire). However the lack of factual evidence is balanced by an abundance of folklore 'evidence' to explain the appearance of holy wells. According to this, their creation was usually spontaneous and miraculous, and it may be possible that at least some of the tales conceal the use of water-divining. As it was most often a saint who caused a spring to arise from the bare earth, possibly many saints were skilled in the use of water-divining and, this skill being inexplicable to the people, they interpreted the finding of water as a miraculous event, to be embodied in the kind of tales which follow.

The simplest explanation for the appearance of a holy well was that the saint prayed for water and a spring miraculously appeared. The saint always had a reason for needing the water. When St Torranan landed on Benbecula (Outer Hebrides) he was very thirsty after his

St Edith's Well, Stoke Edith, Hereford & Worcester

St Augustine's
Well, Cerne
Abbas, Dorset

long journey from Ireland. He could find no fresh water, so he prayed for a spring and one appeared at his feet. St Torranan blessed it, drank from it, and after giving thanks he prayed that it might never dry up. It later became a place of pilgrimage. St Margaret's holy well at Binsey (Oxford) is attributed to St Frideswide, a nun who settled at Binsey after having fled from a determined suitor. On her arrival she found a desolate place without water, so she prayed to God and a pure spring was found among the grass. Six wells at Stourton (Wiltshire) are said to have arisen when King Alfred prayed for water for his men during their wars with the Danes. St Alban prayed for water to quench his thirst while on his way to his execution on 23 June 303, and thus arose St Alban's Well at St Albans (Hertford). St Edith prayed for water when she was helping to build the church at Stoke Edith (Hereford & Worcester), because it was a long way to the brook to fetch water to mix the mortar. The well close by the church is still flowing strongly. There are many other similar examples, including Ffynnon Elian at Llanelian-yn-Rhos (Denbigh), St Ailbe's Well in the old graveyard at Kilroot (Antrim), St Keyna's Well at Llangenon (Monmouth), and a spring which arose in St Cuthbert's cell on Farne Island (Northumberland) in answer to his prayer for fresh water. This miraculous spring was described by Bede, the eighth-century historian and scholar:

This water, by a most remarkable quality, never overflowed its first limits, so as to flood the floor, nor yet ever failed, however much of it might be taken out; so that it never exceeded or fell short of the daily wants of him who used it for his sustenance.

As a variation on the stories of saints praying for water there are tales of saints striking the ground with a staff. St Augustine is said to have done this at Cerne Abbas (Dorset) in order to find water for refreshment, as did St John at Harpham (Humberside) and Archbishop Thomas à Becket at Otford (Kent). On the Isle of Skye where two groups of people were arguing over the use of the local well, St Turog struck the well and caused it to dry up. His anger and the loss of their well caused the parties to appeal to the saint to help him. Separating them into two groups he struck the ground in front of each group, and two new wells flowed. The famous well at North Marston (Buckingham) was created by Sir John Schorne, rector during the years 1290–1314, at a time of drought. Moved by the prayers of his congregation, he stuck his staff in the ground and a spring burst forth. The Shropshire saint St Milburga caused her horse to create one of the wells dedicated to her, St Milborough's Well at Stoke St Milborough. While fleeing from her enemies, she fell from her horse and struck her head on a stone. Two men sowing barley nearby ran to help her, but there was no water to bathe her wound. She commanded her horse to strike the rock with its hoof, and a spring gushed forth. Another well reputedly formed in a similar way is Anne Boleyn's Well at Carshalton (Surrey), which began to flow where Anne Boleyn's horse struck the ground with its hoof. Several other wells were formed by secular persons, sometimes accidentally, as Anne Boleyn's Well seems to have been. A spring began to flow at Prestwick (Ayr) where Robert the Bruce stuck his spear into the sand when he lay down to rest, and he found that the water cured his leprosy. Two Sisters Well

St Oswald's Well,
Oswestry,
Shropshire

between Hoton and Wymeswold (Leicester) came about as a result of a dream. During a period of drought several hundred years ago, Gertrude and Grace Lacy both dreamt the same dream: that they caused a stream to flow by digging a pilgrim's staff into the earth. Next morning the sisters went to the spot they had dreamt about, accompanied by some villagers, and where they prodded at the ground with the staff, a stream began to flow. The villagers built a well at the spot, and the water never dried up.

In some of these stories drought is specifically mentioned, and there are so many accounts of saints needing a water supply that it has been suggested that there may have been more frequent drought conditions or at least a drier climate in Britain in the early centuries AD, when Christianity was gaining a foothold. Some lives of the saints also suggest this, with references to water shortages and the need to travel distances to fetch water. In such conditions free-flowing springs would certainly be of great importance, and anyone able to bring them into being would be looked on as a miracle worker. If missionaries were indeed able to use divination to find water, this could only have helped in their efforts to convert the population to Christianity.

However, there exists another group of tales in which hints of paganism are mixed in with the Christian aspects, showing that pagan practice was not immediately eradicated. In these tales a holy well sprang up where a saint was murdered, where his (or her) severed head fell, or where his (or her) body lay. St Oswald's Well is located where the saint died in 642 following a battle with Penda, King of Mercia, at Winwick (Cheshire), and according to the sixteenth-century antiquary John Leland, his death also led to the formation of another St Oswald's Well, at Oswestry (Shropshire): 'an eagle snatched away an arm of Oswald from the stake, but let it fall in that place where now the spring is'. St Edward's Well arose at Wareham (Dorset) where St Edward the Martyr, King of England, died in 979; while in Kidwelly (Carmarthen) Ffynnon Sul was said to mark the place where a prince named Benisel was murdered. In Norfolk, St Withburga's Well in East Dereham churchyard marks the place where the saint lay buried for more than three hundred years, before her body was removed by the Abbot of Ely in the tenth century to a grave in Ely Cathedral. A pure spring of healing water began to flow at the site of the empty grave, and an inscription still commemorates St Withburga.

In other instances, wells sprang up where saints' bodies were only briefly laid during their last journey. Two wells mark the death of Ethelbert, King of East Anglia, who was murdered by order of King Offa of Mercia while Ethelbert was his guest, as a suitor of Offa's daughter. Miracles were soon reported at Ethelbert's grave at Marden

St Withburga's
Well, East
Dereham, Norfolk

(Hereford & Worcester), and when the body was removed to Hereford, a spring began to flow in the empty grave. At the place in
Hereford where the body briefly lay, St Ethelbert's Well began to flow,
and King Offa, regretting the murder, had a shrine erected to
Ethelbert's memory in 795, on the site of which now stands Hereford
Cathedral, of which Ethelbert is the patron saint. Two wells also
originated from the murder of the child-king Kenelm of Mercia early
in the ninth century. He was murdered in the Clent Hills (Hereford &
Worcester) at the instigation, so it was said, of his elder sister
Quendreda, but from his severed head a dove flew up and away to
Rome, where it dropped a scroll at the Pope's feet. This was
deciphered, and was found to contain the message:

> In Clent Cow-pasture under a thorn
> Of head bereft lies Kenelm, King born.

The body was found and taken away to Winchcombe (Gloucester) for
burial, where Kenelm's father King Kenulf had founded an abbey. At
the spot in the Clent Hills where the body had lain, a spring began to
flow, as also happened near Winchcombe, where the body was rested
before burial. The legend of St Kenelm, as he became, was first written
down in the eleventh century, by which time many miracles had been

recorded at the saint's shrine. When the foundations of the abbey church were excavated in 1815, two stone coffins were found, one containing a man and the other a child, which may possibly have been the remains of Kenulf and Kenelm. Leland had recorded in the sixteenth century that they were buried together in the church.

St Walstan, son of King Benedict of East Anglia who became the patron saint of agricultural workers and sick animals, died in 1016 in Norfolk while engaged in his chosen work as a farmhand, but he had foreseen his own death and asked that his body be placed on a cart and the two oxen which drew it should be allowed to go where they wished. They passed through Costessey Wood, and at the point where they briefly stopped on a hilltop, St Walstan's Well arose. They stopped again at Bawburgh, where a second spring began to flow, and Walstan was buried not far away, where the church now stands. Some time after the death of St Cuthbert in the seventh century, according to legend his body was carried north from Yorkshire, and on three occasions where the coffin was rested a spring arose.

That the presence of a saint's corpse should cause a spring to flow where none flowed before may indicate primarily the awe in which the saints were held, especially by those living in later centuries: a person's reputation is usually enhanced by time, as his story gains legendary accretions. All these tales illustrate this. Although most of them describe people who actually lived, and although they may have been murdered, most of the content of these tales is obvious fiction. The well-links are there to give an interesting explanation for a well or spring which in all probability had been in existence for many centuries before the saint was born. But when the death legend involves a severed head, we are clearly hearing echoes of the Celtic head cult. Several of the murder legends specifically mention severed heads, with the spring flowing where the head fell. The best-known example is St Winefride, who was decapitated at Holywell (Flint) by Caradoc, a persistent suitor. The severed head was replaced by St Beuno, who breathed new life into the girl; and the famous holy well has developed from the spring which flowed where the head fell. This is not the only tale in which a spurned lover chases and beheads a virgin, though most were not as fortunate as was Winefride, for their heads were not restored to them. St Lludd was beheaded at Pencefn-gaer (Brecon) in the same circumstances, Penginger Well marking the spot where her head rested. Women were also beheaded for other reasons. St Sidwella was beheaded in the eighth century on the order of her stepmother who desired some land which Sidwella had inherited. While she was at prayer, a reaper killed her with a scythe, and where her head fell, a spring began to flow, now St Sidwell's Well

A print of St Winefride's Well at Holywell (compare this with the present-day photograph on page 32), which also shows the saint's moss and seal, the latter depicting her decapitation at the hands of Caradoc

near Exeter (Devon). St Osyth was an abbess in seventh-century Essex when the Danes raided her convent and cut off her head. She promptly picked it up and carried it to the nearest church, where she died. St Osyth's Well flowed where she was attacked, and there was at one time a belief that her ghost haunted the well and the church, both at St Osyth (Essex).

Two male saints who were beheaded, with two holy wells resulting from each of their deaths, were St Decuman and St Justinian. Decuman was a Welsh saint who crossed to Somerset and established a hermitage at Watchet, but he was attacked and beheaded by the local pagans, St Decuman's Well springing up where his head fell (or, in another version, the well was already there and St Decuman washed his head in its water). St Decuman gathered up his head and returned to Wales, where another St Decuman's Well arose near Rhoscrowther church (Pembroke). St Justinian was beheaded on Ramsey Island (Pembroke), and he immediately crossed to the mainland with his head, being buried at St Justinian's Chapel where there is another holy well dedicated to him. St Decuman was killed as a result of conflict between paganism and Christianity, and so too was the female Christian saint Columba, who was pursued by her pagan lover, and, refusing to renounce Christianity, beheaded by him at Ruthvoes (Cornwall) where her holy well began to flow.

Only hinted at in some of these tales, and clearly stated in others, it is apparent that there was a long and continuing conflict between paganism and Christianity in the early centuries AD. This may also be the explanation behind other well creation tales, such as the slaying by St Barry of a 'great serpent' in County Roscommon. The saint thrust his crozier at it before it disappeared into Lough Lagan, and where his knee touched the ground, a holy well, Tobar Barry, sprang up. Although the serpent may represent paganism, and the saint's victory is therefore the victory of Christianity over paganism, we cannot entirely ignore the possibility that some of the serpents in similar Irish tales may have been real water monsters, which are still seen from time to time in the lakes of Ireland and Scotland. These eerie ugly monsters, with their aura of primeval mystery, appropriately symbolise the uncouth savagery which the Christians attributed to all non-Christian beliefs; but that is not to say that the monsters were totally symbolic and did not have a reality of their own.

As always, there are some well creation legends which do not fit into our earlier categories, though most of them do involve saints as the instigators of wells and springs. Chibbyr Vaghal or St Maughold's Well sprang up on the Isle of Man at the place where St Maughold's horse's knee touched the ground as horse and saint crossed over from Ireland. A similar story is told of another Manx well, this one having three names – Chibbyr Pherick (St Patrick's Well), Chibbyr Sheeant (Blessed Well) or Chibbyr yn Argid (Well of the Silver), near Peel. St Patrick was being chased by a sea-monster as he came to the island and he sent his horse up a steep hill in order to escape. They rested at the top and a spring flowed at their feet. In an alternative story, the spring flowed where St Patrick made the sign of the cross on the ground. Ffynnon Ddewi (St David's Well) was actually located inside a cottage in Llanddewibrefi parish (Cardigan), and was said to have burst forth to mark the spot where the saint restored the cottager's son to life. Ffynnon Ddewi at Brawdy (Pembroke) flowed where the saint's tears fell. St George's Well at Padstow (Cornwall) gushed forth where the saint had trodden, and St Moorin's Well marked the place under the cliff at Morwenstowe (Cornwall) where the saint rested while choosing a stone for the font of the church when it was being built. She then carried the stone to the church, which feat shows that she was an amazon or endowed with supernatural power, because the font is large and heavy. It is apparently a very early font, and probably Saxon. The story continues with the information that the church site had to be changed because all the building materials were being mysteriously moved overnight to a new site, a common theme in folklore, and one which we have already discussed at greater length in our earlier book *The Secret Country*. Such tales may be based on the conflict between the old religion and the new, with the victory of Christianity in the siting of the church here being reinforced by both the miraculous appearance of a holy well and the saint's provision of a font for Christian baptism.

Several wells in Ballyboy parish (Offaly) arose as a result of the sad fate which overtook St Cormac. He believed he would be attacked and killed by wolves, following a prediction to this effect by another saint. So he lived in a tower, shut away from the world, until one day he saw two black snails creeping up the wall, and they appeared to be changing into wolves. Cormac ran from the tower and was chased by the wolves, and at each place where he fell down, a pure spring began to flow. Finally the wolves caught and killed him. At Ardagh (Longford) a holy well sprang up where St Brigid dropped a hot coal, a miracle which she performed in order to impress St Patrick. Another Irish saint, St Caolainn, used even more dramatic means to create a well in Kilkeerin parish (Roscommon). When a suitor told her that he admired her eyes, she pulled them out and threw them at his feet. She plucked two rushes and a well began to flow, where by bathing her eye-sockets she was able to restore her sight. A similar story was told of St Brigid, but she used an existing well, St Brigid's Well in Killinagh parish (Cavan), to restore her sight. Over the sea in Scotland, St Medana's Well at Glasserton (Wigtown) was created by the saint to restore her sight after she too threw her eyes at the feet of a persistent suitor.

St Edmund's Well in a meadow at Oxford began to flow at the spot where St Edmund Rich, a future archbishop of Canterbury then studying at the university, had a vision of Christ. Its healing reputation grew, and there was an annual festivity by the well on the saint's day, until the gatherings were banned in 1291 by the Bishop of Lincoln. He did not approve of the fact that 'the people were besotted with a fond imagination of its vertues and holinesse, and that they did neglect to serve the true God by hankering after the worshipping this well'. Again we see the Christian's fear of resurgent paganism – despite the strong tradition that the well had originated at the site where Christ had appeared in a vision.

Perhaps one of the strangest well creation tales concerns a dream rather than a vision. William Fiddler's friend died of consumption, and in the night following the funeral, Fiddler, who was himself suffering from consumption, dreamed of his friend whose voice said that he would see him at a certain place. Fiddler, still in his dream, went there and waited, but no friend appeared, only a large bee which flew round and round his head. Its buzzing began to sound like words:

'Dig, Willie, and drink.' So he dug in the ground, and a spring of clear water gushed forth. On waking, Fiddler remembered his dream, went to the place and found the spring. He drank from it and regained his health. This miraculous well is Fiddler's Well, two miles from Cromarty (Ross & Cromarty), and can still be seen in the side of a bank near the sea to the east of the town.

Finally, as a reminder that the interpretation of the kind of tales we have been reporting in this chapter is fraught with danger, and that these tales may often be relatively modern and without historical significance, we note that the medicinal waters of Llandrindod Wells (Radnor) which only sprang to fame a century or two ago, also have their creation legend. The three springs supposedly originated when a hero saved a girl from death by killing three monsters, one with a lump of salt, one with a lump of iron, and one with a lump of brimstone, the 'weapons' presumably corresponding to the waters' natures.

The existence of lakes and pools is also sometimes explained by stories describing their creation, and it is interesting to note that the

A spring at Llandrindod Wells, Radnor, where visitors can sample the chalybeate waters

stories fall into two main categories, examples of both being found in many parts of Britain and Ireland. The first category involves wells, the story in brief being that a well, when left uncovered, overflowed and a lake was formed. Loch Awe (Argyll) was formed in this way, because the female guardian of a well on Ben Cruachan fell asleep. She was heir to fertile farmland now covered by the loch, but in order to inherit she had to cover the well with a sacred stone every evening and remove the stone at daybreak. One day, weary from hunting, she fell asleep and did not wake for three days, by which time the well had overflowed and Loch Awe lay below her in the valley. Other Scottish lakes formed from overflowing wells are Loch Ness (Inverness), Loch Tay (Perth), and Loch Eck (Argyll). Loch Ussie (Ross & Cromarty) was formed when a magic stone was thrown into a pond, which promptly expanded into a loch. Close by on Knockfarrel lies Fingal's Well inside the Iron Age hillfort, and according to tradition this well was covered with a large stone to keep the water under control. A seer prophesied that on the third occasion the stone fell, Loch Ussie would force its way up through the well, and flood the valley below, but so far this has not happened. A holy well on Gigha (Argyll), the same one that was used to obtain favourable winds, was kept covered because the islanders believed it could overflow the island.

The traditional version of the overflowing well story is told of Llyn Llech Owain (Carmarthen). A man named Owen kept his well covered with a large stone, until one day he forgot to replace it after having watered his horse. Looking back as he rode home, he was amazed to see that the well water was rapidly overflowing the land. He quickly galloped round the flood and thus stopped the well from drowning the whole district. In another version, Owen was Owen Glyndwr or Owen Lawgoch, famous Welshmen of the past. At one time the banks of the lake were a favourite meeting place for young people on Sunday afternoons, but a Baptist preacher who did not approve put an end to their amusements – echoes of the religious disapproval of gatherings at holy wells. Ffynnon Grassi (Grace's Well) by Llyn Glasfryn at Llangybi (Caernarfon) was walled in and covered, and here too the lake was formed when the well was accidentally left open, perhaps by Grassi herself. It seems often to be the guardian of the well who is responsible for the disaster, and Francis Jones suggests that the stories may refer to a broken taboo, involving women.

At present we know of only one English lake caused by an overflowing well, the Great Mere at Ellesmere (Shropshire), and that was formed as a punishment. At one time the well was used freely by the people of the neighbourhood, but when the tenancy of the farm changed, the new tenant did not like having his land trampled so he stopped the poor folk from using the well. Soon afterwards when the farmer's wife went to the well for water, she found that the whole field was flooded, and it has remained flooded ever since. On the Isle of Wight a water spirit was imprisoned in the Druids' Well, and it was said that the lid should not be lifted under any circumstances, as a dreadful calamity would ensue. As the years passed, this warning was forgotten, and when a knight found the well while clearing woodland, he raised the lid. The resulting deluge drowned the knight and his men, and the forest was submerged by the water.

In Ireland, both Loughs Ree (Roscommon) and Neagh (Northern Ireland) were formed when the female guardian left a well cover off. Lough Sheelin (Meath) was formed when a woman fetching water left the stone cover off the well, and she was forced to run as the floods quickly spread outwards. After about seven miles, a man mowing hay saw her and, realising what was happening, scythed through her legs to stop her running, and in this dramatic way the water stopped flowing. The River Boyne, which rises in County Kildare, is said to have originally flowed from a well in the garden of King Nechtan, which felt itself insulted when the king's wife walked three times round it in an anti-clockwise direction. The well water rose up and chased her, sweeping her out to sea. A holy well in Columcille parish (Longford) was insulted when a woman washed her clothes in it. A calf which lived in the well jumped out and ran towards the valley, followed by the well water, and thus was Lough Gamhna formed.

In the foregoing tales there is a close link between wells and lakes. However, the other main category of lake formation lore has no link

Semer Water,
North Yorkshire

with holy wells. These tales are all variations on the theme of a settlement being drowned as a punishment for some transgression. In the north of England, Tarn Wadling and Mockerkin Tarn (both in Cumbria) contain villages whose inhabitants were drowned for some unknown misdemeanour, while Semer Water and Lake Gormire (both in North Yorkshire) conceal sizeable towns. The town in Lake Gormire was destroyed by an earthquake before the water flooded into the valley. At Semer Water, in Raydale, the flooding is explained as a punishment on the townspeople who would not help a poor old man (in some versions Christ, or a witch, or an angel, St Paul, or Joseph of Arimathea) who needed food. He pronounced a watery curse on the place, except for one small cottage on a hill where they had made him welcome. Two Shropshire pools complete the English drowned settlements: Bomere Pool near Shrewsbury, which was a village in a hollow whose inhabitants turned back to paganism until heavy rains at Christmas-time brought floods which engulfed them; and Llynclys Pool near Oswestry, where there was a palace which was drowned when the king refused to listen to a sermon preached by St Germanus − or alternatively, the court of the Llynclys family was submerged as a punishment for their riotous living.

The majority of legends of drowned settlements come from Wales, and there is factual evidence that in the past ages certain land areas of Wales, especially around the coasts, have become submerged in reality. At the low spring tides tree stumps can still be seen on the foreshore, for example in Cardigan Bay and.at Rhyl. It is possible that

Bala Lake,
Merioneth

Llyn Gwyn,
Nantmel, Radnor

some of the legends may have been inspired by these ancient events. Nearer to the present day, valley settlements have been sacrificed to reservoirs. Llanwddyn was submerged when Lake Vyrnwy (Montgomery) was formed at the end of the nineteenth century, and houses were also drowned in the flooding of valleys to form the four reservoirs in the Elan Valley (Radnor) at the turn of the century and in the 1950s. According to the legends, there are many more drowned settlements in Wales. Llyn Tegid/Bala Lake (Merioneth) hides a palace where lived a cruel prince, while Llyn-y-Maes/Tregaron Lake (Cardigan) hides the original town of Tregaron, the people's excessive revelry resulting in a lightning strike followed by flooding. Pencarreg Lake near Llanybyther (Carmarthen) covers a village, and Talley Lakes (Carmarthen) cover a town. At Llangadog (Carmarthen) a church sank into a pool, Pwll y Clychan, and bells could sometimes be heard there. The original town of Mathry (Pembroke) is said to lie beneath the waters of Llyn Llanbedr-y-Moch. One Breconshire lake has several names, Llangorse Lake/Savaddan Lake/Lake of Brycheiniog/Llyn Syfaddon, and there are several traditions to account for its presence, but all include the theme of vengeance for wrongdoing. Llyn Gwyn (Radnor) is reputedly the site of an important town, and an unusual semi-circular earthwork beside the lake adds to the mystery of the place. However, the earthwork is likely to be of later date than the lake, which is itself too small to cover a town. Kenfig Pool in the dunes near Porthcawl (Glamorgan) conceals a city drowned in vengeance for murder, and Crymlyn or Crumlin Pool is said to conceal the old town of Swansea (Glamorgan). Three existing towns will one day also be drowned, if the prophecies are fulfilled.

These are the present town of Bala (Merioneth), which will join the old town under the lake, Welshpool (Montgomery) which is threatened by the waters of Llyn Du, a pool near Powis Castle, and Carmarthen, about which one of Merlin's prophecies was:

> Carmarthen, a cold morn awaits thee;
> Earth gapes, and water in thy place will be.

The folklorist the Reverend John O'Hanlon commented in 1865 that 'subaqueous cities are supposed to lie under the surface of nearly all Irish lakes', but he gave no examples, only adding that this belief was probably caused by the reflections of mountains and clouds in the still water. Only Lough Ree (Roscommon) has a well recorded tradition, which tells of an underwater city with a cathedral or monastery. It was said to be often visited by people from the land above, and Caon Comrac, an ancient Bishop of Clonmacnoise, decided to go and see it for himself, but he never returned.

7. Water Divinities

It seems natural that our ancestors should have regarded water as a living creature with the power to bestow the life force, health and energy. The traditions described earlier show that belief in the supernatural power of water was strong and it was accepted that the spirit of the well could, if insulted, withhold her favours, causing the water to lose its power or to disappear altogether. The people prayed to her, and followed complex rituals in an attempt to please her and persuade her to grant a cure or whatever else they desired. We designate the spirit of the well as 'she' because in most of her personifications she takes a female form, though not invariably. She appears in many guises — ghost, witch, saint, mermaid, fairy, and sometimes in animal form, often as a sacred fish — and her presence permeates well lore, and indeed water lore generally. Some rivers were believed to have indwelling spirits, though they were usually feared and demonstrate the evil aspect of water divinities which we will explore at the end of this chapter.

Lakes, especially in Scotland, were endowed with water goddesses, one lake in Strathspey (Inverness) being called Loch-nan-Spoiradan, or Lake of Spirits. The *fideal* was a 'female impersonation of entangling grasses' which haunted Loch na Fideil in Gairloch (Ross & Cromarty), and a female demon known as the *Luideag*, the Rag, referring to her slovenly dress, haunted the shores of Lochan nan dubh bhreac in Skye. The *glaistig* was a half-woman, half-goat, a supernatural being widely accepted in Scotland, which was believed to live in caves or behind waterfalls, or at fords. She was usually invisible, but when she allowed herself to be seen she was dressed in green like the fairies. She could travel great distances at speed, and was generally feared. Indeed it seems that the majority of water divinities were held in awe, and were definitely not to be trifled with. The Irish 'Lady of the Lake' was more beneficent, and each July a twelve-day festival around Lower Lough Erne, particularly in the Irvinestown area (Fermanagh) celebrates the legend of the lady who walked through the mists on the lough, surrounded by light and carrying wild flowers. Her appearance signified good weather and good crops.

There are many accounts of female ghosts, often clad in white or green, appearing close to water. Some of these are vague folktales, and some are recent factual accounts, and it is difficult to avoid interpreting them as manifestations of the water divinity. An Irishwoman's dream, here related by the folklorist Lady Gregory, demonstrates how the image of the water spirit as a woman in white was deeply ingrained in the subconscious minds of the peasant people who used the holy wells.

There was Leary's son in Gort had bad eyes and no doctor could cure him. And one night his mother had a dream that she got up and took a half-blanket with her, and went away to a blessed well a little outside Gort, and there she saw a woman dressed all in white, and she gave her some of the water, and when she brought it to her son he got well. So the next day she went there and got the water, and after putting it three times on his eyes, he was as well as ever he was.[1]

This figure may still be part of our subconscious imagery, even at the present time, thus accounting for many of today's ghostly white ladies. As there are so many accounts of these ghosts, we will describe them in detail in the following chapter.

After ghostly women in white, the supernatural world is most strongly represented by the Little People, or fairies. Some holy wells were believed to be inhabited by the fairies, or to lead to their underworld homes. These fairies were in control of the well's powers and could cure illness and grant wishes. One such well was on the slopes of Schiehallion, the Fairy Hill of Caledonia, on Rannoch Moor (Perth); another was St Cuthbert's Well at Edenhall (Cumbria). Fairies danced on Midsummer Eve around the Trellech wells (Monmouth), and many other wells have names suggestive of a fairy presence: Fairies' Well near Hardhorn (Lancaster), a Fairy Well on Irby Heath (Cheshire), the Fairy Well at Laugharne (Carmarthen), and another on Fordoun Hill (Kincardine), a Pixy Well near Cothelstone (Somerset), and the Piskies' Well (also called St Nun's Well) at Pelynt (Cornwall). The name of a spring at Harlestone (Northampton), Mother Red Cap, suggests a fairy connection, as Redcap is a name once associated with certain Little People. A well beside the River Rhiw at Llanllugan (Montgomery) was the haunt of a sprite called the Bwgan, who lived among the roots of a tree over the well.

Pins, buttons and suchlike were sometimes thrown into a well as a gift to the fairies. At the Cheese Well, Minchmoor (Peebles), bits of cheese were dropped into the water for the fairies living there. A bowl of milk or other offering was left at Fuaran a chreigain bhreac (Well of the Spotted Rock) at Inverness by any woman who believed her baby was a changeling. She would also leave the child there overnight, hoping that when she returned in the morning, she would find her own healthy child, the changeling having been taken back by the fairies.

St Nun's Well,
Pelynt, Cornwall

Some people even claimed to have seen the fairies, as did an old man and his wife living in the Wicklow Mountains who described them to W. B. Yeats and Lady Gregory. Peacock Well was one of the places where they gathered. Another Irishman talked of the fairies seen at St Patrick's Well at Burren, after the priest had put a stop to the regular gatherings or patterns. The first year after they had been stopped, a girl was held up by her father on to a high wall near the well and, looking down, 'she saw the whole place full of the gentry [fairies], and they playing and dancing and having their own games, they were in such joy to have done away with the pattern. I suppose the well belonged to them before it got the name of St Patrick.' In about 1815, William Butterfield saw the fairies at Ilkley Wells (West Yorkshire) where he was the bathman. One midsummer morning when he went to open the door, the key turned round and round in the lock and when he managed to get the door open he saw an unexpected sight:

. . . all over the water and dipping into it was a lot of little creatures dressed in green from head to foot, none of them more than eighteen inches high, and making a chatter and a jabber thoroughly unintelligible. They seemed to be taking a bath, only they bathed with all their clothes on. Soon, however, one or two of them began to make off, bounding over the walls like squirrels.

Finding they were all making ready for decamping, and wanting to have a word with them, he shouted at the top of his voice – indeed, he declared afterwards he couldn't find anything else to say or do – 'Hallo there!' Then away the whole tribe went, helter skelter, toppling and tumbling, heads over heels, heels over heads, and all the while making a noise not unlike that of a disturbed nest of young partridges. The sight was so unusual, that he declared he either couldn't or daren't attempt to rush after them . . . When the well had got quite clear of these strange beings he ran to the door and looked to see where they had fled, but nothing was to be seen. He ran back into the bath to see if they had left anything behind; but there was nothing; the water lay still and clear just as he had left it the previous night.²

At first he told no one of his strange encounter, but later, after no ill luck had befallen him, he told his wife, who told her friends, and so the tale spread. Our account of it came from an Ilkley man who knew William Butterfield. It is impossible to determine exactly what it was he saw, but before dismissing his experience as an hallucination, it should be realised that there are many other people who also claim to have seen the Little People and other inexplicable beings.

Back in the realms of folklore, we find accounts of people who actually visited fairyland. Near the river called Afon Mynach not far from Bala (Merioneth) some men were cutting turf on the moors. One of them washed his face in a well which was known to be a fairy well. At dinner time this youth went to fetch the box of food for them all to share, but he never returned. The others suspected that the fairies had had a hand in his disappearance, but did not know what to do. They consulted a local wise man, and on his advice they returned to the place at full moon in June, and saw the moor covered with thousands of dancing fairies. Among them was their friend, and they managed to pull him free. In Pembrokeshire, a shepherd boy was taken by the fairies from Frenni Fawr to a magnificent fairy palace, where he was well treated but told not to drink from a fountain in the garden. But he disobeyed and drank, and instantly the palace disappeared and he found himself back on the hillside.

Not only holy wells were frequented by or associated with the Little People. They were sometimes seen at lakes, pools and rivers, such as the 'fairy pool' near Brington (Northampton) where they could be seen gambolling among the water plants. An island in the middle of Llyn Cwm Llwch (Brecon) was believed to be the garden of the fairies, though it could not be seen by anyone on the lake shore, except as an indistinct mass. There are many other stories linking the Little People with Welsh lakes, far too many to detail here. Perhaps the best known tells of Llyn y Fan Fach (Carmarthen) where a beautiful fairy maiden from the lake became the wife of a man from Llanddeusant. They lived happily near Myddfai for many years, having three sons, but the wife in due time returned to the lake followed by the cattle she had brought from the lake as her dowry. She later returned to teach her sons medicine and the use of herbs, and this is the origin of the famous Physicians of Myddfai whose remedies have been preserved in manuscript form. A similar story of a fairy/human marriage was told of other lakes such as Llyn Nelfarch/Elfarch/Alfarch/Llyn y Forwyn (Glamorgan) and Llyn Cwellyn (Caernarfon). The Reverend Elias Owen suggested that the great number of Welsh fairytales associated with lakes may possibly indicate a memory of our lake-dwelling prehistoric ancestors. Scottish lakes likewise had their fair share of indwelling fairies, who like the Little People everywhere strongly objected to any interference with their territory. At Lochan-nan-deaan between Corgarff and Tomintoul (Aberdeen) the attempt by a group of local men to drain the loch was met by a great shout from a little man wearing a red cap who appeared before them. The men fled in terror, and the water spirit returned satisfied to his home.

Mermaids are usually thought of as belonging only to the wide open spaces of the sea, but there are a few inland lakes, some quite small, which have legends of mermaids, and this may be simply another form adopted by the water divinity. Some degree of overlap between the different types of lake-dwelling maidens is suggested, because the Welsh fairy maidens' habit of emerging from the water and combing

Llyn Cwellyn, Caernarfon, an area with fairy associations. As well as the story of a fairy caught at the lake one night, who married her human captor, another story tells of a young man who stepped into a fairy circle by the lake, and found himself in fairyland. On returning after seven years, he died of a broken heart on finding his parents dead and his sweetheart married to another

their hair is exactly the behaviour one expects from a mermaid. One of the water spirits of Loch-nan-Spoiradan, mentioned earlier, is supposed to take the form of a mermaid. Except for this lake and also Loch Sin, where a mermaid washing bloody garments foreshadowed the tragic collapse in 1742 of the roof of Fearn Abbey church killing about forty people, the Scottish mermaids seem to prefer the sea. Most of the inland lakes with mermaid legends are in England, some examples being the Mermaid's Pool near Hayfield (Derby), whose mermaid will confer immortality on anyone lucky enough to see her while bathing; Rostherne Mere (Cheshire), where the mermaid would ring a bell on the lake floor and then sit on it singing; the inland pools of East Anglia, haunted by mermaids which were likely to pull people into the water and were used as a threat to keep children away from the pools; Black Mere/Blake Mere/Mermaid's Pool at Morridge (Stafford), whose mermaid also wanted to lure people to their deaths; and Aqualate Mere (Stafford), whose mermaid threatened to drown local settlements if her lake was drained. Some mermaids made their homes in rivers, such as the River Lugg at Marden (Hereford & Worcester), whose mermaid held a bell from the church and could not be outwitted by the people who tried to get it back. In 1848 an ancient bronze bell was actually discovered in a pond at Marden. The River Mersey also had a mermaid, who could be seen on moonlit nights near Leasowe Castle (Cheshire).

It is clear that the water divinity rarely took the form of a witch, as there is very little lore linking witches with wells or other water sources. Sometimes there is a vague reference to a witch at a well, as for example Ffynnon y Wrach, which means Witch's Well, on the slope of Moel Bentyrch (Montgomery), and other similarly named wells and pools in Wales. There is also a Witch's Well in Kilve parish (Somerset), and a Witch's Pool at Sandhill (Somerset), where the ghost of a notorious witch had reputedly been laid, giving it an unpleasant atmosphere. Occasionally witches were believed to practise their witchcraft at wells, such as the Skimmington Well near Curry Rivel (Somerset), where they were said to dance at May Eve and Midsummer, and the Witch's Well at Irongray (Kirkcudbright), where in the seventeenth century a witch was said to be in the habit of walking widdershins round the well by her cottage, for which crime she was rolled downhill in a blazing tar barrel. It has been suggested that the witch's bubbling cauldron symbolised the sacred well which had an important role in the witch's religion.

In fact very little is known of the practices of genuine witches, who undoubtedly did exist in earlier centuries. Today they have a bad reputation, being connected in people's minds with black magic and evil spells, but these much-maligned women probably played an invaluable role as shamans in their communities, supplying many needs from herbal medicines to psychological counselling, as well as possibly being the inheritors and custodians of the ancient religion of the pre-Christian Celts. There are hints, and only hints, of this more esoteric side to their practices, and one of the hints is in the occasional references to witches acting as keepers of sacred wells. Ffynnon Sarah (also known as Ffynnon Deg) at Caerwys (Flint) was in the control of a witch named Sarah, without whose help no benefits could be obtained from the well. More often the well custodian was simply referred to as an old woman, but she had the knowledge and power necessary to keep the well functioning, and in many cases we can assume that her position was hereditary and may have been so since the time when wells played an important part in the pre-Christian religious practices. At Bernera in Glenelg (Inverness) the White Well was kept clean and pure by Anne MacRae, who also looked after the sacred trout in the well. This disappeared at her death around the turn of the century. St Mary's Well at Culloden (Inverness) also had a female guardian, who provided drinking dishes and kept the place tidy. Gulval Well (Cornwall) had a female custodian, though she died in the mid-eighteenth century and seems to have been the last of her line. From the evidence recorded at the time, 'she seems to have known all the mystic endowments of the fountain, and to have been for a long time its high priestess and dispenser of its virtues.'

Francis Jones points out the difficulty in estimating which of the well custodians were really priestesses with links back to pagan times, and which were merely old women living in cottages near the wells, who would help visitors in return for small payments. Sometimes a cottage was built at the well, presumably to house the custodian, as at St Cybi's Well, Llangybi (Caernarfon), but there can be no certainty that his or her role was anything more than helping people who wanted to bathe in the well. Where a ritual was involved, and the position was known to be hereditary, we can feel more certain of the custodian's role as a representative of the pagan priesthood. On the island of Lewis (Outer Hebrides) the water from St Ronan's Well was conveyed to the patient in a jar in the hereditary custody of a certain family, known as 'the clerk of the temple'. A case with particularly strong pagan connections was reported by Dr Anne Ross from Wester Ross, where she met the present hereditary guardian of Tobar a' Chinn (The Well of the Head). The water is said to cure epilepsy, and a complex ritual must be followed under the guardian's direction, during which the patient drinks the well water from a human skull. In this discussion we have travelled some way from our suggestion that

St Cybi's Well,
Llangybi,
Caernarfon. The
cottage was the
building at the
right, adjoining
the well buildings

some tales of witches at holy wells may be one way of referring to the spirit or divinity of the well, but the ensuing discussion helps to show the complexity of the material we are dealing with, and how it is open to a number of interpretations.

In addition to the female entities we have already discussed, there are others who are mentioned in only a small number of tales, but who may also represent the goddess of the well. In this connection the role of the saints should not be overlooked. In the peasant's mind they may not have been distinguishable from the deities, most especially the female saints such as Brigid or Bride (who was originally a Celtic goddess) and the Virgin Mary. According to tradition she has appeared to people seeking a cure at her well at Dunsfold (Surrey), and indeed in strongly Catholic countries such as France, Spain and Portugal, there are a number of locations where healing springs are associated with visions of the Virgin Mary. This is also the case at Walsingham (Norfolk), which became a shrine following a vision of the Virgin Mary, and where a holy well plays an important part in modern pilgrimages. It is also probable that male saints were often confused with the deity of the well, so that although the Christian priests may have had in their parishes holy wells dedicated to saints, the people who visited them may have felt more comfortable offering their prayers to a pre-Christian deity. A story from Ireland shows how the elements can become confused, when a creature sounding like one of the Little People is described as a saint. A little boy fell into a well at Kilmacduagh and was found when people went to draw water. He was standing in the water, and he told them that 'a little grey man, that was St Colman, came to him in the well and put his hand under his chin, and kept his head up over the water.'

Another example of pre-Christian beliefs surviving to the present century, albeit cloaked in a Christian garb, concerns the well Tobar na mBan Naomh (Well of the Holy Women) near Teelin (Donegal). It was believed that three women grew up at the well and became nuns. They gave their blessing to the well, and fishermen sailing in Teelin Bay would ask the blessing of the holy women. This trio is very reminiscent of the trios of goddesses worshipped in the Celtic religion. In Wales a memory of Gwenhudw, a water goddess, has been preserved at two holy wells. One was Ffynnon Gwenhudw/Gnidiw/ Cridiw between Dolgellau and Garneddwen (Merioneth), and in the same county was also a standing stone known as Maen Gwynhudw. The *hudw* part of her name indicates a connection with primitive magic, and this, together with the water connection and a standing stone, shows the survival of elements of pagan religion, with Gwenhudw representing the water divinity. Any female personality connected with a well may represent a deity rather than a real person. Two examples are Lady Wulfruna's Spring at Wolverhampton (West Midlands) and the Viking princess Beothail who died of grief on Lismore island (Argyll) when her lover died in battle. Her spirit was restless, and so her corpse was exhumed and after being washed in a sacred well, was taken to her home at Lochlann. The well where the corpse was washed became known as the Well of Beothail's Bones.

Fishes can be seen as a phallic symbol, and they are also symbolic of fecundity, procreation, life renewed and sustained. Salmon and trout were sacred creatures to the Celts, and may have represented the gods of the underworld. Traces of these beliefs remain in the form of sacred fishes in holy wells, which in some instances were present until recent times. All the examples we have discovered come from areas under Celtic influence. Martin Martin mentions a well he saw at Kilbride on Skye during his tour of the western islands of Scotland in the 1690s where there was a sacred trout: 'the natives are very tender of it, and though they often chance to catch it in their wooden pales, they are very careful to preserve it from being destroyed; it has been there for many years.'[3] This well was, appropriately enough, called the Well of the Trout. Near Glenelg (Inverness) there were two wells with sacred trout, while St Bean's Well at Kilmore (Argyll) used to contain two black fishes, known as *Easg Siant* or Holy Fishes. Loch Siant on Skye was rich in fish but none were ever caught because the people held the water in such great esteem that they dared not touch the fish living there.

From England we know of only two places where sacred fishes were kept, but there were very probably others. A trout with a golden chain around its neck lived in the Golden Well at Peterchurch (Hereford &

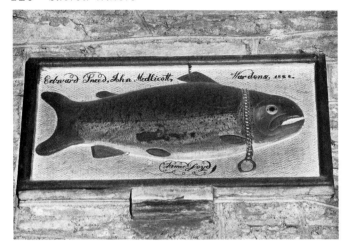

The fish with a golden chain around its neck still to be seen in Peterchurch church, Hereford & Worcester

Worcester), and is now commemorated on a tablet still to be seen in the church. Francis Jones reports that in medieval times fishes in ponds and wells often had rings placed round them, while at Versailles and Fontainebleau silver rings on the fishes marked the birth of princes and princesses. In Cornwall, St Neot's Well once contained three fishes, whose existence an angel told to the saint, with the added information that if he took only one for his daily meal, the supply would remain constant. But when he was lying sick in bed, his servant took two of the fishes, cooking each in a different way in order to please his master's palate. The saint, on realising what had happened, immediately ordered him to throw both cooked fishes back into the well, whereupon they were restored to life.

The best-known Welsh well containing sacred fishes was Ffynnon Beris near Llanberis (Caernarfon), where the appearance or non-appearance of the fishes could be used as guides to the future. Two new fishes were put into the well as late as 1896, as was reported in the *Liverpool Mercury* of 18 November 1896. The report is worth quoting in full, as it demonstrates the strength of the well cult in some areas less than a century ago.

Two new fishes have just been put in the 'Sacred Well', Ffynnon y Sant, at Tyn y Ffynnon, in the village of Nant Peris, Llanberis. Invalids in large numbers came, during the last century and the first half of the present century, to this well to drink of its 'miraculous Waters'; and the oak box, where the contributions of those who visited the spot were kept, is still in its place at the side of the well. There have always been two 'sacred fishes' in this well; and there is a tradition in the village to the effect that if one of the Tyn y Ffynnon fishes came out of its hiding-place when an invalid took some of the water for drinking or for bathing purposes, cure was certain; but if the fishes remained in their den, the water would do those who took it no good. Two fishes only are to be put in the well at a time, and they generally live in its waters for about half a century. If one dies before the other, it would be of no use to put in a new fish, for the old fish would not associate with it, and it would die. The experiment has been tried. The last of the two fishes put in the well about fifty years ago died last August. It had been blind for some time previous to its death. When taken out of the water it measured seventeen inches, and was buried in the garden adjoining the well. It is stated in a document of the year 1776 that the parish clerk was to receive the money put in the box of the well by visitors. This money, together with the amount of 6s 4d, was his annual stipend.

Other Welsh wells known to contain sacred fishes included Ffynnon Fair, Llanddwyn (Anglesey), where the movements of the fishes predicted the course of true love for the young people, Ffynnon Wennog (Cardigan) whose trout wore golden chains, Ffynnon Bryn Fendigaid, Aberffraw (Anglesey) where a fish was used for divination, St Peter's Well, Llantwit Major (Glamorgan), and Ffynnon Gwyfan near Disserth (Radnor).

There were also many wells with sacred fishes in Ireland, for example St Ciaran's Well, Castlekeeran (Meath), where the sacred trout could only be seen at midnight on the first Sunday in August, and the pilgrims used lights to try and catch a glimpse of them. The trout in the well of Tubbernalt (Sligo) were invisible to most people, and visitors regularly threw in pieces of bread to feed them. A blind man

Ffynnon Beris
near Llanberis,
Caernarfon

claimed to have regained his sight at the well: 'Oh look on me; I was blind from my birth, and saw no light till I came to the blessed well; now I see the water and the speckled trout down at the bottom, with the white cross on his back.' The sacred fishes were also the subject of stories and beliefs, one of which explained the dark markings some-times seen on their sides. A fish was caught by unbelievers and placed on a gridiron to fry, but was miraculously transported back to the well, though retaining the marks of the hot gridiron on its body.

The well's guardian spirit would sometimes be embodied in another animal form, such as an eel. That in Ffynnon Gybi, Llangybi (Caernarfon), would coil round the legs of a patient standing in the well, if he was to be cured. When the eel was removed, people believed that the well had lost much of its power. The movements of an eel in Ffynnon Elaeth (Anglesey) were interpreted by someone skilled in the art, and people waited for the eel to appear, and to learn what was predicted. Other Welsh wells with sacred eels included Ffynnon Gybi at Holyhead (Anglesey) and the churchyard well at Llandeloy (Pem-broke). Ffynnon Sarff at Llangian (Caernarfon) was said to be the home of a serpent, and a winged serpent flew from St Edrin church tower and curled up at night in Grinston Well at Brawdy (Pembroke). Giraldus Cambrensis wrote of a Pembrokeshire well with a serpent which guarded a golden torque, and would bite anyone trying to retrieve it. Treasure was also concealed in Ffynnon Digyn, Clynnog (Caernarfon), perhaps guarded by the creatures looking like hedge-hogs which a woman once claimed to have seen in the well. Several frogs said to dwell in the Frog Well at Acton Burnell (Shropshire) represented the Devil and his imps, while a well on a hill in Strathdon parish (Aberdeen) contained a worm which predicted the patient's recovery.

Perhaps the strangest embodiment of the well's divinity was in the form of a fly, which would skim across the water in St Michael's Well, Kirkmichael (Banff). It was believed to be immortal, and pilgrims would anxiously watch its movements for a sign as to the outcome of their concerns. The well was visited by pilgrims from far and wide, and its popularity brought about two attempts in the seventeenth century to stop the pilgrimages. It finally lost its reputation as a healing centre at the end of the eighteenth century.

The preceding tales indicate a healthy respect for the guardian of the well: she/he will only react favourably if the pilgrim makes the correct deferential approach. In some instances, the guardian is of a malicious or evil nature, and a belief concerning a well near Corgarff (Aberdeen) demonstrates clearly how the evil side of the guardian's nature can be triggered off by the pilgrim's inattention to the correct ritual. A Little Grey Man (*Duine-glase-beg*) living in a small knoll nearby was the guardian of Tobar-na-glas (the Well in the Grey Wood) and everyone taking a drink had to drop a pin or other piece of metal into the well. If they omitted to do this, and later tried to take water from the well, the spirit would not allow it, and the victim would eventually die of thirst. People who drowned while trying to cross the River Ribble by the Bungerley stepping stones near Waddow Hall (Lancaster) were seen as victims of Peg, the evil spirit of Peg's Well nearby. Sometimes the evil spirit was seen as the Devil, who was said to haunt several wells, including one near St Lawrence (Pembroke).

The spirits of lakes and rivers seem to have usually been evil in nature. In Scotland the Cailleach (Old Wife) was a prominent supernatural figure with many abilities, one of them being the power to cause storms, and in the early nineteenth century she was believed to be living around Lochan na Cailliche (Moray) in the form of a heron. Her home was said to be a cairn of stones at the end of the loch. She had been 'spreading sickness and death among man and beast', and attempts by the clergy to control her had failed. Finally an ex-soldier shot down a heron using a gun loaded with a crooked sixpence and some silver buttons, and everyone believed that the Cailleach had been defeated. As a local gillie told a traveller, *c.* 150 years ago, 'She hasna' done much harm since yon, but her ghaist is still to the fore, and the loch side is no canny after the gloaming.' The Cailleach also haunted river fords and drowned unwary travellers. The River Conon (Ross & Cromarty) was believed to be haunted by an evil spirit, and one story tells of a young man who began to cross at a ford on horseback. Halfway across the horse started to struggle and the man cried out in terror. His horrified companions watched as a tall dark figure rose out of the water and dragged the man off his horse. The animal struggled to the bank, but the man disappeared into the river.

We have space only for these brief examples of Scottish lake and river spirits, belief in which was very widespread in the rural areas. Likewise in England and Wales, one example picked from many being the 'Torrent Spectre', here described by the Welsh folklorist the Reverend Elias Owen:

This spectre was supposed to be an old man, or malignant spirit, who directed, and ruled over, the mountain torrents. He delighted in devastating the lands. His appearance was horrible to behold, and it was believed that in the midst of the rushing stream his terrible form could be discerned apparently moving with the torrent, but in reality remaining stationary. Now he would raise himself half out of the water, and ascend like a mist half as high as the near mountain, and then he would dwindle down to the size of a man. His laugh accorded with his savage visage, and his long hair stood on end, and a mist always surrounded him.[4]

Jenny Greenteeth was one evil entity who might have a factual existence, of a kind. She was until recently widely used as a threat to keep children away from water, especially in the Lancashire/Cheshire/ north Shropshire area. She was said to pull children into the water, and was most likely to be found in stagnant pools covered with green slime. This, and her name, give a clue to her identity, for it has been suggested that 'Jenny Greenteeth' is simply a name for the green duckweed which covers the surface of some pools and from which the victims would find it very difficult to disentangle themselves.

Human deaths are never very far away from the lore of rivers and lakes, for it was widely believed that the water divinities demanded regular human sacrifice. In Scotland the River Spey was said to require one life a year, while

> Bloodthirsty Dee, each year needs three;
> But bonny Don, she needs none.

The river spirit would also decide whether or not to release the body of a drowned person. A search failed to find the body of a basket-maker drowned in the Dee, so his wife took her husband's plaid and knelt on the river bank to pray to the spirit to give back her dead. She threw the plaid into the water, and next morning the corpse was found, wrapped in the plaid. Similarly, a biscuit was placed in the River Don as a gift to the spirit of the river, which then released the body of a drowned man.

Some Scottish lochs also demanded a sacrifice, such as Loch Ness in which sacrifices of cattle used to be made, or even of children in withy baskets. Otta Swire wrote of the loch:

I used to hear in my childhood, when we often visited Glen Urquhart, that this 'thing' was still sometimes seen, a great dark shapeless mass, brooding over the waters, dreaming of evil. And its dreams worked, for if it was seen, however faint and formless an apparition, shortly afterwards someone would be drowned and their body would never be found.[5]

Loch Wan (Lamb's Loch) (Aberdeen/Banff border) required the first lamb of each of the flocks grazing around the loch, else half of the flock would drown. An attempt to drain the loch met with failure, for the channel dug each day was mysteriously filled in again at night. After three days the men stayed to watch in secret, and at midnight saw hundreds of small black creatures rise from the loch and with their spades undo the men's work for the day in the course of a few minutes.

The Welsh River Dee was the home of the war goddess Aerfen, who was said to need three human sacrifices each year in order to ensure success in battle. Llyn Gwernan and Llyn Cynwch (both Merioneth)

The spirit of Llyn Cynwch, Merioneth, was said to demand an annual sacrifice

are the subjects of similar stories describing how the lakes need annual sacrifices, and when another year has passed a voice is heard crying: 'The hour is come but the man is not!' Whereupon a man is seen rushing headlong into the lake, having experienced what could be called 'a compulsion to suicide' in answer to the call of the spirit of the lake.

A number of English rivers (but apparently no lakes) required sacrifices. In Devon the Dart's need was well known, as told in a couplet which has several slight variations, one version being:

> Dart, Dart, cruel Dart,
> Every year thou claim'st a heart.

Other Devon rivers demanding human lives are the Tavy and the East Okement. Recently a man told how he had heard a voice from the latter river calling 'The hour has come, but not the man' as he hurried to join a man he saw standing on the riverbank, as if about to throw himself in. The assumption in this instance, contrary to that shown in the Welsh example given above, is that the water spirit was rejecting the victim who presented himself. Other southern rivers include the Parrett (Somerset) and Wye (Hereford & Worcester), both of which demanded an annual victim. In the north, the Trent, Ure and Ribble all required periodic sacrifices, the Ribble (Lancaster) every seventh year, the Ure (Yorkshire) annually, and the Trent (Lincoln) three times a year.

Sometimes it is the compulsion to suicide which assures a victim, as was suggested by the coroner following the apparently accidental drowning of a young soldier in 1968 at Lydford Gorge (Devon):

The River Ure at
Aysgarth, North
Yorkshire

He could have been overcome by the atmosphere of the Gorge which I personally think is no cheerful place even in daytime. In the gloom and damp he may have been overcome by the eeriness and had a certain compulsion to jump in . . . but there is no evidence of premeditation.

Of another Devon water, Bradmere Pool, believed to be haunted, a young woman recently said: 'It's as if there's something in there that makes you want to throw yourself into the water.' Feelings such as these may have helped to shape the earlier beliefs in evil spirits living in the lakes and rivers.

8.   Ghosts at Wells, Lakes and Rivers

'I dunna believe in ghosses, for I've bin about the church and churchyard, day an' night, for the last fifty years, an' I never seed none.'

Despite this plain speaking from Molly Daniel, sexton at Llandysilio church (Montgomery) in the first half of the nineteenth century, ghost stories abound, and many people evidently did (and still do) believe in the existence of ghosts. We have collected over thirty ghost stories connected with wells, and more than a hundred haunted lakes, pools, rivers and streams. These stories can be roughly divided into four categories:
1. representations of water divinities;
2. modern folklore;
3. recent first-hand sightings of ghosts; and
4. cases on the borderline between fact and fancy, that is, those with a possible factual basis, though it is not possible at this stage to decide for certain whether the tale is a true story, and we are lacking a first-hand account.

As well as the possible overlap between categories 2 and 3, there is often uncertainty as to whether category 1 or 2 is more appropriate for a particular story: although we suspect that a story of a 'white lady' might have originated in a belief in water divinities, we can never be sure that it is not a relatively modern expression of a feeling that a certain stretch of water is 'haunted'.

Bearing these problems in mind, we shall describe the well ghosts first of all. Over half of them may be tentatively interpreted as describing water divinities. The phantom hand sometimes seen stretched over those drinking at the Well of the Outstretched Hand near Dores (Inverness) was said to belong to the spirit of the well. Also in Scotland, a ghostly nun was in charge of a well in a haunted hollow near Loch Ness (Inverness). The white lady which haunted St Julian's Well at Wellow (Avon) was the family ghost of the Hungerfords who lived in the Manor House, and she would appear beside the well whenever a calamity was about to befall the family. The ghost of St Osyth, who was beheaded by Danish raiders at her nunnery, was said to appear by her well at St Osyth (Essex), carrying her head in her hand. Marian's Well at Uttoxeter (Stafford) was haunted by the ghost of a young woman, and the Lady or Lady's Well near Whittingham

(Northumberland) by a white lady. Another white lady appeared by the Cattle Well at Detchant near Belford (Northumberland). Also in Northumberland, Meg of Meldon, said to be a witch and miser, had placed a bull's hide full of gold in a well near Meldon Tower, and her ghost haunted the well. Peg o' Nell's Well (or simply Peg's Well) near Waddow Hall (Lancaster) was the haunt of a former servant at the hall, who is said to have died while fetching water from the well after her master or mistress angrily wished that she might fall and break her neck.

There are a number of haunted Welsh wells, a grey lady being a frequent visitor, or so it was said, to Taff's Well near Cardiff (Glamorgan). She once asked a man to hold her tight by the hands until she asked to be released, but a sharp pain made him let go, and the ghost cried that she must now remain in bondage for a further hundred years. Not far away, a grey lady haunted St Denis's Well near Llanishen (Glamorgan), while at Penylan Well, Cardiff (Glamorgan), a woman in dark clothes was seen at twilight, and a similar story of bondage and her attempt to be released is told. The eye well at Marcross near St Donat's (Glamorgan) was the haunt of a green lady, who used to watch people as they fastened rags to the thorn-bushes. The area of Ffynnon Gwenno at Cynwyl Gaio (Carmarthen) is haunted by Gwenno's ghost. She was exploring caves nearby when she was taken by spirits, and her ghost is now seen as a wreath of mist hanging over the rocks. The white ghost of the Boiling Well between Grasswell and Hay (Radnor) once jumped up on to the back of a horse behind a farmer's wife who was riding by, and stayed there until she arrived home. Jack-y-Cap-Coch (Jack with the Red Cap) was the name of the ghost sometimes seen at Jack Cap Coch's Well in Llandysilio parish (Montgomery), Jack being a boy who was murdered nearby and his ghost eventually captured and placed in a bottle at the bottom of the well, to stop it haunting the family mansion at the Rhysnant.

To digress briefly, laying them in water, sometimes in a bottle, seems to have been a favourite method of dealing with troublesome ghosts in Wales. They were often ejected from churches, as was the ghost which disrupted services at Llanfor church (Merioneth) and was with great difficulty persuaded to remove itself to Llyn-y-Geulan-Goch, a pool in the River Dee. The ghost of Llandegla's old rectory (Flint) was captured in the shape of a fly, placed in a small box and buried under a large stone in a mountain stream, while the ghost of Lady Jeffrey was enticed into a bottle and thrown into the river at Llanidloes (Montgomery). There are several other stories of this kind, with some of the spirits being laid behind waterfalls. Over the border in Shropshire, the ghost of old Diggory of Huglith near Pulverbatch

The Swallow Falls at Betws-y-Coed, Caernarfon, where the spirit of wicked Sir John Wynne is said to be held fast to the bottom of the fall, his cries of anger as he tries to break free sounding from the rushing water

was laid in a well, called Diggory's Well, where he was occasionally said to show himself, just as Jack-y-Cap-Coch still put in occasional appearances at his well, even though he was supposedly securely imprisoned at the bottom of it. The ghost imprisoned inside St David's Well at Henfynuw (Cardigan) tried unsuccessfully to escape. An old man visiting the well on Midsummer Eve heard a voice shouting for help, and saw a hand reaching from under the well. The voice asked him to clasp it and hold tight, but it slipped free and as it vanished the voice cried that it was bound for another fifty years.

Some more Welsh wells haunted by ghosts include Ffynnon y Bwci near Newcastle Emlyn (Cardigan), a well at Llanwddyn (Montgomery), and Ffynnon Digwg (Caernarfon), the field nearby being haunted by the ghost of a crying child. Sometimes the ghosts take the form of animals, especially horses, and a white horse was seen walking on its hind legs towards the churchyard well at Oxwich (Glamorgan), finally disappearing into the well. Anyone visiting the well at Gerddi Bach Trewilym (Pembroke) at night would hear the sound of a horse galloping closer, though nothing was ever seen.

These ghost stories may be the scanty remains of a once-strong belief in the spirit of the well, though as we emphasised earlier, they are usually so vague as to be difficult to interpret with any degree of certainty. A ghostly white lady may seem to be the ideal embodiment for a water goddess, but another feasible explanation is that the name of a well may sometimes be the cause of the ghost story, so that a well called Lady Well, the name originating with a dedication to the Virgin Mary, is likely to acquire a white lady ghost legend, and indeed there are two such wells in our account: Lady Well at Whittingham, and Marian's Well at Uttoxeter.

Later folklore or an active local imagination may have given rise to the following ghost stories, though there is also a possibility that the murders mentioned did actually take place. A well at Everton (Merseyside) was haunted as a result of a murder, while the Well of the Spectre at Dunlichty (Inverness) was named for the ghost of a packman murdered there. A white lady, stained with blood, used to haunt a tree by Three-Tree Well, Glasgow; she was said to be Catherine Clark, murdered by her lover and buried near the tree. Two lovers haunt a spring near Aconbury (Hereford & Worcester), the girl having murdered her lover in a fit of jealousy, then dying herself of a broken heart when she learned he was innocent. Ghosts identified as representing known people may indeed be the ghosts of those people, or, as Francis Jones has suggested, they may be 'ancient well spirits reappearing as ghosts of once living men'. Ffynnon Feirad (Cardigan) was haunted by the ghost of a parson from centuries past, and Pistyll Cwyn in Llandyssul parish (Cardigan) by Dafis Castell Hywel who died in 1827.

We have no first-hand accounts of ghosts seen at wells, but there are a few tales which may possibly be based on fact, for they contain details which we have also found in factual accounts. Still in Wales,

Three Tree Well, Glasgow, as it used to be

Ffynnon yr Yspryd (the Well of the Spirit) in Trefethin parish (Monmouth) was known to be haunted, as its name suggests. Anne Jenkins was going to milk cows near the well when she saw a horrible-looking black man standing by a holly tree. Her dog ran barking towards the man, whereupon he stretched out a long black tongue and the dog ran back cringing with fear. Anne was also afraid, but she continued on her way after the straying cows, and when passing the tree on her way back she looked again and saw the man, or monster. It walked away with heavy tread, towards the well in the field, whistling loudly before vanishing. This strange tale defies explanation, but Anne could certainly have had a genuine brush with the supernatural.

The remaining ghosts are rather more conventional, that at the Flass Well on the North Road in Durham being of Jane Ramshaw who was murdered in the late eighteenth century, though her murderer was never found. She was also often seen by pitmen in the neighbouring fields and on the road to Brancepeth. A murder was also perpetrated at Happisburgh (Norfolk), the victim being a sailor whose decomposed body was found at the bottom of a well after a legless ghost with its head hanging down its back had been regularly seen in the village, around 1800. Two farmers who saw the ghost decided one night to follow it, and watched as it threw a bundle it was carrying down a well at Well Corner, then disappeared down the well itself. A search revealed the man's remains. The bundle the ghost had carried was a pair of boots which still contained the sailor's legs. Later finds on the beach suggested that the man had been one of a group of smugglers who had quarrelled. A 'crisis apparition' was seen at a well at Auchloa (Perth). A man dying in a cottage in the area repeatedly called for water, and he wanted the water from this particular well. Two women set off for the well, which was some distance away, and evening was coming on when they arrived. As they were descending the steps into the well, they saw the ghost of the man for whom they were fetching the water. He wore a nightshirt, and had a grey blanket wrapped round his waist. The ghost was drinking water from the well in his cupped hands. The women quickly returned to the cottage, and as they entered the old man was just at the point of death. During the preparations for the funeral, a grey blanket was found in a chest, identical to the blanket the ghost had worn, though until that moment no one knew that there was such a blanket in the cottage.

Water was believed to give access to the world of spirits, and it is this belief which may have led to the practice of laying ghosts in water, as described earlier. There is certainly plenty of evidence linking ghosts with water, and from stories of ghosts at wells we now move to other water sources. The great majority of ghosts we have recorded tend to follow the same pattern as the well ghosts, so we will again begin with those ghosts which may possibly represent ancient water divinities, though still bearing in mind the pitfalls that lie in the path to a certain identification. In Warwickshire, a brook at Shottery was haunted by a female ghost, and by a white horse, which would be seen tramping around an old mill by the brook. In the same county, a pool in Charlecote Park is haunted by the ghost of a woman who is said to have drowned herself there: she is seen gliding into the water and sinking; while a headless lady haunts a stream at Wellesbourne. A white lady ghost in Ragley Park (Warwick) was seen at the spot where in 1833 a skeleton was found buried, the accompanying brooches and dagger dating the interment to the Anglo-Saxon period. The burial was close to a spring, and in one version the ghost was seen drinking from a spring.

Vague tales of female ghosts abound: a ghost with green hair close to Wilton stream at Taunton (Somerset); a white lady at Morton Gymes (a water-filled pit) (Lincoln); a lady on a grey horse at the Haugh Pool, Eaton Bishop (Hereford & Worcester), now laid so no longer seen; the ghost of old Kitty by the haunted pool known as Kit's Steps at Lydford Gorge (Devon); the woman in black with a long black veil on the banks of the River Teifi (Cardigan), pointing to a bend in the river; the woman in white on the surface of a pond at Rendlesham (Suffolk); the woman in white carrying a baby and rising from Swan Pool at Redbrook (Gloucester); and a tall woman dressed in green, 'distinguished chiefly by her withered meagre countenance, ever distorted by a malignant scowl'[1] who haunted the River Conon (Ross & Cromarty).

Sometimes these ladies are described in such a way as to make their identification as water divinities almost certain. The last example, for instance, sounds like the traditional fearsome hag who is never far away in Scottish folklore, whatever name she goes by, like the Cailleach of the previous chapter, or the Bean-nighe, the Washer at the Ford, who would be seen at night at fords, lochs, burns and river pools, a ghostly woman washing the shrouds of those fated to die. Legends of washers-at-fords also survive in Wales, for example at a bridge where there was probably once a ford between Old Colwyn and Betws-yn-Rhos (Denbigh), where in the last decades of the nineteenth century a story was current of little old women seen washing clothes in the stream. The hag-like ghost known as the Gwrach-y-rhibyn, with long black hair, bat's wings and long talons, may also be a descendant of a water divinity. She haunted the Caerphilly swamp (Glamorgan), which became a lake when the stream overflowed during wet weather, and she would rise from the water, wailing and groaning, and fly off to the castle nearby. This tale also carries a strong suggestion of embellishment in subsequent retellings, and in this way many traditional beliefs may have been perpetuated, hence we have an overlap between our categories 1 and 2, that is, genuine folk memories of a belief in water divinities overlain by more modern folklore.

The following tales may also have originated in the same way, a good example being the story of the girl in a green cloak who haunted the fifteenth-century Old Ferry Inn on the River Bure at Horning (Norfolk) and was seen to disappear into the river. Sometimes she was seen on the river bank near an abbey, and one explanation for her presence was that she had been raped and murdered by drunken monks who had thrown her body into the river. Here a possible water divinity, a female dressed in green, is 'identified' as a murder victim. Similarly the maidens of Llyn y Morynion (Maidens' Lake) near Ffestiniog (Merioneth) were 'explained' by an unlikely story, that the local men had gone to the Vale of Clwyd seeking wives and had brought back a number of maidens, but were followed by the men of the Vale, and near the lake a battle was fought in which the raiders died. The maidens drowned themselves in the lake. One local man swore that he had seen them often during his youth early in the nineteenth century: they came out of the lake in the early morning and combed their hair: echoes of the mermaids described in the previous chapter.

Sometimes female ghosts are given the identity of a known person, as for example the White Lady of Kilsall who was said to be the ghost of one of the Whiston family, one-time owners of the mansion named Kilsall near Albrighton (Shropshire). She walked near a pool in the grounds. Elaborate tales were concocted to explain two Welsh lady ghosts. A woman in black who used to haunt Pwllhelig Pool in the Vale of Glamorgan was said to be the wife of the owner of a house which used to stand where the pool was. The house was buried in a landslip as a result of the owner's evil ways, and the ghost was looking for her lost money and jewels. A man who spoke to her early in the nineteenth century received no answer, only a sad smile. Riches were also involved in a ghost story from the River Teifi (Cardigan), where a girl dressed in green and carrying golden objects about her person was seen filling a tub bound with gold in the river. She was said to be guarding treasure in a mound nearby.

Ghost stories about females seen beside water, and dressed in white, green or black, are likely to have somewhere in their ancestry a belief in water divinities, however elaborate and unlikely the accompanying 'explanation' may be, the last two stories being vivid examples of this. Sometimes, however, a ghost story does not contain this giveaway element, and we must for safety's sake assign it to the category of relatively recent folklore, though a thorough analysis of such tales by someone able to separate the elements and relate them to ancient folklore patterns would probably conclude that some of these also have their origins in the distant past. What, for example, can we make of the story of ghosts leaving the River Ness on Hallowe'en and making their way to the High Church at Inverness, seen only by those with psychic vision? Or the tales of ghostly coaches, like the one drawn by four horses which would plunge into the River Teme at Leigh (Hereford & Worcester), or the one which was followed into a lake near Scawby (Humberside) by a man who then drowned? The most dramatic of the coach-and-horses hauntings involved Squire Blount of Kinlet (Shropshire) whose spirit was said to live in a pool at Kinlet, restless after his daughter made a poor match (or so Squire Blount thought) to a page-boy, all his property automatically passing to the couple after his death. The Squire's restlessness caused him to haunt his family, and he would emerge from the pool in his coach drawn by four white horses, even driving into the hall and across the dinner-table! Eventually the ghost was laid in the sea; but the story also mentions a little bottle kept under the Squire's monument in Kinlet church, the point being that if it were broken, Squire Blount's ghost would again be free. Until around the mid-nineteenth century this was used as a threat to misbehaving children in the Kinlet area.

There are many of these unfathomable hauntings, and their great variety is demonstrated in the following examples. Dartmoor's Cranmere Pool (Devon) is the site of many ghost stories, including one which describes how an attempt was made by twenty-three clergymen to exorcise the restless spirit of a local merchant at Okehampton. The spirit fled into the body of an unbroken colt which was then galloped to Cranmere Pool, where it vanished into the water. The River Wye at Goodrich Castle (Hereford & Worcester) is haunted on the anniversary of their deaths by a woman and her lover who drowned while attempting to escape from the castle during a siege, while the River Trent between Wildsworth and Owston Ferry (Humberside), at a bend called the Jenny Hurn, is the location for a number of strange happenings, one being the crossing of the river in a tiny craft by a manlike pygmy with long hair and the face of a seal. On reaching the shore, he browses in a field, as does another strange river creature, with large eyes, long hair and walrus tusks.

Two troublesome Shropshire ghosts were laid in pools – Madam Sandford who haunted the Prees area was laid in Black Pool, but she escaped and would tease the lads who took their horses to water at the pool, so she was captured in a bottle which was thrown into the Red Sea, and the pool was filled in too, just to make sure. Madam Pigott, who terrorised Chetwynd and Edgmond, was laid in Chetwynd Pool, but she too escaped and had to be laid in the Red Sea, despite her pleas not to be thrown there. Chwythlyn, a lake near Llanrwst (Denbigh), was haunted by the noise of men fighting, and a couple who heard it afterwards became ill and died. A dramatic death overtook the last Earl of Desmond who practised magic at his castle in County Limerick. His wife once witnessed his magical performance, and was so shocked that instead of keeping silent as the Earl had instructed her, she screamed loudly, whereupon they and their castle sank into Lough Gur. Now every seventh year they are seen on the lake, riding on a black horse, until dawn overtakes them.

Although the majority of ghosts seen beside water are women, which is to be expected if they represent water divinities, usually assumed to take female form, occasionally male ghosts are recorded in folklore, and there is a possibility that some of these, too, may have been the ghostly personifications of water divinities. The saints to whom the holy wells were dedicated were often male, and these may have been confused in people's minds with the water divinities, so it is not surprising to find reports of ghostly male figures who may represent water divinities. Such may be the Old Man of Inverfarigaig, or the Bodach, a ghost of Loch Ness (Inverness), who was heard more often than seen, especially shrieking in the trees during the winter storms. The Pool of the Harper in the River Teifi near Llandyssul (Cardigan) commemorates an old harper who was said to have drowned there, and whose music could still sometimes be heard at the pool. A green man (the familiar colour which has connections with the fairy folk and nature spirits, and therefore usually indicates an ancient origin) haunted a lake in the grounds of Bramshill House at Basingstoke (Hampshire), the Black Prince having drowned in that same lake, according to legend. All these tales may have originated as legends of water divinities.

There is no such obvious explanation for the stories of ghostly boats which carried ghosts both male and female over our waterways, though here again beliefs in water divinities may be at the heart of some of these tales – it is impossible to tell. A ghostly barge on the Little Ouse River near Ely (Cambridge) carried the body of St Withburga, which was snatched from her grave at East Dereham on the instructions of the Abbot and taken to his cathedral at Ely. A boat on the River Wye carried a woman, every evening at eight pm, from Hereford towards Ross-on-Wye (Hereford & Worcester), and it travelled fast even against the wind, landing about seven miles from Hereford at the place where there was once a village. After weeping and wailing for a while, the ghost would return to the boat and sail back towards Hereford, disappearing as she approached the city. Local boatmen believed that anyone meeting her would soon die, and the stretch of river where the boat sailed was known as the Spectre's Voyage. A ghostly sailing ship haunted Croft Pasco Pool on the Lizard (Cornwall), while an apparently empty boat rowed across Lough Derg (on the borders of Clare, Galway and Tipperary). Sometimes when the boat cannot be seen, the sounds of music and voices, and the splash of the oars, are heard. A man who threw a stone at the empty boat had it thrown back at him, followed by mocking laughter. Phantom white-robed ladies crossed the River Towy near Carmarthen in two boats, watched by a young man who returned to see them again. Bright moonlight showed him that the boats were cockleshells, and the white ladies on reaching the shore turned into black cats – they were the white witches of Carmarthen.

From these highly imaginative tales we come down to earth with some factual reports which at first sight do not appear to have much to do with ghosts, but whose relevance will later become clear. The reports describe balls of light seen at various stretches of water, especially on the Scottish lochs, but also elsewhere. A light was reported from time to time in Upper Loch Torridon (Ross & Cromarty), looking like the light carried on a ship riding at anchor. But it was not always stationary, sometimes being seen moving quickly towards the head of the loch. Another light would rise from Balliveolan House at the head of Loch Creran (Argyll), travel along the loch for about a mile, and then drop into the water, this having been seen many times by local residents. In Scotland such lights were thought to foretell death, and local lads would not go fishing aboard a boat based in Loch Carloway (Lewis, Outer Hebrides) because a weird light had been seen hovering above it. The death association reappears in an account from Loch Tay (Perth), where two bright balls of light were seen moving rapidly along the surface of the loch following the route that on the next day was taken by a boat carrying two bodies for reburial at Killin. Today such balls of light are interpreted as UFOs. A young chef living beside Loch Ryan (Wigtown) awoke early one morning in June 1973 with a compulsion to look out of the window. He saw hovering over the water three yellowish-orange spheres, which then shot up at a fantastic speed. A group of coloured lights seen hovering over a reservoir at Golbourne near Wigan (Greater Manchester) in August 1980 were interpreted by the witnesses as a helicopter, though this could not have hovered for twenty-five minutes, which was the length of the observation. In March 1983 the people of Belfast were seeing red, white and yellow lights over Lough Neagh and the surrounding countryside, these again being interpreted as UFOs.

A light seen at Broadford, on the Isle of Skye (Inverness) could also be called a UFO – until one reads the end of the account. The witness was a doctor, who was strolling by the bay one evening when he saw a bright light. He thought it was a flare lit by fishermen, until he realised that it was approaching him. It looked like a light globe, and when it reached the water's edge it went out. Then the doctor briefly saw a cloaked woman carrying a baby. She hurried across the sands and was gone. On making enquiries, he learned that a dead woman and child had been washed ashore from a shipwreck at the place where he had seen their ghosts. This was reported as a factual story; whether there are factual events behind the next story is less certain. An encounter took place between a lady in white and a young man who was walking from Dyserth to Rhyl (Flint), and they walked together for a while, talking, until they reached a pool. Here the lady suddenly disappeared into the water, in the form of a ball of fire. A ghost that haunted Llyn-Nad-y-Forwyn (Caernarfon) sometimes appeared as a ball of fire, rolling along the River Colwyn, and sometimes it appeared in various female guises, being the ghost of a girl drowned in the lake by her lover. Male, and identified as the Devil himself, was a phantom angler seen beside Loch Shin (Sutherland), who disappeared in a mass of flame when spoken to by a child seeking some fish.

These accounts and stories show that basically similar phenomena, in this case balls of light (which may in fact be ball lightning or some similar natural phenomenon), are interpreted in a variety of ways according to the period and place of the sighting, and to the beliefs of the witnesses, an interesting observation which also applies more widely to the whole range of ghost stories we have recounted. After all, it has been suggested that the tales of white ladies haunting stretches of water, some of them simple tales, others very elaborate, may all have originated in patches of white mist which often form over water, especially in valleys and on still nights. Seen by a superstitious, and perhaps drunken, late-night traveller, might they not seem to resemble ghostly ladies in flowing robes? In some cases this may be an acceptable explanation, but all cases are not equally explicable, as is demonstrated by the first-hand accounts of ghosts which will close this chapter.

Another complexity in these stories is the frequent inclusion of bridges. Many of the hauntings (twenty-five, or almost a quarter of those in our collection) take place near or on bridges – why should this be? The Bogle's Bridge near Dingwall (Ross & Cromarty) was haunted, and people avoided it after nightfall; a story of a murder by a

The bridge over the River Dee at Farndon, Cheshire, said to be haunted by the ghosts of two murdered children

jealous lover had been concocted to 'explain' the haunting. Another dramatic story explains the haunting of the bridge at Farndon (Cheshire) where the River Dee forms the England/Wales border. Two children were dropped from the bridge and drowned in the river, their cries being heard on stormy nights and their ghosts haunting the bridge arches. Cuckoo Bridge near Castle Douglas (Kirkcudbright) is also haunted by a crying child, murdered and buried there. A bridge near Prenton (Merseyside), made of a whale's jawbone, was guarded by the ghosts of two drowned men, while it was a phantom piper whose music could be heard at Elvet Bridge in Durham. A man walking across the Denbighshire hills saw a ghostly figure, a gentleman in grey clothes fastened with yellow or gold, at the bridge known as Pont Brenig, the ghost disappearing into a bog. Phantom battles are re-enacted at a haunted bridge at Gidleigh (Devon), and two other haunted bridges in Devon are on the River Bovey between Chudleigh and Stover, and between Warren House Inn and Chagford.

Many bridges are haunted by female ghosts, like that of Ann Hawtrey, a servant who murdered her mistress in 1820 and was hanged at Warwick. She, or rather a figure in white identified as her, haunts Chesford Bridge over the River Avon (Warwick). Not far away is the village of Leek Wootton, where in the 1920s a man walking home late at night saw a girl in a long pale dress at the bridge crossing the Cattle Brook. He later saw her twice more, and on all three occasions she was sitting on the end of the bridge. As he approached, she crossed the road and went into the trees. Her history is unknown, but the white lady seen at Kirkdale Bridge (Kirkcudbright) has half her head cut off, and was murdered by a gipsy. Further east near Dundrennan, a headless lady haunted Buckland Glen, and there is a story that on one occasion she appeared to a farmer who was returning home late at night, just as he was about to cross a small bridge over the burn. He turned back and continued by a different route, and later learned that two men had been lying in wait to steal his money. Had the ghost not appeared, the farmer would have been robbed and perhaps murdered. A female ghost in Dunkenhalgh Park, Clayton-le-Moors (Lancaster) haunted the bridge where she had thrown herself into the river in the mistaken belief that her lover had abandoned her. The veracity of this tale is not known, but an early nineteenth-century ghost seen on a bridge near Skipsea (Humberside) was claimed to be genuine. The witness saw a woman in white walk down a lane towards the brook and then, 'to my great astonishment, when she approached the brook, instead of turning to the right to gain the bridge, she vanished from my sight at the very time my eyes were fixed upon her.' The seven-foot-long Sagranus Stone, an important fifth-sixth century Ogham stone now on display in St Dogmaels church (Cardigan), was at one time used as a bridge across a brook, and was reputedly haunted at midnight by a white lady. A grey lady haunted a bridge over the River Taff in Cardiff (Glamorgan), which was at the end of her route through the town, and she would vanish at the bridge after signalling to someone unseen. The Nun's Bridge at Hinchingbrooke (Cambridge) is haunted by a nun accompanied by an old woman dressed as a nurse, and they were seen as recently as 1965 by a woman and her husband who were driving across the bridge. On their return journey, they saw the ghosts again. A bridge over the River Cam near Harston (Cambridge) is haunted by a woman in white

The haunted bridge over the Cattle Brook at Leek Wootton, Warwick

who jumps into the water. The white lady of Longnor emerges out of a pool at Leebotwood (Shropshire), and was reportedly seen by a young man crossing a footbridge beside the ford over Longnor Brook some time in the mid-nineteenth century. He later described his encounter:

I sid 'er a-cummin, an' I thinks, 'ere's a nice young wench. Well, thinks I, who she be, I'll gi'e 'er a fright. I was a young fellow then, yo' know – an' I waited till 'er come close up to me, right i' the middle o' the bridge, an' I stretched out my arms, *so* – an' I clasped 'er in 'em, tight – *so*. An' theer was nothin'![2]

Since he was recalling the events of his youth in old age, this witness may have been exaggerating, or even concocting a lively tale to please the enquiring folklorist.

Our final bridge ghost, the white lady of Corfe Hill bridge at Corfe Castle (Dorset), was reportedly seen on 4 July 1967 by 22-year-old John Seager, who was driving home in the early hours of the morning. We quote from a report in the *Swanage Times*:[3]

. . . as I rounded the corner on Corfe Hill, by the Bankes Arms, I saw it. In front of me was this figure. At first, I thought it was a woman in a nightgown out late at night with the dog. But I was wrong. As I drove closer I braked hard. There it was. A white figure, headless, and seemingly wearing a long nightgown, drifted across the road in front of me. It moved on and down the path at the foot of the castle hill near the bakery. I trembled and came over cold. In fact I felt frozen. It was an experience I would never want again.

After this report was published, it became known that this ghost had also been seen on at least one other occasion.

The bridge which features so often in these ghost stories, legendary and factual alike, may symbolise the connection between this life and the next. At death one crosses the bridge into unknown realms, but these ghosts do not usually cross over, they hover on the bridge, or else vanish as they approach it. As ghosts they are tied to this world, unable to pass to the next and be freed from their ghostly state, however much they may wish to cross. Also of possible relevance is the belief that spirits and supernatural beings were unable to cross running water. Why should such beliefs arise, and why should ghosts be seen so often near water? If there is any physical basis to these beliefs, it may lie in the energy fields created by running water, which under certain circumstances may perhaps produce strange effects, including triggering off hauntings. These are speculative thoughts, but the ghost sightings, and the strange sensations experienced by some people in reputedly haunted places, need explaining, which no one has so far been able to do. Disbelievers will put all sightings of ghosts down to lying, drunkenness, and misidentification (of mist, trees, etc), but we do the witnesses an injustice if we reject their sincere testimony without further consideration. In this book we have no space to explore the nature of a ghost sighting in all its complexity, but we shall close this chapter with some intriguing first-hand reports of ghosts seen beside water.

One summer's day not too long ago, Mr Barlow and a friend were visiting the lake and marshland near Wolston (Warwick) and after a peaceful morning they were eating their lunch and planning a little fishing when Mr Barlow noticed about eight figures across the water. They seemed to be wearing the clothes of Elizabethan times, the women in long dresses and ruffs, the men in doublets and leggings, carrying swords and wearing plumed hats. The couples were strolling arm-in-arm – but a couple of feet above ground level. As the two men watched, the figures disappeared into the bushes. The ghost of Bagwell Lane at Winchfield (Hampshire) was thought to be only a legend until 1968 when a motorcyclist saw her, and later three men walking along the lane saw her vanish beside a pond in a nearby field. She is said to have drowned there, either accidentally or as a suicide victim. It was thought to be unlucky to see the ghost of a farmer who had drowned himself in Pinkworthy Pond on Exmoor (Somerset). In 1906 a man who saw a figure standing beside the pond asked him the way, but got no answer, and the figure then disappeared. The walker was staying at a nearby farm, and fell ill with pneumonia on his return, since he had gone astray into a bog. His illness was attributed to his having seen the ghost. Two monks are sometimes seen near a stream at Beenham Common (Berkshire), one 1977 witness believing them to be fishermen in dufflecoats until he realised that they had vanished. Two ponds beside Bodiam Road, Sandhurst (Kent), were both the scene of suicides, and a ghostly man seen in 1973, standing in the hedge beside one of the ponds, may have been the ghost of one of the suicide victims. He followed the two witnesses for a short distance, and then vanished.

Several people have seen ghosts by the lake in Witton Lakes Park at Upper Witton, Erdington, Birmingham, West Midlands. Late at night in August 1974 two men exercising their greyhounds saw a

swirling white shape floating on the grass verge some 50 yards away. One of the dogs . . . ran towards it, stopped suddenly, turned and raced back past us at a speed he never achieved on the trials . . . As the shape drew nearer I realised it was a ghost of a rather young woman. I wanted to run, but my legs went numb and she actually passed within a couple of inches of me. I'll never forget this as long as I live.

The other witness tried to describe the ghost:

She wasn't old-fashioned, just like an everyday woman, only very white . . . I wanted to touch her as she passed us, but at the last minute I closed my eyes. When I opened them again she was floating towards a tree and as she reached it she vanished.[4]

In February 1926 a Miss Godley of Killegar (Leitrim) went to visit one of her former farm labourers, an old man who had been ill but was not known to be dying. She talked to him and then set out for home in her donkey trap. As she and her companions passed the lake, they saw

an old man with a long white beard which floated in the wind, crossing to the other side of the lake. He appeared to be moving his arms, as though working a punt, he was standing up and gliding across but I saw no boat . . . The figure crossed the lake and disappeared in among the reeds and trees at the far side.[5]

They were puzzled, and thought the man had looked like the labourer they had just visited. When they arrived home, they learned that he had just died. His ghost was never seen again.

A woman in black was seen in August 1899 by a family (husband, wife and two children) as they walked along the bank of the Monmouthshire canal near Abergavenny. It was a moonlit evening, and they were going to see their aunt. When they were about forty yards from a bridge over the canal, with the children running ahead, they all saw a solitary female figure gliding towards them. She wore black, with a shawl covering her head. The children thought it was their aunt, but the adults realised it could not be her, as she would be unlikely to come out on her own at night. They watched as the ghost, for they had now realised that was what it was, kept gliding in front of them, eventually vanishing. Nearly forty years later, one of the child witnesses wrote:

I am very pleased to corroborate the evidence my father has given you concerning the lady in black we saw walking along the canal bank in Monmouthshire. I was a child of twelve at the time but have never forgotten the weird experience of seeing a woman appear suddenly in front of us, first walk towards us, then away, and disappear into nothingness before our very eyes. I was the first of the party to see the apparition, which I took to be my aunt coming to meet us, and was dashing towards her when my father called me back. It was the sudden disappearance as we watched her, which specially disconcerted me.[6]

The ghost which crossed the road in front of two surprised witnesses in May 1912 was following the course of a stream which flowed beneath the road. The place was just outside Paddock Wood (Kent), near the vicarage, and Mr Fuller and Mr Luck were cycling home from work just before dusk. Mr Luck described what happened:

As we approached the stream, we saw the figure of an elderly lady wearing a rusty black or dark brown coat and skirt, and a bonnet like those we see on some pictures of Queen Victoria. The bonnet was also a rusty black colour, and the light was good enough to see her face distinctly; she had made up her mind to go somewhere, and two hedges and a ditch were not enough to stop her. She moved from east to west, along the south bank of the stream, and passed through the hedge about four feet from me, while I was riding close in on the left of the road.

At that time I was a teetotaller, so I knew I was sober, but I should not have mentioned the apparition to a soul except for the fact that Mr Fuller asked me why I slowed up and reached for my bell. Then I told him what I had seen, and he replied that was exactly what he had seen himself, so we both turned round on the road, and went to the spot on the west side of the road where the figure had disappeared through the hedge. The long grass was unmarked, and the hedge intact, but we found the remains of an old gateway beneath the brambles, which is still there.

I was in a better position than Mr Fuller to have a good look at the old lady's face, and I was so impressed that I feel I could pick her out of a crowd of grannies even if they were all dressed alike, after all these years. The apparition was too plain, and the movements too distinct, and the light too good, for either of us to have made a mistake over a shadow.[7]

A similar ghost has been reported elsewhere in Kent, at Oxney Bottom near Dover. A ghostly grey lady would drift across the A258 road at a bend, possibly causing the several fatal accidents which have occurred there. A ruined church stands in woods beside the road, and a stream runs beneath it. In 1973 a couple of young engineers who were on the look-out for ghosts actually saw her for themselves.

The coincidence of ghosts seen near running water has been remarked upon before, particularly by T. C. Lethbridge, archaeologist and dowser, who published his speculations on the subject in three of his books, *Ghost and Ghoul*, *Ghost and Divining Rod* and *A Step in the Dark*. Briefly, he postulated that running water will generate fields of electromagnetic energy which are capable of recording sense impressions emitted by a human psyche in moments of extreme emotion. At a later date a suitably attuned human, in the right place, at the right time, will unwittingly 'tune in' to the recorded impression and thereby experience a 'ghost'. Space restrictions preclude our giving more details of a complex and potentially valuable theory, but we suggest that readers pursue these ideas further in Lethbridge's own books. This subject demands serious scientific study but has so far been neglected. Perhaps a future generation of scientists will have sufficient curiosity and courage to pursue these and similar aspects of the paranormal.

9. The Past – and the Future

Our journey through British and Irish water lore has shown us many aspects of an active water cult, which clearly had a strong influence on the population for many hundreds, possibly thousands, of years, and which in some minor ways continues to the present day. If we examine the unconscious symbolism of water and wells, we can perhaps obtain some understanding of the power of the water cult.

Water symbolises the Great Mother. Through her life is assured. The well or spring itself symbolises the womb of the Great Mother, and therefore has a special significance for birth and children. Immersion in the sacred water purifies and regenerates, hence the belief in the water's value as a healer. In this connection, the great emphasis on cures for eye troubles may suggest that the still pool of water at the well was sometimes interpreted as the eye of the Great Mother or water divinity. There are folktales which tell how an intruder who looked into a forbidden well would be punished by the ruin of his eyes, because he had incurred the wrath of the divinity by gazing into her eye. Wells were also a point of contact with the underworld, which meant that they were populated by supernatural beings. When the wells and springs were adopted by the Christians and dedicated to the saints, these beings became absorbed into the lore along with the spirits and goddesses of paganism.

The significance of water was known intuitively by the people who frequented the wells, the attitudes and beliefs being transmitted through successive generations, acquiring many embellishments on the way but often retaining identifiable links with their origins. An inherent belief in the power of water was in many cases probably sufficient for the pilgrim to achieve positive results from a visit to a sacred well or spring. But the reaction may not have simply been a psychological one, the power of the unconscious mind over the body. Water is not an inert substance. It contains many characteristics which can be analysed, hence the use of iron- or sulphur-rich waters at the relatively recent spas, for such characteristics are easily noticeable. Water contains other elements which are far more subtle and in fact undiscernible, but which react with that highly sensitive organism the human (or animal) body, and there is an energy transference which is beneficial to the recipient. Therefore the pilgrim visiting a sacred well or spring will receive benefit both spiritually and physically when he partakes of the living water.

Evidence for the existence and nature of energies contained within water is as yet slight, because little research has been undertaken. That water emits some form of detectable radiation is indicated by the success of dowsers in tracing underground water. The evidence relating to the appearance of ghosts which we presented in the previous chapter also suggests the involvement of some form of energy given off by the water which somehow reacts with a latent image imprinted on the aura of the haunted place, bringing a ghost into manifestation. One researcher who took readings at springs was able to measure very weak electrical potentials, which varied from week to week, but he was unable to say why or how the electrical fields were generated. It is likely that our ancestors who first began to make use of the sacred water springing from the earth had a much more highly developed sensitivity to natural phenomena and instinctively appreciated the qualities in the living water of which we are only beginning to be aware. Now it may be too late: whatever value the pure spring water had will today be overshadowed, perhaps even cancelled out, by the ever-present pollution caused by modern man's greedy grabbing at ever more profit, even at the expense of a healthy environment. The two main hazards affecting our water supplies are acid rain, now scientifically shown to be widespread throughout Europe, including Britain, and modern farming methods, in the form of excess fertilizers and pesticides applied to the land and crops.

In addition to the wells used for a community water supply it is most likely that each community had its own sacred spring or holy well, which was much used and very important to the life of the community. There would probably be legends attached to the well, it would almost certainly be endowed with healing properties, and the correct rituals would have to be performed by pilgrims. In some places, particularly in Ireland, the present rituals are patterned on the current dominant religious beliefs, but everywhere the surviving customs hint of paganism, as we have shown in earlier chapters. Now, in the late twentieth century, although holy wells and sacred springs have no relevance in the lives of most people, they have not been entirely abandoned. Some of the major wells have survived and are still visited by a considerable number of pilgrims. The most active well is also the one most recently developed, at Little Walsingham in Norfolk, which is now visited by over 100,000 pilgrims every year. St Winefride's Well at Holywell (Flint) is also still much visited by people seeking cures as well as by those who just wish to see the well, and probably some of the smaller country wells are also still quietly visited by local people. Certainly during the 1914–18 war people visited Ffynnon Deilo (Pembroke) to drink the well water from the saint's skull, in the hope of bringing the war to an end. More recently, Ruth and Frank Morris found some evidence of the continued use of holy wells in Scotland while researching in the 1970s for their book *Scottish Healing Wells*. St Mary's Well, Culloden (Inverness), was visited by as many as a dozen busloads of pilgrims from Inverness on the first Sunday in May as recently as the 1930s, and the Morrises found newly placed rags on the trees there when they visited the well in 1979. They also met people at the well at Scotlandwell (Kinross) in 1978 who had travelled from Edinburgh for some of the water. Many holy wells in Ireland are still visited by pilgrims, and the pilgrimages to famous sites such as Croagh Patrick (Mayo), Knock (Mayo), Lady's Island (Wexford), Tobar an Ailt (Sligo), and Lough Derg (Donegal) seem to be more popular than ever, despite the changes brought about by the sophistications of modern life.

This evidence of survival of the water cult, however, is very small when we consider the great number of holy wells which were once in existence. In Chapter 2 we suggested that there may once have been at least 2000 holy wells in England and 1200 in Wales. Only a small proportion of these now survives, as we discovered when we tried to track down the surviving wells for our Gazetteer. The story told by Edward Jones in 1984 concerning Ffynnon Tudno at Llandudno (Caernarfon) is typical of many ancient wells.

It was a very popular meeting place when I was young. They used to take us to it from school on St Tudno's Day. Also Sunday School teachers used to take the children to visit it. This has not happened for many years. Probably

St Patrick's Well, Mám Éan, County Galway, is still very popular with pilgrims and has recently been 'modernised', as the carved stone name-plate shows. Water is now piped from a nearby stream to supplement the spring water

my 38-year-old son was one of the last lot of children to see it with his Sunday School teacher. It seems to me that it is now almost unknown by the locals. I have asked people who were born just half a mile away from it and they had never heard of it. It's amazing when you think. Anyway it was quite a pleasant thing to look at. Unfortunately it is now enclosed in farm fields. This was done about 1959–60. I told the church authorities what was happening but they didn't do anything about it . . . I cannot say what sort of condition it's in now, but I know cattle are often near it. It's a great pity, I think. I have not seen it myself for many years as I have been retired some years and am in my seventies.[1]

Unless a well has a caring owner, or is adopted by the villagers, it is nowadays very likely to disappear, as has happened all too often. However, caring owners and concerned villagers do happily exist, and as a result a number of ancient wells have been restored and again play a part in village life. Many of Cornwall's beautiful holy wells have been particularly well restored, and several examples are given in our Gazetteer. This report from the *Daily Mail* for 20 September 1899 describes the then newly restored well at St Clether.

The rededication service of the restored well-chapel of St Clether . . . was a very interesting function. The chapel which had long been in ruins, was situated in a bog, and last year, when the castle was cleared away, suddenly the water resumed its old course and flowed by a subterranean channel under the east wall and bubbled up beneath the altar, and then was carried away by a second subterranean conduit into the second holy well. The chapel has been completely restored. Almost all the old stones were found, and its reconstruction was like the putting together of a puzzle. The situation is one of extraordinary beauty among prongs of volcanic rock rising above the Inney. Sunday was a fine day. There was a procession from the parish church, headed by a cross, consisting of masons and carpenters who had rebuilt the chapel, the Sunday school children, choir, and clergy singing 'O Word of God above' and the 'Exurgat Deus.' The effect of the many coloured banners borne by the procession winding among the rocks and tufts of gorse and heather under a brilliant sun was very striking. On arriving at the west door a collect was said, and the choir entered singing the 'Urbs Beata.' The procession passed round the chapel singing 'A living stream as crystal clear', when suddenly a striking incident occurred. A couple of poor people arrived, and asked for their child to be baptised at the well; and this was done, the name given being 'Clether'. The Rev. Sabine Baring-Gould gave an address on the saint's history. The 'Nunc Dimittis' concluded an interesting service.

Elsewhere in England, new festivals have been instituted which are now held annually and involve the village holy well in their proceedings. For example, since 1929 at Harpham (Humberside) St John's Well has been decorated and a ceremony held to celebrate the festival of St John of Beverley. It is now held on the Thursday nearest to 7

May, and includes a procession to the well, a blessing ceremony, and a service in the church. Similarly at Kemsing (Kent) an annual procession to St Edith's Well on or near the saint's day (16 September) was revived in 1926, then lapsed during the war, and was again revived in 1961. The attractive custom of well-dressing also continues to be adopted at village wells around the country, inspired by the magnificent example of the Derbyshire wells.

Now in the late twentieth century, as concern for our environment and the conservation of our surviving historic buildings and other antiquities increases, more holy wells are being rediscovered and restored. Three very recent examples which have come to our notice are the Penegoes health wells (Montgomery) and Lady Wulfruna's Well, Wolverhampton (West Midlands), both restored by local civic societies, and an eye well beside a farm lane at Forden (Montgomery), in danger of total obliteration and dug out of a high bank by the landowner. It is to be hoped that this recovery and restoration work will continue, though for many wells it is already too late. It would be sad if we were to lose many more of our holy wells, forming as they do a valuable and little appreciated link with our ancient past.

A Gazetteer of 200 Ancient and Holy Wells Which Still Survive in England, Wales, Scotland and Ireland

ENGLAND

Our research into the present (1980s) state of English holy wells has revealed many lost and forgotten, many overgrown and rapidly being lost, but a surprising number still extant and being maintained. This gazetteer includes wells that are easily accessible and in a relatively good state of repair, but makes no claim to be comprehensive. Readers are invited to notify us (in care of the publishers) of any other surviving wells in England or Wales. There is no modern published guide to English holy wells, though a few guides to the wells of individual counties have been published (*see* Bibliography). The wells are presented in alphabetical order of the new counties.

Bedfordshire

Holy well at Stevington (TL991536) : Stevington is 5 miles north-west of Bedford, and the holy well is close to the church, reached by following the path at the side of the church. The area around the well is a small nature conservation plot and therefore may look slightly overgrown in summer. The well issues from the limestone rock on which the church is built, and has never been known to run dry or freeze.

Nell's Well, Turvey : Turvey is 7 miles west of Bedford, and the well is in Newton Lane. The water has been covered over, but the well-arch and a poetic inscription can still be seen. Nell's Well was last restored in the 1870s, and may soon be restored again.

Berkshire

St Anne's Well, Caversham, Reading : The well is at the top of Priest Hill in Caversham, less than a quarter of a mile away from the shopping area, where there are car parking facilities. A plaque placed on the well in 1908 reads: 'The Holy Well of St Anne, the healing waters of which brought many pilgrims to Caversham in the Middle Ages.' There is a tradition that people buried their valuables beside the well to hide them from the Roundheads and others, and earlier this century some gold coins are said to have been discovered near the well. A Celtic stone head has also been found in a garden not far away, which is now in Reading Museum, and it is tempting to speculate on a link between head and well, with the head providing possible evidence for the well's antiquity.

Buckinghamshire

Schorne Well, North Marston (SP777226) : The village is 6 miles north-west of Aylesbury, and the well is in the centre of the village, in Schorne Lane.

which is off Church Street. Originally the well was a pit 10 feet deep and 10 feet square, with steps leading down into it, but it now has a wooden cover and the water, which is no longer suitable for consumption, comes from a pump beside the well. Traditionally the well was created by Sir John Schorne, who was rector of North Marston from 1290 to 1314. During a drought he struck the ground with his staff and a spring began to flow. Pilgrims visited the well seeking cures for ague, gout and sore eyes, and after his death they also visited Sir John's tomb in the church. This was such a popular pilgrimage in the fifteenth century that his bones were moved in 1480 to the newly built St George's Chapel at Windsor, where they were one of the main attractions until overshadowed by King Henry VI's remains.

Cambridgeshire

Holy well at Holywell near St Ives (TL336707) : This holy well is easy to find, tucked away behind the church. An annual well-dressing ceremony has recently been introduced here.

Holy well at
Holywell,
Cambridgeshire

The wishing well at Alderley Edge, Cheshire

Cheshire

Wishing well on Alderley Edge (SJ858778) : The B5087 runs north-west from Macclesfield through the woods of Alderley Edge, and to the right of this road a sign points to 'The Edge'. Follow this path into the woods, and down to where another path runs at right angles; here turn left and follow the path by rocky outcrops, from one of which water drips into a stone trough. Above on the rock-face is an inscription: 'Drink of this and take thy fill for the water falls by the wizards will', the wizard being Merlin. A face is also carved in the rock. The connection with Arthurian legend is that King Arthur and his knights were believed to lie sleeping till their country needs them, in a cave on the Edge. Merlin once tried to buy a white horse from a local farmer to add to the knights' horses. There are still caves to be seen elsewhere on the Edge, and the remains of old mines.

Hampston's Well, Burton, Wirral (SJ311743) : Burton is 8 miles north-west of Chester, and the well is beside a lane to the west of the village. In the earliest written record, of 1602–3, it was referred to as Patrick's Well. It was cleaned each year by the able-bodied men of Burton, who were required to help under pain of a fine of sixpence. Washing clothes there was prohibited, and funds were raised from the villagers for its maintenance. By the nineteenth century this well, which may have served the Iron Age and Saxon settlements around Burton, was known as Hampston's Well after a local family.

St Oswald's Well, Winwick (SJ958942) : Winwick is just north of Warrington, and the well is to be found about 1½ miles north of the village, in the grounds of Woodhead Farm at Hermitage Green. Anyone wishing to visit the well is requested to contact Mr and Mrs Cooper of Woodhead Farm in advance. The well is reputed to have flowed at the spot where King Oswald was killed in battle by Penda, King of Mercia, on 5 August 642.

Dupath Well,
Callington,
Cornwall

Cornwall

Dupath Well, Callington (SX375692) : A mile east of Callington, the well is approached through a farm. It is covered by the largest well building in Cornwall, dating from around 1510, but restored from a ruined state in the last century and later transferred to the care of the Department of the Environment.

St Cuby's Well, Duloe (SX241579) : 4 miles south-west of Liskeard, the well is beside the B3254, to the south-east of Duloe village and on the left-hand side for travellers approaching from Looe. The stone well building sits back behind the bank, and was restored by a former rector. There was a strong superstition against moving the well basin, and when the squire wished to move it in the mid nineteenth century, he had to agree to provide pensions for their families if any of the men died while handling the basin.

St Sampson's Well, Golant (SX121551) : Golant is close to the River Fowey, and 2 miles north of Fowey itself. The well adjoins the church, near to the porch, and was restored in 1938 when the church was restored. The church stands on the site of a hermit's cell, built in the sixth century beside a holy well, whose existence for at least 1400 years is clearly shown. On the wall of the holy well is a small black figure representing St Sampson.

Holy well and chapel at Madron (SW445327) : Madron is just to the north-west of Penzance, and the well is a further mile north-west, reached along a path which leaves the lane just west of Madron and passes through a weatherbeaten wood of lichen-covered blackthorn. The chapel is now very ruinous, and the well only a square hole in the ground 50 yards away, but this once-famous well is still much visited and you are likely to find rags tied to the surrounding bushes, as we did. The story of the cure of crippled John Trelille is told in Chapter 3.

Holy well at St Cleer, 2 miles north of Liskeard (SX249683) : The well is easily found in the village, beside the road which leads north-east. There is a cross beside it, and the well itself is covered by a fifteenth-century stone building, the whole site being restored in 1864.

St Clether's holy well and chapel, St Clether (SX202846) : St Clether is 8 miles west of Launceston, and the well and chapel are half a mile north-west of the church, easily found and much visited. They were in a ruinous state until restoration was begun in 1895 by the Reverend Sabine Baring-Gould, writer and antiquarian. The water from the well flows underneath the chapel, where one or two services are held during the summer.

Holy well at St
Cleer, Cornwall

St Levan's Well, St Levan, Cornwall

St Keyne's Well, St Keyne (SX248602) : Half a mile south of St Keyne, which is itself 2 miles south of Liskeard, the well is easily found beside the lane. It was restored in 1936, and its main fame lies in the story perpetuated in Southey's poem, that the first of a newly married couple to drink the well water would be 'master for life'.

St Levan's Well, St Levan (SW382219) : Not far from Land's End, this well would be difficult to beat for grandeur of location. It sits on the cliff above the bay, and is reached by a path opposite St Levan church. Unfortunately the restored well somehow lacks the atmosphere of other Cornish wells. Close by are also a few remains of St Levan's cell, and it was once the practice to sleep in the saint's 'bed' after washing in the well.

St Anne's Well, Whitstone (SX263985) : The well is in the churchyard on the south side of the church, in the village of Whitstone 9 miles north-west of Launceston. It has been carefully restored, the small stone building hugging the bank, and is well maintained.

Cumbria

St Ninian's Well, Brisco (NY423520) : Brisco is just south of Carlisle, and a worn path leads off the main street to the well, which is now somewhat neglected and overgrown.

St Helen's Well, Great Asby (NY685133) : 4 miles south of Appleby, this powerful spring issues from limestone into a deep basin walled on three sides; it has never been known to fail.

St Oswald's Well, Kirkoswald (NY555409) : Kirkoswald is 7 miles northeast of Penrith, and the well is easily found outside the church, at the west end. The church itself is to the south of the village.

St Patrick's Well, Patterdale (NY387166) : This well is easy to find, being at the head of Ullswater and beside the main road. It is covered by a small stone building with a pointed roof.

St Patrick's Well,
Patterdale,
Cumbria

St Helen's Well,
Great Asby,
Cumbria

Mompesson's
Well, Eyam,
Derbyshire

Derbyshire

St Ann's Well, Buxton : The medicinal springs at Buxton were known to the Romans, and later St Ann's Well was visited by thousands of pilgrims. Despite Henry VIII's attempts to close the well down, it retained its reputation and eventually Buxton became famous as a spa town. Water still flows from St Ann's Well, in The Crescent (across the road from the Tourist Information Centre which is housed in the Natural Baths Building). Next to the well is the Micrarium, which was originally the Pump Room where water was served until 1981. It is now a private museum.

Mompesson's Well, Eyam (SK222772) : Eyam is 8 miles south-west of the outskirts of Sheffield, and the well is in a junction of the lanes just to the north of the village. Eyam is famous as the place which isolated itself when the plague struck in the 1660s, thus preventing the disease from spreading further afield. William Mompesson was the rector at that time, and he it was who persuaded his flock to stay, though in a few months 80 per cent of the villagers were dead, including Mompesson's wife, whose grave can be seen in the churchyard. The villagers left money at Mompesson's Well in payment for the goods brought to them from outside.

Five wells at Tissington (SK176522) : Four miles north of Ashbourne is Tissington, the village where the custom of well-dressing is said to have started around 1350. The village's five wells (Town Well, Coffin Well, Yew Tree Well, Hands Well, Hall Well) are beautifully decorated every Ascension Day, but are worth seeing at any time of the year.

Devon

St Gudula's Well, Ashburton : A small park off Old Totnes Road, marked by an old cross, contains St Gudula's Well, whose water was once believed to be beneficial for weak eyes.

Fitz's Well, Okehampton (SX591939) : The well is on the northern edge of Dartmoor, above Okehampton Park, just south of the town, beside an old pilgrim footpath that led to Canterbury. It was latterly visited by the young people of Okehampton on Easter Sunday, who hoped to learn their matrimonial prospects from the state of the water.

St Nectan's Well, Stoke, near Hartland (SS236247) : 1½ miles west of Hartland, the well is just off Stoke's main street, down a steep path, alongside a garden and enclosed in a stone building.

St Nectan's Well, Welcombe (SS228184) : This tiny village is 4 miles south-west of Hartland, and the well is near the church, at a junction of lanes. It is housed in a stone building set amongst bushes and flowers.

Dorset

St Augustine's Well, Cerne Abbas (ST665016) : Cerne Abbas north of Dorchester is well known for its hillside giant, but a holy well can also be found there, at one time the abbey's only water supply. It is approached through the churchyard and then down to the right, along an ancient cobbled path between tall lime trees. Traditionally the well was formed where St Augustine struck the ground with his staff.

Holy well at Holwell near Sherborne (ST699121) : The well is near to St Laurence's church, just over the bridge which crosses the River Caundle. When it was excavated in 1968 seven stone steps were found and a covered dip well fed by a pipe on the north side and drained by another pipe on the south. As the river floods the area very easily, the well quickly silts over. This must be a recent development, for into living memory the well was used for baptisms and as a domestic water supply, also as an eye well.

Wishing well at Upwey (SY661852) : Upwey is halfway between Dorchester and Weymouth, and the well is close to the church, in the corner of a garden and approached through a small shop; there is a small admission charge. To make a wish you are instructed to fill a glass with water, stand with your back to the well, sip the water and wish, then throw the rest of the water over your shoulder into the well.

Wishing well at
Upwey, Dorset

Essex

Running Well, Runwell : The well is 2 miles north of Wickford and is reached along footpaths from Poplars Farm, which is along a lane running west–east a mile to the north of Runwell village. Poplars Farm is signposted on the lane, and you should turn into this private road, drive to the farm and then carry on for 30 yards to an area of concrete where you can park your car. To the east is a gate leading into a field. Go through this and follow the pathway across the field to a gap through the hedge on the opposite side. Once through this gap, immediately turn left and then after 20 yards you will come to a corner of the field, beyond which is a triangular piece of land, within which is the well. Although the well is on private land, it is accessible along public footpaths and the occupants of Poplars Farm should not be disturbed as they have nothing to do with the well.

The Running Well has recently been cleaned out and restored, following its rediscovery by Andrew Collins. His enthusiastic researches into the history of this well are described in his book *The Running Well Mystery* (published 1983 by The Supernaturalist, 19 St David's Way, Wickford). The annual Boxing Day walk along the footpaths of Runwell, ending at the well, has also been revived, and in 1983 over 200 people took part.

Gloucestershire

Seven Wells, Bisley (SO903059) : Bisley is 4 miles east of Stroud, and Seven Wells is easily found by the roadside south of the church. The structure dates from 1863, when the Reverend Thomas Keble, church builder and restorer and vicar of Bisley, restored the wells, which once provided the local water supply. He also established the custom of blessing the wells and dressing them with flowers each year on Ascension Day, and this custom continues.

St Anthony's Well, Forest of Dean, Gloucestershire (photo early twentieth century)

St Anthony's Well, Forest of Dean (SO657158) : This well is tucked away in the woods north of Cinderford. It is best approached from the A4136; at Plump Hill take the lane south, and then take the turning along Jubilee Road and continue until you come to a timber yard. Here bear right along the track for about 300 yards, bear right again into the wood, and follow the stream and the noise of running water until you reach the well. The water from the spring is led into a large bathing pool 3 feet deep, which was made at the beginning of the last century. Skin diseases were treated at this well, and the treatment ritual involved the rising sun, the month of May, and nine successive visits.

Lady's Well, Hempsted, near Gloucester (SO815173) : Hempsted lies to the west of the city, on the east bank of the River Severn, and the well is best approached from the fifteenth-century church of St Swithun. Enter the main gates of the church and immediately turn right, across the churchyard. At the end of the path, leave the churchyard, cross a field and enter a partly overgrown footpath. Pass Bank Cottage on the left and enter a field straight ahead. In the middle of this field, the well-house can be seen on a bank. The small stone building may have been built in the fourteenth century by the Canons of Llanthony Priory a short distance to the north.

St Bride's Well, St Briavels (SO559046) : St Briavels is a small village 7 miles north of Chepstow, and the well can be seen on Lower Road, below the Tump with the flagpole, and not very far from the church.

Hampshire

Springs at Holybourne (SU732412) : There is not a holy well as such at Holybourne (north-east of Alton), but the church is sited close to, and on top of, several springs which feed a pond by the side of the church, which in turn is the source of the Holy Bourne, the stream from which the village is named. It is clear that this was a holy place even before the church was started late in the eleventh century, and its origin as a site for Christian worship probably goes back to the seventh century when missionaries came from Canterbury. We can speculate that even earlier this was a sacred place. In much later times, the water was still used as a cure for eye troubles.

Hereford & Worcester

St Kenelm's Well, Clent Hills (SO945808) : A footpath beside St Kenelm's church, Romsley (a mile north-west of the village) leads to a valley behind the church where, in the left-hand bank, the small well can be found. Here is said to have lain the body of the murdered Kenelm, a youthful king of Mercia in the early ninth century.

St Ethelbert's Well, Hereford : The site of this well can be seen near the entrance to Castle Green, not far from the cathedral. The well is said to have flowed at the spot where the murdered King Ethelbert's body briefly lay, while being carried from Marden to Hereford. The cathedral stands on the site of a shrine erected to the memory of the dead king by his murderer, King Offa of Mercia, in AD 795.

St Ethelbert's
Well, Hereford

Holy well at
Malvern Wells,
Hereford &
Worcester

'Holy well' and St Ann's Well, Malvern (Holy well, SO770423; St Ann's Well, SO772458) : The famous spa town of Malvern still retains two ancient holy wells, both nestled into the eastern side of the ridge of the Malvern Hills. The 'holy well' is actually at Malvern Wells, to the south of the main town of Great Malvern, and is approached along a minor road which runs roughly parallel to the main A449. An elaborate well-house, recently restored, covers the well, where the water can be sampled. Further north, a steep climb up a path from Great Malvern (follow the lane opposite the former Pump Room, now the Nationwide Building Society) brings you to St Ann's Well, again inside a large well-house, the older part of which dates back to 1813. The spring is said to have been discovered by a monk in 1086, but only became well known when the town began to be promoted as a spa.

St Ethelbert's Well, Marden (SO512471) : Marden church is on the east bank of the River Lugg, 4 miles north of Hereford, and the well is one of the few to be found inside a church. It is of course covered, and is located towards the rear of the nave. This well is said to mark the spot where the body of the murdered King Ethelbert was buried, treacherously slain in AD 794 by order of King Offa of Mercia. The body was later removed to Hereford.

St Edith's Well, Stoke Edith (SO604406) : This well is 6 miles east of Hereford, in the bank below the church. According to legend St Edith prayed for the water she needed in building the church, and this spring began to flow; it still flows strongly. The water was later credited with healing properties.

St Edith's Well, Stoke Edith, Hereford & Worcester

Hertfordshire

Chadwell Spring, Hertford : Chadwell Spring and Amwell were the two sources of the New River which was constructed in 1613 by Sir Hugh Myddelton to carry drinking water to London. The name 'Chadwell' does not refer to St Chad, but means 'cold spring'. In the Middle Ages it was known as 'chaldewelle' or 'caldewelle', only being called Chadwell from 1727. Nevertheless the water was used for the treatment of eye diseases. Today the spring is a circular pool, which sometimes dries up, to be seen below the main Hertford–Ware road, opposite the Chadwell Golf Club, and there are some seventeenth-eighteenth century stone monuments close by. The land is owned by the Thames Water Authority, and permission to enter should be sought from the officials at the nearby linesman's house.

The other source of the New River was Amwell, an ancient spring in the parish of Great Amwell. It is now an island in the New River, just below Great Amwell church (a mile south of Ware), and can be visited.

Humberside

St John's Well, Harpham (TA095617) : The lane east from Crossgates leads to the well, which is just outside the village. Since 1929, a ceremony has been held on the Thursday nearest 7 May (St John of Beverley's Day), and this includes a procession to the well. St John of Beverley was, according to tradition, born in Harpham. The well water was credited with miraculous powers, including the ability to subdue fierce animals. Harpham is 7 miles south-west of Bridlington.

Isle of Man

Chibbyr Vaghal/St Maughold's Well, Maughold Head : Maughold is 3 miles south-east of Ramsey, and the well is about half a mile from the village. From the east end of the churchyard, proceed for 100 yards on the road to the lighthouse, turn left on to Manx National Trust property, and at the end of the track proceed on the pathway straight across the field to the north side of the headland. A wicket gate gives access to the track leading to the well. It is about halfway down a steep grassy slope, and is said to have been formed where the saint's horse landed. Its water was believed to cure many ailments, including sore eyes and infertility. Barren women would sit in the 'saint's chair' nearby (no longer to be seen) and drink a glass of the well water. Pilgrims would drop a pin, bead or button into the well before leaving.

Isle of Wight

Well at Carisbrooke Castle (SZ488878) : A sixteenth-century building houses the well which was sunk in 1150 and which for 750 years was the main means of supplying water to the castle. The wheel is worked by donkey power, each of five donkeys at the castle working for an hour in the wheel-house and then resting. This is not by any stretch of the imagination a holy well, but it is worth seeing for its unusual method of raising the water.

Holy well at St Lawrence : For many years this well was by the roadside between Ventnor and St Lawrence, but when a new road had to be made because of cliff falls the old road became part of a private entrance to a cottage. The well is a small Gothic shrine and is on the edge of Lisle Court grounds and the grounds of The Cottage, on the left-hand side if approaching from Ventnor.

Kent

Black Prince's Well, Harbledown : Harbledown is just west of Canterbury, and visitors should take the main A2 road from Canterbury towards London and proceed along the dual carriageway marked Rheims Way. After the roundabout marked Harbledown Bypass, take the first turning on the left by the Highfield Hotel. Go up Summer Hill, then down Church Hill, and St Nicholas Hospital and church are on the left-hand side. The well is behind the hospital at the foot of the hill. The well was also known as Leper's Well for its ability to cure leprosy, and the hospital at Harbledown was founded for the relief of lepers in 1084 by Archbishop Lanfranc. Edward, the Black Prince, is said to have drunk the well water, and even to have called for water to be sent to him on his deathbed in 1376. The three feathers carved on a stone over the well are the Prince of Wales feathers, a badge the Prince took from the King of Bohemia at the Battle of Crécy.

St Edith's Well, Kemsing : Kemsing is 3 miles north-east of Sevenoaks, and the well is in the village, near The Bell. St Edith was a tenth-century Saxon princess born in Kemsing, where a shrine was erected to her memory in the twelfth or thirteenth century. The well water was believed to cure eye troubles and is still sought by visitors. The custom of a procession to the well was revived in 1961, the year of St Edith's millenary, and continues annually on or near her day, 16 September.

St Eustace's Well, Withersdane, Wye (TR062459) : The well is close to Withersdane Cottages, ¾ mile south-east of Wye and reached along a lane by Withersdane Hall. The well now has an air of neglect, but in medieval times it was famous, because it was believed to have been blessed by St Eustace when he was visiting this country. People especially visited it for eye cures.

Lancashire

Peg's Well, Bungerley Bridge, near Clitheroe : The well is in a field owned by Waddow Hall (on the road between Clitheroe and Waddington), which is now the North of England Training Centre of the Girl Guide Movement. Visitors should call at the Hall to obtain permission to visit the well, and also to obtain directions. Peg was said to have been a servant employed at Waddow Hall, who drowned in the River Ribble and now haunts the area, claiming a human victim every seven years.

Holy well at Fernyhalgh (SD555340) : Fernyhalgh is a hamlet hidden away halfway between the villages of Broughton and Grimsargh, just north of Preston. Although there was a chapel there at least as early as 1348, it was in

Holy well at
Fernyhalgh,
Lancashire

1471 that the shrine at Fernyhalgh became established, as a result of a storm at sea. A merchant sailing across the Irish Sea vowed that if he were saved, he would undertake a work of great devotion. Finding himself on the Lancashire coast, a voice told him to go to Fernyhalgh, where he would find near a spring a crab tree bearing fruit without cores, and there he must establish a chapel. Several days later by a lucky chance he found Fernyhalgh, the tree, the spring, and an undiscovered statue of the Virgin Mary, and he set about his work. In time the holy well became famous for curing illness, and many pilgrims came to drink the water. The well is now in the garden of a house which incorporates a chapel built in 1685, but visitors can approach the well from the adjacent lane. The present church was built in 1796, 400 yards away from the old chapel and holy well.

Leicestershire

King Richard's Well, Bosworth Battlefield (SK402000) : This is not a holy well, but is famous for its historic connection, King Richard III being said to have drunk from it during the Battle of Bosworth (1485) where he was killed. The battlefield is 2 miles south of Market Bosworth and well signposted. Make for the Battlefield Centre, and from the car park the well is only a short walk away towards the woods.

St John's Well, Lutterworth : The well is named from John Wycliffe who was not a saint but was regarded as such by the local people. He was Rector at Lutterworth in the fourteenth century and while there he translated the Bible into English. He died on New Year's Eve 1384 and was buried in the churchyard. In 1425 the Council of Constance ordered that his remains should be dug up and publicly burnt. This was done, and his ashes thrown into the River Swift. According to the legend, when the remains were being transported by cart, a bone fell on to the ground and the spring began to flow at that spot. The well became known for its ability to cure eye troubles. It is now situated in the garden of a private house, but can be visited by making an appointment with the owner, John Daniell, of The Springs, Stony Hollow, Lutterworth, LE17 4BL (Tel. Lutterworth 2370). To find the well, on entering Lutterworth from the M1 or along the Rugby road A426, you cross the Swift Bridge and come to an old white house called The Springs on your left, on the corner of Stony Hollow.

St Withburga's Well, East Dereham, Norfolk

Norfolk

St Withburga's Well, East Dereham (TF986134) : This well is easy to find, being situated in the churchyard close to St Nicholas' church and on the west side. It is well maintained, and marks the spot where the saint's body was buried before being stolen and taken away to Ely in AD 974. The remains of the walls of a chapel which once stood over the well can still be seen, but there are no signs of the bath-house which was built in the late eighteenth century.

Wishing wells, Walsingham Abbey, Little Walsingham : In the eleventh century, Richeldis de Faverches, a rich widow, had a vision of the Blessed Virgin Mary who told her to build a replica of the Holy House of Nazareth. The original site chosen for the building, though it could not be built there because it was the wrong size, was close to two holy wells. The wells were believed to have healing powers, especially for headaches and stomach troubles. Later they degenerated into wishing wells, the wisher kneeling on a stone between them and dipping a hand into each well while silently making his wish, and finally drinking a little water from each well. The wells can be visited in the abbey grounds, and they are close to a Norman archway. The grounds are open in the afternoons of certain days of the week in the summer, not at all in the winter. Entrance is through the main gateway in the High Street. When closed, admission may be gained during office hours by application to the Estate Office at 10 Common Place. An admission fee is payable.

St John's Spring, Boughton, Northamptonshire

Holy well in the Anglican Shrine, Little Walsingham : Since the first shrine of Our Lady of Walsingham was founded over 900 years ago, Walsingham has been the destination of countless pilgrims, many kings and queens among them. The shrine's fortunes have changed along with changes in the religious and political climates, but it has survived all vicissitudes. In 1931 it was decided to build a new home for the shrine, and when the ground was being prepared for the foundations, an ancient well was unearthed. Clear water soon filled it to a depth of five or six feet. It was discovered that this well was directly linked to the two wells in the abbey ruins. The holy well was incorporated in the new shrine, and now plays an important part in the pilgrimages. Over 100,000 pilgrims a year now visit Walsingham, and most of them are sprinkled at the holy well. The water is drawn out of the well in a long silver spoon, a cross is marked on the pilgrim's forehead, he drinks some of the water, and the rest is poured over the hands or any afflicted part of the body. This newly restored holy well can safely claim to be the most active holy well in England, probably in Britain.

Northamptonshire

St John's Spring, Boughton (SP765656) : Boughton is 3 miles north of Northampton town centre, and St John's Spring is close to the ruined St John's church, at Boughton Green, ¾ mile east of the village. The spring rises in a steep bank at the south corner of the east end of the ruins, only 4 yards from the church. When the church was in use, water from the well was used for baptisms.

Becket's Well, Northampton (SP761602) : Becket's Well is on Bedford Road and near the General Hospital. It faces Becket's Park across the road, and is 50 yards along Bedford Road from the Bedford Road/Victoria Promenade/Derngate/Cheyne Walk crossroads. It is well preserved and has recently been renovated; a fresco by the local children depicting St Thomas à Becket's life is to be installed.

Well at Scaldwell (SP769725) : Little is known about the history of this old well on the village green, but that it is certainly ancient is shown by the name of the village, derived from Caldwell.

North Yorkshire

The Ebbing and Flowing Well, Giggleswick (SO805654) : This once-famous well can be seen at the foot of Giggleswick Scar, beside the A65 a mile north-west of Giggleswick which is itself just west of Settle. Sadly the well no longer ebbs and flows.

St Hilda's Well, Hinderwell (NZ791170) : Hinderwell is 8 miles north-west of Whitby, and the well can be found in the churchyard. It has recently been cleaned up and rebuilt. In past centuries, children would make liquorice water there on Ascension Day.

The Ebbing and
Flowing Well,
Giggleswick,
North Yorkshire

The Dropping Well, Knaresborough (SE348565) : This famous petrifying well is in the Long Walk, a wooded grove near Low Bridge. The limestone content of its water solidifies objects placed in it. Nearby is the cave where the sixteenth-century prophet Mother Shipton lived.

St Cedd's Well, Lastingham (SE729904) : Lastingham is an attractive village on the moors 6 miles north-west of Pickering, and no visitor should miss seeing the church crypt, built in the eleventh century as a shrine to St Cedd, who founded the abbey at Lastingham. His well is about 100 yards east of the crypt, beside a small stream; and opposite the Post Office, set in a wall, there is another well, to St Chad, who was St Cedd's brother and succeeded him as abbot of Lastingham. Both men lived in the seventh century, and St Chad also had connections with Lichfield, where his well can also be visited.

Our Lady's Well, Threshfield (SD998636) : The well is between Threshfield and Grassington, close to the west bank of the River Wharfe, and is reached from the Grassington to Linton road near Grassington Bridge. A stile and a flight of steps lead to the well.

Northumberland

St Cuthbert's Well/Cuddy's Well, Bellingham (NY837833) : This well can be seen in a grassy lane just outside the churchyard wall. Tradition tells us that St Cuthbert was a dowser who found and consecrated this pure spring in the seventh century. The small upright stone structure with a spout from which the water flows is known as a pant, many of these being built in Northumberland in the eighteenth century as an improvement on dipping wells. The water from this well is still used in the church, for baptisms, at the Eucharist, and on other occasions.

Our Lady's Well,
Threshfield, North
Yorkshire

St Cuthbert's
Well, Bellingham,
Northumberland

Lady's Well, Holystone (NT953029) : Holystone is 7 miles west of Rothbury, and the well is a short distance to the north of the village, reached by a footpath. The well is a large pool, with a Celtic cross standing in the middle. It is now in the care of the National Trust, and open at all times, free of charge.

Pin Well, Wooler (NT986271) : The well is to the south of the town, reached on foot as follows: 300 yards up Ramsey Lane, Common Road, branch off to a footpath leading to Waud House. This path leads on to the Pin Well, and then to Yearle Road, from where it is possible to return to Wooler by the road and Cheviot Street. Lovers would go to the Pin Well at midnight and throw a bent pin into the water, wishing for 'a speedy marriage or some other lover-like wish'. Also there was a May Day procession to the well, when those present would also drop a bent pin into the water and make a wish.

Oxfordshire

St Margaret's Well, Binsey (SP486080) : The well is close to Binsey church, which is 2 miles north-west of the centre of Oxford, and reached by a lane leading north off the A420 at Osney. The well is reputed to have been founded by St Frideswide, who built a chapel by it and performed miracles there. Many people came on pilgrimages in the Middle Ages, two of the more famous visitors being King Henry VIII and Katherine of Aragon. The water was used to cure eye troubles and to promote fertility in barren women, but it has today degenerated into a wishing well.

Fair Rosamond's Well, Blenheim Park, Woodstock (SP436164) : Blenheim Park is open daily (9–5) throughout the year, on payment of an admission charge, and visitors can find Fair Rosamond's Well on the north bank of Blenheim Lake. It was once known as Everswell, its present name deriving from the legend of Rosamond Clifford, the lover of King Henry II, found dead in her bower and thought to have been killed by the jealous Queen Eleanor, although the bower was protected by a labyrinth whose path only the King knew. The water still flows quietly into a large pool in a rustic setting, plans for an elaborate bathing-house in the late eighteenth century never having been put into execution.

Ladywell, Wilcote, Finstock (SP374148) : The well is 3 miles north of Witney and is approached through Wilcote Grange Farm, where the key to the well is kept. A path leads straight from the farm to the well along an avenue of ash trees. Until only a few decades ago, a large number of local people would visit the well on Palm Sunday to make liquorice water. The well has never been known to run dry, not even during the 1976 drought.

Shropshire

St Cuthbert's Well, Donington, near Albrighton (SJ808045) : Just below Donington church, a wooded area with a lake and a stream is laid out for the public's enjoyment, and the well, with a stone canopy, will be found beside the path. It was for many years used to bathe weak eyes.

St Cuthbert's
Well, Donington,
Shropshire

St Oswald's Well, Oswestry (SJ284293) : At the crossroads with traffic lights near the church, take the Trefonen road westwards, then turn right into Oswald Place and follow this road for a short distance. The well is on the left-hand side, by the school grounds, close to the road but hidden from view in a hollow. The name of both well and town commemorate Oswald, King of Northumbria, who was killed in battle in 642 at Maserfeld, which may have been Oswestry. Whatever uses were made of the well water in earlier centuries, it has latterly declined to the status of a wishing well.

St Winifred's Well, Woolston (SJ322244) : This is a rare example of a well covered by a secular building, in this case a half-timbered cottage originally used as a court-house. The present sixteenth- or seventeenth-century building may have succeeded a chapel. It is tucked away behind the hamlet of Woolston, 4 miles south-east of Oswestry. From Maesbury Marsh turn left into Woolston, then where the road turns right you should follow the lane to the left. It shortly comes to an end, but a gate on the right in worn letters announces St Winifred's Well. Through the gate a path soon reaches the well cottage, and the well itself and the pool into which it flows are seen behind the cottage. The various stone troughs through which the water flows could be dammed up to form bathing pools. The well water was said to be very good for healing wounds and bruises and broken bones, while another spring lower down was good for the eyes. An alternative approach from Maesbury Marsh is to walk along the canal bank as far as the ruined bridge, then turn right across the fields to Woolston.

Somerset

St Aldhelm's Well, Doulting (ST647432) : Doulting is just to the east of Shepton Mallet on the A361, and the well is at the bottom of the garden of the house adjoining the church; it is signposted from the church. Bishop Aldhelm died at Doulting in 709, and the well which bears his name was once a popular healing well. A long stone channel was probably used for bathing, and both well and channel were probably roofed.

Holy well at Edington (ST388399) : Edington is 7 miles east of Bridgwater, and the well is beside a lane in the village: if travelling north, turn right at the T junction, towards Burtle, and at the left-hand bend a few hundred yards further on, the well can be seen on your right. It is maintained by the Parish Council, and produces a nasty-smelling sulphurous water which was used as a cure for skin diseases.

Chalice Well, Glastonbury (ST507385) : Chalice Well is at the foot of the Tor, on the western side, and is in the care of the Chalice Well Trust. It is situated in a well-tended garden, to which an admission charge is payable. The antiquity of the well was shown by archaeological excavations in the early 1960s, but its documented history is scanty. The reddish tinge of the water gave rise to the name Blood Spring, with a later embellishment that it is the blood of Christ from the Holy Grail. The well is covered by a wrought-iron lid designed by Frederick Bligh Bond who carried out excavations at the abbey, but the water can be sampled at a fountain elsewhere in the garden.

Chalice Well,
Glastonbury,
Somerset

St Bertram's Well,
Ilam, Staffordshire

St Andrew's Well, Stogursey (ST203428) : Stogursey is 7 miles north-west of Bridgwater, and the well is in the centre of the village: from the priory church go up High Street and turn left at the stump of the market cross; the well is a few yards ahead of you. It is in good condition, having been recently renovated by the Parish Council. There are two cisterns and three lead spouts, and the water continues to flow even in a drought. The right-hand spring was said to give a softer water, and was at one time used for washing clothes. Today the well water is still used in the church for baptisms.

St Decuman's Well, Watchet (ST064426) : Watchet is on the north Somerset coast, south-east of Minehead, and the well can be found 200 yards west of St Decuman's church, overlooking the town. The hillside spring is covered by a small stone shelter, and the water flows into three connecting basins. It never dries up. According to the legend, St Decuman, having been decapitated by local pagans, picked up his head and washed it in the well.

Staffordshire

Egg Well, Bradnop (SK006541) : Bradnop is 2 miles south-east of Leek, and the well is a mile south of the village, close to a footpath. The well's name may derive from the oval shape of the masonry which surrounds it. The stone basin carries the following inscription: 'Renibus et Speni Cordi, Jecorique Medetur, Mille Maelis Prodest Ista Salubris Aqua' – The liver, kidneys, heart's disease these waters remedy, and by their healing powers assuage full many a malady.

St Edith's Well, Church Eaton (SJ835165) : Church Eaton is 5 miles east of Newport, and the well can be found a mile to the south-west of the village, south of the road to High Onn. As it is on private land, permission to visit it should be sought at the nearby farm. The rectangular stone basin is covered by a thatched timber structure. The well was visited for eye problems and the king's evil, and visitors still throw coins into the water.

St Bertram's Well, Ilam (SK137514) : The village of Ilam is 4 miles north-west of Ashbourne, and the well, which is in fact a small spring beneath a tree (St Bertram's Ash), can be found halfway up the hillside to the north of the village, along a footpath past Townend Farm. It is not easy to find, because it has no well-house and is little more than a hole in the ground. Ilam was a centre of pilgrimage in the Middle Ages because of the saint's tomb in the church, and pilgrimages are still made today. In Ilam another well or spring can be seen between the church and St Bertram's Bridge over the River Manifold, about 20 yards from the latter.

St Chad's Well, Stowe, Lichfield (SK122103) : Stowe church is on the north side of Lichfield town centre, on the northern edge of Stowe Pool, and the well is in the churchyard behind the church. St Chad was the first bishop of Lichfield in 669, and is closely associated with Stowe, where he founded a monastery and built a church. He was buried here in 672. He baptised his converts at a spring somewhere near the place where his well now stands. On Ascension Day in past centuries the well was regularly decorated with flowers and greenery.

Surrey

Anne Boleyn's Well, Carshalton : Now enclosed in railings, this well can be seen near the old churchyard, where Church Hill joins the High Street. An alternative name for it is Queen Anne's Well and it was probably originally named for St Anne, the Anne Boleyn connection deriving from a story that a spring began to flow at the spot where her horse's hoof struck the ground, when she was riding with King Henry VIII.

St Mary the Virgin's Well, Dunsfold (SU997363) : A lane leads from the church to the well at Dunsfold, a village 5 miles south-east of Godalming. An elaborate oak canopy has covered the well since 1933, in which year it was dedicated by the Bishop of Guildford. The well water was used to treat eye troubles, and it was believed that the Virgin Mary had appeared to pilgrims seeking cures at the well.

Holy well at Burton Dassett, Warwickshire

Berks Well, Berkswell, West Midlands

St Edward's Well, Sutton Park, Guildford : Sutton Park is a private park just to the north of Guildford, but there is public access to the well and St Edward's Roman Catholic church. There is no public entrance to the park through the gates on the A3. Access is from a minor road between the villages of Jacobs Well and Sutton Green, through the gates of Sutton Place. St Edward's Well is in an area known as the Manor Field, and on the site of a hunting lodge of King Edward the Confessor who was canonised in 1161, being venerated after his death in 1066 for his works of charity and healing powers.

Warwickshire

Holy well at Burton Dassett (SP398515) : The church is all that now remains at Burton Dassett, once a market town which was depopulated in the fourteenth century by order of St Edward Belknap, who wished to turn the land into sheep pasture. Now the open hills form a country park with fine views over the surrounding countryside, 8 miles north-west of Banbury. The holy well with its stone cover will be seen on the left-hand side of the lane as you approach the church. Its water was once used for baptisms, and probably also was credited with healing properties and much used when Burton was a thriving community. The area's history stretches back to Saxon times, several skeletons from this period having been discovered near Pleasant Hill. We can speculate also that the holy well has been in existence at least since Saxon times.

West Midlands

Berks Well, Berkswell (SP244790) : Berkswell is 5 miles west of Coventry, and the well is just south of the church, outside the main gate and beside a footpath. It is in fact a large stone tank 16 feet square, which was probably used for immersion baptisms.

Three wells in Sutton Park, Sutton Coldfield : Sutton Park is a very large open space to the west of the town, open twenty-four hours a day to pedestrians but with some night-time restrictions on vehicles. The three wells are: Rowton Well in Long Moor Valley, a spring with a low sandstone wall; Keeper's Well on the feeder stream to Keeper's Pool; and Druid's Well/St Mary's Well close to Bracebridge Pool and Bracebridge restaurant. The park guidebook is out of print at the time of writing, but may be available again by the time you wish to visit the park, and it should give more information on the wells and their location.

Lady Wulfruna's Well, Wolverhampton : To find this well, follow the A449 road towards Stafford from Wolverhampton town centre. After about 1½ miles, take Gorsebrook Road which leads to the racecourse. After 200 yards the road passes under a railway bridge, and shortly afterwards the well-head is on the left, opposite the racecourse fence. The original Lady Wulfruna's Well was probably situated near St Peter's church, Wolverhampton, where the Lady Wulfruna founded a monastery in the tenth century. The history of the spring at present called Lady Wulfruna's Well is not known, but the stone well-head with a small drinking trough for dogs and a drinking cup above was erected in 1901. Until recently the area was badly overgrown, being cleared in the early 1980s by members of the Wolverhampton Civic Society; the vegetation may have regained control by the time you visit the well.

Wiltshire

Daniel's Well, Malmesbury (ST931871) : Located in the meadows by the river, to the south of the abbey church, and reached by a footpath, the well is in fact a spring which flows into a pool. Bishop Daniel of Malmesbury used to immerse his body to the shoulders in all weathers as a penance.

Well at Tollard Royal : A 300-year-old well opposite Chase Cottage on the B3081 7 miles south-east of Shaftesbury has been restored and planted with spring flowers, and although not a holy well but simply the cottage's original water supply, is worth seeing for its picturesque appearance. It is now used to collect money for the Save the Children Fund. At Chase Cottage is a fascinating Museum of Chimney Pots, around two hundred of them being on display.

WALES

The holy well researcher's 'Bible', Francis Jones's *The Holy Wells of Wales*, lists just about every holy well that ever existed in Wales, but there is little indication as to which have survived to the present day, and in any case the book is long out of print. We have discovered relatively few surviving wells, somewhat to our surprise, and should be glad to learn of others not mentioned below. The wells are presented in alphabetical order of the old counties.

Anglesey

St Seiriol's Well, Penmon (SH631808) : The well is located near the easterly tip of the island, near to Penmon Priory. A footpath opposite the dovecot leads in a few yards to the well, which is attractively sited below a cliff. It is believed to date back at least as far as the sixth century, when St Seiriol settled here, and the ring of boulders on the left may be the foundations of his cell. The well-house is probably only eighteenth-century.

St Seiriol's Well,
Penmon, Anglesey

Brecon

Bishop Gower's Well, Llanddew (SO055308) : A Celtic Christian community, or *clas*, was established at Llanddew, and Giraldus Cambrensis, then Archdeacon of Brecon, came to live at the Bishop's Palace, now ruined, in 1175. Bishop Gower's Well dates from around 1340, and can be seen beside a lane near the church.

St Ishow's Well, Partrishow (SO278223) : Partrishow is tucked away in the Black Mountains, and is reached by country lanes to the north-east of Crickhowell. The well is situated at the bottom of the hill, below the church, where a stream passes beneath the road. If you are facing uphill, the well is a short distance off the road to your right, on the church side of the stream. This well was obviously closely linked to the church, which dates back to pre-Norman times and is well worth visiting, though the only item remaining from the ancient church is the font dating from the mid-eleventh century.

Caernarfon

Ffynnon Beuno, Clynnog Fawr (SH414495) : Clynnog Fawr is 9 miles south-west of Caernarfon, on the coast road into the Lleyn Peninsula, and the well is beside the road but set back, and therefore easily missed if passed at speed. It is on the opposite side of the road from the church, and south of the church, just outside the small village. The water-filled stone tank has stone seats and alcoves round it; it is not roofed.

The history of the very interesting church at Clynnog Fawr is bound up with St Beuno, who is said to have built his original church where St Beuno's Chapel now stands, adjoining the present sixteenth-century church. He was also believed to have been buried there, and his tombstone played a part in the holy well cures. Children and adults suffering from epilepsy and fits would bathe in the well, and then sleep overnight on a bed of rushes on the saint's tombstone. Scrapings from the columns of the chapel were also added to the holy well water, as a cure for sore eyes, and at one time heifers were reputedly sacrificed to St Beuno.

Ffynnon Gelynin/St Celynin's Well, Llangelynin old church, near Henryd (SH751738) : This small stone church in the hills south of Conway must surely be one of the most isolated in Britain. It is approached along steep and narrow lanes from Henryd, being signposted at some points. There is no signpost at the last junction, so fork left at this point (where there is a telephone kiosk and a house bearing the date 1902). Go through the gate with the café sign, and you will find plenty of parking space. The church is a short walk across the fields and rocky outcrops. The well is in the south-west corner of the churchyard, under a tree, and is sadly not looked after. It was once covered by a building, but no traces of this remain. The water was used in the church for baptisms, and sick children were bathed there, afterwards being wrapped in blankets and taken to a nearby farm to spend the night. The children's chances of recovery were predicted from the behaviour of clothes placed on the water: if they floated, the child would recover; if they sank, death would occur.

Bishop Gower's
Well, Llanddew,
Brecon

St Ishow's Well,
Partrishow,
Brecon

Ffynnon Gybi/St Cybi's Well, Llangybi (SH427413) : Llangybi is 5 miles north-east of Pwllheli, and the well is approached along a path through the churchyard and across a field into the valley. There a group of ruined stone buildings will be seen. That on the right was a cottage for the custodian, built about 1750. On its left is an older building, but no earlier than the twelfth century, which encloses the main pool; the actual well is hidden away behind. This was obviously once an important healing centre, dating back to the time of St Cybi in the mid-sixth century. The water was reputed to cure warts, lameness, blindness, scrofula, scurvy and rheumatism. At one time an eel lived in the well, and anyone seeking a cure would consider it a good sign if the eel coiled around his legs as he stood in the water. Young girls would also use the well for love divination. They would spread a handkerchief on the water and if it moved to the south, they knew that their lover's intentions were honourable; but the contrary if it moved to the north. A Welsh Office leaflet gives more detailed information on this well and its history.

Ffynnon Beris/St Peris's Well, Nant Peris (SH609584) : Nant Peris is in the Llanberis Pass, a short distance south-east of Llanberis, and the well can be found to the north-east of the church. Look for the group of houses called Nant Ffynnon, park there, and walk through the gate just to the right of the houses, up the track for a short distance to a low white cottage on the right. The well is in the front garden, so ask for permission to visit it.

This once-popular well was reputed to cure many ailments, including rickets, scrofula, rheumatism, wens and warts. People visiting the well would place offerings in an alms box in the church, from which money the parish clerk was paid. Until the turn of the century, sacred fishes were kept in this well, as described earlier in Chapter 7. There are still fishes in it today, according to its owner, but they are no longer regarded with the reverence bestowed on those of earlier centuries.

Llangelynin old church, Caernarfon: Ffynnon Gelynin is in the corner of the churchyard, at the right of the picture

St Cybi's Well,
Llangybi,
Caernarfon

Ffynnon Beris,
Nant Peris,
Caernarfon

Carmarthen

St Anthony's Well, Llansteffan (SN346099) : Llansteffan is 7 miles south-west of Carmarthen, a small village by the Tywi estuary. To visit the well, which is twenty minutes' walk away, park near the church and walk along the road past the church, heading towards the castle. At the car turning-circle, walk straight on through the wood, and continue all the way along the cliff-top path to St Anthony's Bay. There you will see one house, and you should walk away from the sea towards the house. The well is down some steps in the garden wall, about 50 yards along. This once-popular well was famed for its healing qualities, but later degenerated into a wishing well.

In Llansteffan village can also be seen Mary's Well. From the church, walk up the hill past The Castle and The Sticks Motel, and Well House is 30 yards further along, on the right. An arched niche in the garden wall contains Mary's Well, also reputed to have healing properties.

Denbigh

Ffynnon Gynhafal, Llangynhafal (SJ133638) : The village is 7 miles west of Mold, and the well is to be found in the orchard/garden of Plas Dolben, a farm whose driveway forks right off the lane leading north from Llangynhafal. Visitors are requested to call at the house for directions to the well. It had a reputation for curing warts, which were pricked with a pin, the pin then being thrown into the water.

Ffynnon Ddyfnog, Llanrhaeadr (SJ081633) : From Llanrhaeadr church, 2 miles south-east of Denbigh, a path behind the church and to the left of the almshouses leads through a wood and along a stream for a short distance to a large stone-edged pool, all that now remains of the once famous holy well of St Dyfnog. This pool was once covered by a roofed building, where people bathed in hopes of a cure, especially from 'scabs and itch'.

Flint

Ffynnon Beuno, near Tremeirchion (SJ083723) : Tremeirchion is 3 miles east of St Asaph, and the well is half a mile south of the village, beside the B5429. When travelling south, it is on the left-hand side, and in front of a single house set back from the road. A high stone wall encloses a large bathing pool, and the water issues through a stone head low down on the wall which faces the road.

St Winefride's Well, Holywell (SJ185763) : The well is situated below the church, and beside the B5121. An admission charge is payable. The main features visible today are a large open-air bathing pool and the elaborate stone chapel set over the well itself. We have made several references to this famous well in the body of the book (*see* Index).

Glamorgan

St David's Well and St John's Well at Newton Nottage (St David's, SS820785; St John's, SS837774) : The parish of Newton Nottage, formed from the villages of Newton and Nottage, is just inland from Porthcawl. The two wells are only a mile or so apart, and can be found as follows. From The Cross in Nottage (the central crossroads), take the road leading north down Cradocks Hill, and halfway down turn left into Moor Lane. St David's Well is 300 yards down on the left. St David is reputed to have rested at Nottage on his way to Llantwit Major. The well is in a good state of repair, being looked after by the local Scouts.

Starting again from The Cross, take the road east for just over a mile to Newton church. St John's Well is on the south side, 100 yards away. It is also known as Stanford's Well, de Stanford being a Knight Hospitaller who built Newton church.

Taff's Well, near Tongwynlais (ST119837) : Beside the River Taff just to the north-west of Cardiff, this well used to be almost in the river bed, before the development of a flood prevention scheme. The derelict buildings of this once famous well are to be seen between the river and the A4054. People would bathe in the water in order to cure rheumatic complaints.

Monmouth

St Tewdric's Well, Mathern, near Chepstow (ST523910) : The well is near Mathern church, and near the north-east corner of Mathern House. Tewdric, King of Glamorgan, was wounded in battle near Tintern around AD 470, and his wounds were washed in the water of this well. He died close by, having asked that a church be built where he died.

St Anne's Well/Virtuous Well, Trellech (SO503051) : Trellech is a village full of interest, with three large standing stones called Harold's Stones, a large mound called Tump Terret, and the holy well, all three being depicted on an ancient sundial now kept in the church. There were once said to be nine wells altogether, each curing different illnesses. St Anne's Well was also used to

St Anne's Well,
Trellech,
Monmouth

make wishes, a pebble being dropped into the water and a plentiful uprush of bubbles signifying that the wish would be granted. A few bubbles meant a delay; none meant a failed wish. The well, with its stone surround, is in a field beside a lane just to the south-east of the village.

Wishing well at Wilcrick (ST409879) : If approaching on the M4, leave at the Magor exit (junction 23), turn on to the B4245 in the direction of Llanmartin and Langstone, take the first turning on the left after passing the large brewery, and after a couple of hundred yards the road turns sharp right. On the right is Church Farm; on the left is Wilcrick Hill (an ancient hillfort) topped by St Mary's church. The well and a duck pond are at the foot of the hill, by the side of the road.

Montgomery

Ffynnon Fair/St Mary's Well, Llanfair Caereinion (SJ104065) : The well, now sadly neglected, is in the churchyard, reached by walking up towards the church, then going left round it and down the slope towards the river. The stone walls of the well enclosure will be seen below. Its water was once used to cure many illnesses, and people would bathe in it to cure rheumatism and skin diseases. Water was taken to the church for baptisms, and it was also believed to act as a protective against curses and witchcraft.

Health wells at Penegoes (SH767009) : Two wells side by side, one said to be of a higher temperature than the other, are enclosed by low walls and were once covered by a roof. They can be seen in a field beside the A489, on the opposite side of the road from the church, 100 yards further on towards Machynlleth, which town is a mile to the west. The wells can clearly be seen over the hedge. They were cleared out in the early 1980s by the Machynlleth and District Civic Society. Once the accumulated debris (about 24 tons of it!) was removed, the water soon began to flow again, filling the wells to a depth of about two feet.

St Mary's Well, Llanfair Caereinion, Montgomery

Llanlawer holy
well, Pembroke

Pembroke

Llanlawer holy well, Llanlawer (SM987360) : Llanlawer church is 2 miles south-east of Fishguard, and reached by a steep lane north from Llanychaer Bridge. A cottage stands by the roadside, with the church a short distance above it in a field. Park by the first gate beyond the cottage and you will see the well to your right as you enter the field; it is covered by a newly restored stone canopy. The water still flows, and was once regarded as a cure for sore eyes. Coins and pins were left in the well, bent pins being thrown in to accompany ill-wishing against any person.

Ffynnon Fair/St Mary's Well, Maenclochog (SN076271) : Maenclochog is 10 miles south-east of Fishguard, and the well is beside the lane leading west from the village. It is on the north side of the lane, just beyond the last house, and the water now issues from a modern pipe in a brick surround. Even during the spring drought of 1984, there was a steady flow of water. The well was once visited by people suffering from rheumatism. There are large stones nearby, possibly the remains of a cromlech, and a legend connecting the well with the stones suggests that this may be a very ancient well once the focus of pagan water-worship.

St Leonard's Well, Rudbaxton (SM985188) : This well is 2 miles north-east of Haverfordwest, just off a minor road leading to Clarbeston Road and on top of a tree-lined hill called The Rath. It has a stone cover with the inscription 'Fons Leonardis' carved on it, and close by once stood St Leonard's Chapel or Hospice, though nothing of this can now be seen. It was visited for the treatment of sore eyes.

Ffynnon Fair,
Maenclochog,
Pembroke

St Non's Well,
St David's,
Pembroke

St Madoc's Well, Rudbaxton (SM961205) : This well is close to Great Rudbaxton church, which is 3 miles north of Haverfordwest and beside a lane just to the east of the A40. Although now dedicated to St Michael, the church was originally dedicated to St Madoc. The well is just outside the south wall but it is not enclosed in any stonework and its location is shown by water bubbling from the ground.

St Non's Well, St David's (SM751243) : From St David's a lane leads south to St Non's Bay, and the well is off to the right, just before the lane ends. Close by is the ruined St Non's Chapel, with around it a few scant remains of a stone circle. Legend tells how St Non (or St Nonna) in the sixth century came here when a violent storm was raging, but she found summer weather, with sunlight and blue skies, within the stone circle. She bore St David there, near the well, and from that time the waters were said to have healing powers. A nearby stone was said to bear the mark of St Non's hand, when she pressed down hard upon it during her delivery of St David. For centuries the well was visited for healing purposes, and offerings left in the water. Today it is well cared for, and a statuette of Our Lady stands in a niche opposite.

SCOTLAND

The wells described here represent only a small proportion of those still in existence, and anyone wishing to explore Scottish holy wells thoroughly should obtain a copy of *Scottish Healing Wells* by Ruth and Frank Morris, where nearly one thousand wells are described. We are not including wells on the Scottish islands, as we have no reliable information on their location and present condition. The wells are presented in alphabetical order, using the old county names.

Aberdeen

St Michael's Well, Culsalmond (NJ650317) : In a garden centre at Williamston House, where it is the centrepiece of a water garden.

St Drostan's Well, New Aberdour (NJ887646) : To the north of the village, a lane leads down to the seashore and the well. It passes a ruined church, said to be the place where St Drostan landed when he came from Caithness to spread Christianity to the area.

Angus

Silver Well, Arbroath (NO648429) : At Silverwells just north of Arbroath on the A92, recently restored in the corner of a garden centre. According to James Mackinlay the name 'is derived not from the nature of the offerings left there, but from the colour of the scum on its surface'.

Lady Well, Glamis (NO388470) : In woods just beyond the church and close to the river, and also known as St Fergus's Well for this was the place where St Fergus is said to have lived in the eighth century.

Argyll

Holy well, Keil, Kintyre (NR675077) : About 1 mile south-west of Southend, just beyond Keil Hotel and about 20 yards north-west of the ancient chapel of Keil, the well issues from a cliff face. Two footprints carved on rock, known as St Columba's Footsteps, can be seen on a rock outcrop near the chapel.

Banff

St Colm's Well, Portsoy (NJ596663) : In Seatown graveyard a little to the east of Portsoy.

Red Well, Whitehills (NJ662653) : To the east of Whitehills, a lane leads to the shore from the B9038, and this chalybeate well is beside the lane, in a tall circular building.

Berwick

Nun's Well, Abbey St Bathans (NT758622) : Opposite the church, which stands on the site of an ancient nunnery. Its water is believed never to freeze.

Wells at Ladykirk : There are five wells at Ladykirk : Fairy Well (NT880447) beside a footpath along the river; Monk's Well (NT885465) on a hillside near Home Farm; Nun's Well (NT887467) to the east of Monk's Well, marked by an obelisk; St Mary's Well (NT886466) about 200 yards west of Nun's Well; Sybil's Well (NT889463) in the grounds of Ladykirk House and now dry.

Caithness

St Mary's Well, Crosskirk Bay (ND024697) : To the west of the ruined St Mary's Chapel a burn flows into the bay, and the well is at the head of the burn, a quarter-mile inland. There is a Pictish symbol stone at Crosskirk and St Mary's Chapel dates from the twelfth century.

Lady Well,
Glamis, Angus

Brow Well,
Dumfries

Clackmannan

Red Well, Alloa (NS874935) : North of the entrance to the Pleasure Gardens, west of Alloa.

Dumfries

Brow Well, near Clarencefield (NY084675) : To the south of the B725; restored in 1976. Robert Burns spent the last weeks of his life here in an effort to regain his health.

East Lothian

St Baldred's Well, East Linton (NT593779) : A path down to the river starts at the B1407 near the graveyard of Preston parish church. The spring water runs into a stone trough beside the path. Baldred was a seventh-eighth century saint who founded a settlement here.

Rood Well, Stenton (NT624744) : The stone well-house stands beside the main road to the north-east of the village. Also in Stenton is Daw's Well beside the village green, and the Tron Well near the village hall.

Our Lady's Well, Whitekirk (NT598816) : Off the A198 to the north-east of the village. A chapel was built in 1297 by Black Agnes, Countess of Dunbar, in gratitude for the relief from pain she felt on drinking the water. A shrine to the Virgin Mary was built in 1309, and thousands of pilgrims visited the well annually.

Fife

Well in Dunfermline Abbey (NT088872) : In the nave, and still in use.

St Fillan's Well, Pittenweem : Halfway down Cove Wynd a doorway leads into a cave with the well on the far left side. The cave was the home of St Fillan in the seventh century, and in the eighteenth was used by smugglers. It was restored in 1935.

Monk's Well, St Andrews (NO514167) : Under a grassy knoll in the outer cemetery in the grounds of the cathedral.

Inverness

St Mary's Well, Culloden (NH723453) : In Culloden Wood, reached by a footpath from Blackpark. This famous well is still much visited, and rags are still hung in the trees round about. Also at Culloden is the Well of the Dead, beside the grave mounds of the clans, just across the grass from the National Trust for Scotland Centre.

Well of the Heads, Invergarry (NN304993) : South of Invergarry, beside the A82 and Loch Oich. The monument topped by severed heads (*see* Chapter 1) was erected in 1812.

Rood Well, Stenton, East Lothian

Well of the Heads,
Invergarry,
Inverness

Well at
Scotlandwell,
Kinross

Kincardine

St Kieran's/Caran's Well, Stonehaven (NO868868) : Below the Glenury viaduct at the end of Mineral Well Road. This chalybeate spring is now dry, but the carved well-head remains.

Kinross

Well at Scotlandwell (NO185016) : This elaborate well is in the centre of the village, and its water is said to have cured Robert the Bruce of leprosy.

Kirkcudbright

Rutherford's Well, Anwoth (NX584562) : On the hillside behind the ruins of the old church, and reached by a track beside the church.

Lady Well, Terregles (NX928775) : To the north-west of Dumfries, this dry well is close to the site of a Lady Chapel at Bowhouse.

St Queran's/Jergon's Well, Troqueer (NX957722) : To the south of Dumfries, and reached by a footpath off a lane to the south of Islesteps. This well has been visited for several hundred years, as shown by coins discovered in it, and by seventeenth-century documentary evidence. The Morrises found rags on the bushes during their recent visit, which suggests that this well is still active.

Lanark

St Mungo's Well, Glasgow Cathedral (NS602655) : In the south-east corner of the crypt in Jocelin's Court; this well is said to have been used by St Mungo for baptisms.

Midlothian

St Anthony's Well, Holyrood Park, Edinburgh (NT275737) : Near the ruined St Anthony's Chapel above St Margaret's Loch. On May Day mornings it was customary to wash in the dew on Arthur's Seat, and to wish at the well. Also in the park is the Well of the Holy Rood, a spring now covered by the stone well-house which was brought from St Margaret's Well, Restalrig, which is nearby, and rebuilt here.

St Katherine's Well/Balm Well, Liberton, Edinburgh : In the grounds of St Katherine's House, which is itself located within the environs of the Regional Assessment Centre. The complex is on Howdenhall Road (A701) immediately opposite Mortonhall Crematorium. The well is not open to the public, but small parties may visit it, having first made an appointment to do so by telephoning the Regional Assessment Centre on 031 664 8488.

According to legend, the spring flowed where St Katherine dropped some oil she was bringing from Mount Carmel. Scottish kings visited this well, but it was vandalised by the Roundheads, later being restored. The oily water was believed to have curative properties.

St Katherine's
Well, Liberton,
Edinburgh

St Triduana's Well, Restalrig, Edinburgh : In the hexagonal chapel adjoining the parish church. The well is now dry, but was once a famous eye well.

Our Lady's Well, Stow (NT454438) : Our Lady's Chapel site is half a mile south of Stow, between the A7 and Gala Water, and the well is beside the chapel.

Moray

Pictish Well, Burghead (NJ109692) : Steps lead down into an underground chamber cut out of solid rock, at the bottom of which is a large pool. This ancient well may have been used as a baptistery by the Picts when they embraced Christianity. It is within the ancient fortification on Burghead Point, and is now in the care of the Department of the Environment. Being potentially dangerous, the well is kept locked, but the key can be easily obtained.

St Mary's Well, Orton (NJ324553) : In a maze of lanes east of the B9015, this once important well is in the wall of an ancient chapel, and its basin may have once been the chapel font. The water was used to cure whooping cough, diseases of the joints and sore eyes, and large crowds of pilgrims would pay an annual visit to collect some of the water.

Peebles

Cheese Well, Minch Moor, near Traquair (NT356336) : 1500 feet up on the moor, the well is reached by footpath from Traquair 2 miles to the north-west. People passing on the drove road would leave pieces of cheese in the water for the fairies.

Perth

Iron Well, Fortingall (NN720478) : This wishing well is beside the road in Glen Lyon, about 1½ miles west of Fortingall. Its iron-tasting water was believed to have curative properties.

Maiden's Well in the Ochil Hills above Glendevon (NN970014) : The well is actually on the border between Perth and Clackmannan, beside the old drovers' road between Dollar and Glendevon, and can be reached on foot from either of those places.

Renfrew

St Fillan's Well, Kilmacolm (NS384690) : Near the ruined church a mile along the road to Houston. This well was used to bathe children with rickets, and rags were left on the bushes.

Maiden's Well in the Ochil Hills, Perth

Craigie Well/St Bennet's Well, near Avoch, Ross & Cromarty

Cloutie Well, Munlochy, Ross & Cromarty

Ross & Cromarty

Craigie Well or St Bennet's Well near Avoch (NH679532) : This well is located on the north shore of Munlochy Bay, 50 yards above the shoreline, at the foot of a bank with trees. It is still visited by local people, as is shown by the rags tied to the surrounding bushes. Sick people used to try and discover whether they would recover, by placing two straws on the water. If the straws whirled round in opposite directions, recovery was predicted, but if they remained still, the patient would soon die. The time to visit the well was the first Sunday in May, and its water was used to protect pilgrims against disease, witchcraft and fairies.

Fiddler's Well, Cromarty (NH808673) : Two miles along the shore east of Cromarty, the well is to be found in the side of a bank facing inland, near the Sutor. According to legend, it was dug here as a result of a dream (*see* Chapter 6).

St Boniface's Well/Cloutie Well, Munlochy (NH641537) : This famous rag well is now considered to be an eyesore, but because of the belief that anyone destroying the rags will take on the donor's illness, they have remained intact. Today visitors add rags arbitrarily. A recent estimate put the total at 50,000, and this is one well which has definitely got out of hand! It can be found beside the A832 half a mile to the north-west of Munlochy.

Selkirk

Mungo's Well (NT473280) : Just west of the junction of the A7 and A699 to the south of the town, and in the Haining Deer Park.

St Finnan's Well,
Mochrum,
Wigtown

West Lothian

Cross Well, Linlithgow : In the square south of the Palace, the elaborate structure dating from 1807 was built on the site of an earlier well. There were several other wells in the town, inclúding St Michael's Well still to be seen near the station.

Wigtown

St Medana's Well, Glasserton (NX365397) : Half a mile south-east of Monreith a lane leads off the A747 towards a golf course and the sea. The well is on the shore, 100 yards north-west of the old church. It was believed to cure whooping cough.

St Finnan's Well, Mochrum (NX278490) : The ruins of St Finnan's Chapel are beside the A747 about 5 miles north-west of Port William, and the now-insignificant-looking well is in a corner of the ruins. According to the seventeenth-century author of 'Large Description of Galloway', Andrew Symson, Loch Mochrum about 3 miles to the north 'is very famous in many writers, who report that it never freezeth in the greatest frosts'. He had received 'several credible informations' that people had been cured by washing three times there. The first Sundays in February, May, August and November were considered most favourable days, for they marked the new quarters of the ancient year.

IRELAND

Many holy wells have survived in Ireland, of which the following are a small sample. There is no guidebook to Irish holy wells. Travellers exploring ancient Ireland are recommended to use as their guidebook Anthony Weir's thorough survey *Early Ireland: A Field Guide* (Blackstaff Press, 1980), and for information on Irish holy wells, though it does not include a gazetteer, Patrick Logan's *The Holy Wells of Ireland*. The wells are presented here in county alphabetical order, with wells in Northern Ireland in a separate section at the end.

Carlow

St Moling's Well, St Mullins (S 73 38) : The ritual once practised here, made barefoot and including walking through a stream, has now been abandoned and all that remains is the reciting of the rosary. Children's heads also used to be placed under a spout of water on the pattern day, to protect them against illnesses.

Cavan

Toberbride/St Brigid's Well, Killinagh, near Blacklion (H 06 38) : This monastic site is on the shore of Lough Macnean Upper, and in addition to the holy well can be seen St Brigid's House (a megalithic tomb) and St Brigid's Stone (cursing stones in bullauns).

Clare

Holy well on Inishcaltra, an island in Lough Derg (R 70 85) : The island is reached by boat from Mountshannon. A round tower and monastic remains can also be seen.

St Brigid's Well, Liscannor : Formerly visited at Lughnasad, this well is now visited on 15 August, and is still a popular pilgrimage.

Holy well on Scattery Island, River Shannon estuary (Q 97 52) : Reached by boat from Cappagh Pier near Kilrush, the island was a monastic site with churches and a round tower.

St Cronán's Well and the Eye Well, Temple Cronán, 5 miles north of Killinaboy (M 29 00) : The wells can be found two fields south of the small ruined church.

Cork

St Gobnet's Well, Ballyvourney (W 20 77) : Pilgrims still perform the 'pattern' here, where in addition to the well can be seen St Gobnet's House or Kitchen, the remains of an Iron Age house, and St Gobnet's Grave with abandoned crutches and gifts laid across it.

St Ólann's Well, Coolineagh, near Coachford (W 44 78) : North-north-east of the ruined church of Aghabulloge and on the west side of the road from Aghabulloge to Rylane Cross; the well-house has a thorn tree growing from it. Also in this area are St Ólann's Cap (a quartzite stone) and a boulder with the saint's footprints, and a pattern takes place here on 5 September.

Donegal

Doon Well/St Columba's Well, Rock of Doon, Kilmacrennan (C 12 20) : Pilgrims visiting this well have over the years left a large collection of crutches and sticks, as grateful tokens of their cures.

Dublin

Holy well at Jamestown, Stepaside (O 20 24) : North of Stepaside Farm can be seen a cross and the holy well.

St Gobnet's Well,
Ballyvourney,
County Cork

Doon Well,
Kilmacrennan,
County Donegal
(photo some time
between 1910 and
1930)

Lady's Well, Mulhuddart (O 07 41) : This well is still visited on 8 September, and is believed to cure sore eyes, if the pilgrim walks round the well three times before bathing his eyes with the water and drinking some too.

Galway

St Patrick's Well, Mám Éan (L 91 51) : This is a famous mountain-pass well to which pilgrimages are still made to celebrate Lughnasad. St Patrick's Bed is cut out of the rock cliff close by.

St Fechín's Well, Omey Island (L 56 55) : On one of the many small islands off the Connemara coast, nearest mainland settlement Claddaghduff, the well is close to the north shore of the bay on the west coast. It is possible to drive across the sand to the island.

Kerry

St Molaga's Well, Ballineanig near Ballyferriter (Q 35 03) : The well is 400 yards east of the ruined oratory.

St Manchán's Well, Ballymoreagh, west of Dingle (Q 40 02) : The well is close to St Manchán's Grave and Oratory.

St Brendan's Well, Brandon Mountain, north of Dingle (Q 46 13) : The well is near St Brendan's Oratory.

St Buonia's Well, Killabuonia (V 40 70) : The well is near the south-west corner of the monastic remains, and close to it is a large cairn of pebbles, continually added to by pilgrims, who also push offerings into the 'priest's grave' after following the ritual pattern, which includes nine circumambulations of the well.

St Fechín's Well,
Omey Island,
County Galway

Leitrim

St Mogue's Well, Rossinver (G 93 50) : The well can be found near the southern shore of Lough Melvin and not far from the ruined medieval church.

Mayo

St Derivla's Vat, Fallmore, at the southern end of the Mullet Peninsula (F 62 18) : The holy well is about 300 yards north of the ancient granite church, and close by also is St Derivla's Bed.

St Patrick's (or St Brendan's) Well, Lankill, south of Westport (M 01 79) : The well is close to an ancient cemetery.

Meath

St Ciarán's Well, Castlekieran (N 69 77) : This is a famous well, visited on the first Sunday in August, and believed to cure many illnesses. The pilgrims use lights around midnight to try and see the sacred trout, which is not visible during the rest of the year.

Offaly

St Ciarán's Well, Clonmacnoise (N 01 31) : This is the most famous Early Christian site in Ireland and there is much to see, including crosses, grave-slabs, churches and round towers. The pattern day is the first Sunday in September, when pilgrims follow the Short or Long Station, the latter beginning at the well which is not far from the ancient graveyard. A thornless whitethorn tree stands beside the well, on which pilgrims hang offerings, or else throw them into the well.

St Colmcille's Well, Durrow, south of Kilbeggan (N 32 31) : The well, visited on 9 June, is north-east of the derelict church at Durrow Abbey.

St Manchán's Well, Lemanaghan, north-east of Ferbane (N 17 27) : There are decorated grave-slabs at the church, to the east of which can be found the well. A causeway leads from it to a small oratory.

Roscommon

Bride's Well/Tobar Bhride, Brideswell (M 94 44) : Pilgrimage day is the last Sunday of July, when the priest says Mass at a portable altar near the well, and the pilgrims proceed through a number of praying stations.

Lassair Well, Kilronan, west of Drumshanbo (G 90 12) : At the eastern end of Lough Meelagh/Mealey, the well is near the ruined medieval parish church. It is still visited by pilgrims, who carry out a complicated ritual which includes washing the feet, face and hands in the Holy Font of St Ronan, a water-filled hollow in a stone on the right-hand side of the stream which flows from the well. The ritual ends with the pilgrim drinking three sips of water from the well.

Tobar Ogulla, near Tulsk : The pilgrimage to this well has been revived, and takes place on the last Sunday of June. It was formerly visited on St Patrick's Day, as the saint was said to have baptised the daughter of the King of Ireland here.

Sligo

Tobar an Ailt, on the shore of Lough Gill : The well is about 3 miles from Sligo, in a valley running down to the lough. The pilgrimage at the end of July is very popular; Patrick Logan saw hundreds of people there for midday Mass in 1978.

Waterford

St Declan's Well, Ardmore (X 19 77) : The well is south-east of the village, where also can be seen one of the finest round towers in the country, the ruined St Declan's Cathedral, and also the saint's tomb or oratory.

Holy well at Ballyquin, south-east of Carrick-on-Suir (S 41 18) : The well is by the roadside, to the south-east of a collapsed dolmen.

Westmeath

St Brigid's Well, Cullienmore townland, Walshestown parish, just west of Mullinger : A pilgrimage to this well is still a popular family outing on the Station Sunday, the last Sunday in August, and pilgrims follow a route through fourteen praying stations. About 500 people were present when Patrick Logan visited the well on 25 August 1974.

Wexford

St Mogue's Well, Ferns (T 01 50) : There are a number of relics at this important monastic site, and the well is located outside the graveyard of a ruined thirteenth-century church. It has a nineteenth-century well-house with ancient carved heads from Clone church built into it.

NORTHERN IRELAND

Antrim

St Colman's Well, Churchtown (J 05 85) : The well is on the shore of Lough Neagh, east of the ruined Cranfield church. It was visited during May and June, and was part of a pattern which included the church. Sick people would wash the affected parts in the well, and drink the water, and would consider themselves especially favoured if they found any of the amber-like stones, called Cranfield Pebbles, which were believed to save men from drowning and women from pain and danger in childbirth. The well is still visited by the sick hoping for a cure.

Derry

Wart Well, Dungiven Priory (C 69 08) : The church is ¾ mile south of Dungiven, and the well is to the east of the path. It is a large bullaun under a hawthorn on which pilgrims have hung rags.

Bishop Aidan's Well, Tamlaghtard, ½ mile east of Bellarena Railway Station (C 68 32) : The well is in the graveyard of the ruined church, along with a modern Catholic church, the ruined church, and a church-shaped tomb-shrine.

St Colman's Well,
Churchtown,
County Antrim

Bishop Aidan's
Well,
Tamlaghtard,
County Derry

Struell Wells,
Downpatrick,
County Down
(photo some time
between 1910 and
1930)

Down

Mearing Well, Saul (J 50 46) : Two miles north-east of Downpatrick are a church with engraved cross-slabs, and a shrine-tomb or mortuary house. By the roadside, and 300 metres west of the graveyard, can be seen Mearing Well, beside which is a bullaun in the natural rock.

Struell Wells, east of Downpatrick (J 51 44) : A group of buildings are arranged along a stream in a quiet, rocky valley: an unfinished mid-eighteenth century church; the circular Drinking Well with a domed roof; the rectangular Eye Well with a pyramidal corbelled roof: the Men's Bath-house; and the adjacent Women's Bath-house. Until comparatively recently the place was much visited, as described here in 1744:

Hither vast throngs of rich and poor resort on Midsummer Eve and the Friday before Lammas, some in hopes of obtaining health, and others to perform penances enjoined them by the Popish priests from the water blessed by St Patrick. [The wells] are four in number, each covered with a vault of stone, and the water is conveyed by subterraneous aqueducts from one to the other; but the largest of these vaults is the most celebrated [Men's Bath-house] . . . and is more particularly said to have received St Patrick's benediction. In this they bathe the whole body, there being a commodious chamber fitted up for dressing and undressing; and the water of this well may be raised to what height you please, by means of a sluice.

Tyrone

St Patrick's/St Brigid's Well, Altadaven, south-east of Augher (H 60 50) : St Patrick's Chair and Well are in Favour Royal Forest and best approached from the north. The 'chair' is a massive chair-shaped rock, possibly an inauguration seat, and the well is below it. St Patrick or St Brigid was said to have driven devils off the cliff, and Lughnasad celebrations were held here until recently, the site never having been taken over by Christianity like so many of the Irish wells.

St Kieran's Well, Errigal Keerogue, Gort townland, west of Ballygawley (H 58 57) : The well is across the road and to the north-east of the cross and church.

MAPS

WALES

ANGLESEY
Conwy
92 △
96 △
St. Asaph
Denbigh
101 △
Llanberis ● △ 98
95 △ △ CAERNARFON
Pwllheli ● △ 97

8 ● △
Warrington
103 △ Holywell
102
Mold
△ 7
● Chester
Maccles
100 △
FLINT
CHESHIRE

MERIONETH
Llanfair
Caereinion
Machynlleth ● 110
△ 109
MONTGOMERY

● Oswestry
72 △ 73
Newport ●
Shrewsbury
Wolverham
SHROPSHIRE

71 △

38

RADNOR

HEREFORD & WORC

CARDIGAN

BRECON
93 △
94 △
Brecon

△ 41
39 △ △ 42
Hereford ●
GLO
35 △
△ 34
36

Fishguard ● △ 111
PEMBROKE △ 112
114 △ ● St. David's
113 △

CARMARTHEN
● Carmarthen
99 △

MONMOUTH
107 △ 36
Chepstow ●
108 △ 106
AVON

GLAMORGAN
104 △
Porthcawl ●
105 △
Cardiff ●

78 △ 77 △
Watchet ● △
Bridgwater ●
75 △
Glastonbury
76 ● △ 74
● Shepton M
SOMERSET

27 △
28 △ △ Hartland
DEVON

Okehampton ●
△ 26

17 △
14 △ Launceston △
Callington
13 △ △ 9
CORNWALL
10 △ ● Liskeard
△ 15
11 △
Fowey ●

25 △ ● Ashburton

Sherborne ● △ 30
Cerne Abbas ●
DO
31 △ ● Upw

12 △ △ Penzance
△
16

△23
xton

LINCOLNSHIRE

△24
●
Ashbourne
DERBYSHIRE

NOTTS

field

△
82

LEICESTERSHIRE

△56
●
Little Walsingham

on
field

△53 ●Leicester

△55
East Dereham ●

87△ ●Coventry

Lutterworth 54
△
NORTHANTS

CAMBRIDGESHIRE

NORFOLK

△ 59

St. Ives
●
△ 5

/ARWICKSHIRE

57△

SUFFOLK

●△ 58
Northampton

86△

1
△●

△ Bedford
2

BEDS

HERTS

ESSEX

IRE

69 ●Woodstock
70△

Witney ●

△68
●Oxford

4
△ ●
Aylesbury

△32

Hertford ●△43

●
Wickford

S

OXFORDSHIRE

BUCKS

GREATER
LONDON

esbury

3
△
BERKSHIRE ●Reading

'SHIRE

85
△
Guildford ●

Carshalton
●
83△

49
△

48 △ ●Canterbury

SURREY
Sevenoaks ●

Wye
● △ 50

37△
Alton ●

●Godalming
84 △

KENT

HAMPSHIRE

WEST SUSSEX EAST SUSSEX

△46
●
47△ ●Ventnor

ISLE OF WIGHT

ENGLAND

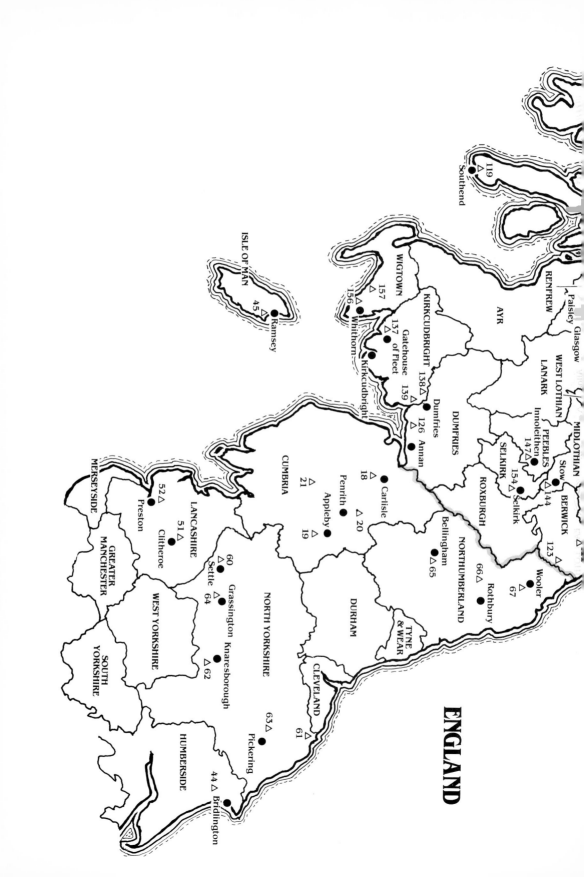

ENGLAND

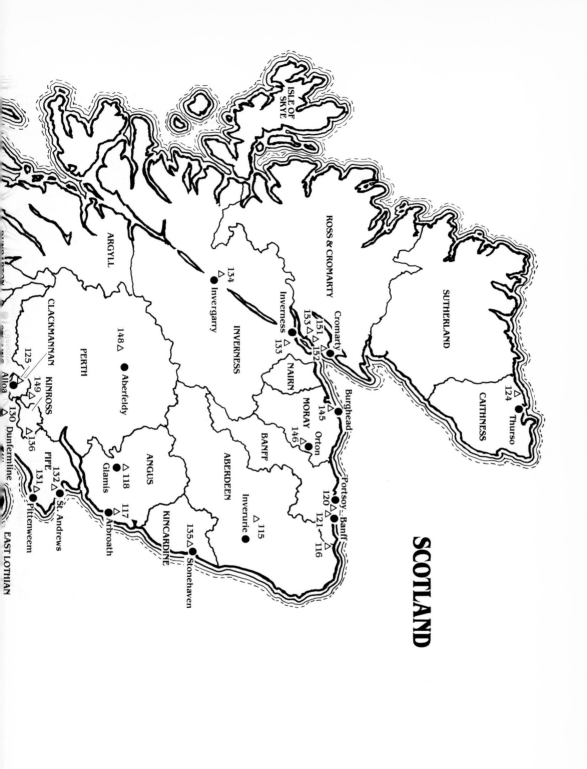

SCOTLAND

ISLE OF
SKYE

ROSS & CROMARTY

SUTHERLAND

CAITHNESS

△ 124
● Thurso

ARGYLL

134
△
● Invergarry

Cromarty
153 △ △ 151
△ 152
●
Inverness
133
△

INVERNESS

NAIRN

Burghead
●

MORAY
146
△ Orton
●
145
△

BANFF

Portsoy - Banff
120
△
●
121 — 116
△

PERTH

148△

● Aberfeldy

CLACKMANNAN
125
Alloa
149
△
KINROSS
130 Dunfermline
△
136
△
FIFE
132△ ● St. Andrews
131
△
● Pittenweem

ANGUS
△ 118
● Glamis
117
△ ● Arbroath

ABERDEEN

● Inverurie

△ 115

KINCARDINE
135△ ● Stonehaven

EAST LOTHIAN

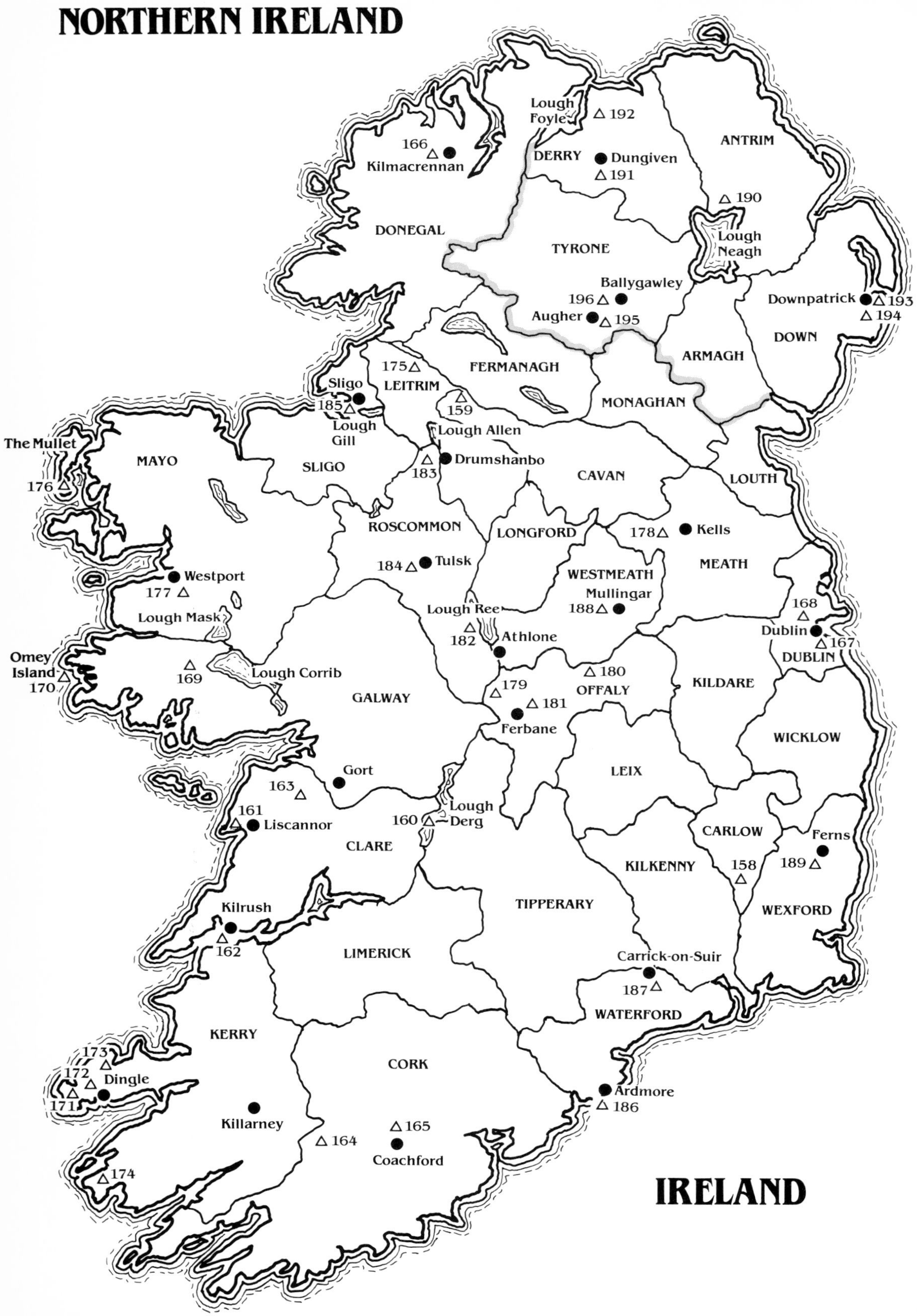

NORTHERN IRELAND

Lough Foyle
△ 192

ANTRIM

166 ●
△ Kilmacrennan

DERRY ● Dungiven
△ 191

DONEGAL

△ 190

TYRONE

Lough Neagh

Ballygawley
196 △ ●

Downpatrick ● △ 193
△ 194

Augher ● △ 195

ARMAGH

DOWN

FERMANAGH

MONAGHAN

175 △

Sligo
185 ≋ LEITRIM
Lough Gill

△ 159

Lough Allen

CAVAN

LOUTH

The Mullet

MAYO

SLIGO

△ 183 ● Drumshanbo

ROSCOMMON

LONGFORD

178 △ ● Kells

MEATH

176 △

Westport ●
177 △

Lough Mask

184 △ ● Tulsk

WESTMEATH
Mullingar
188 △ ●

168
△

Dublin ●
△ 167

Lough Ree

182 △

Athlone

DUBLIN

Omey Island △
170

△ 169

Lough Corrib

GALWAY

179 △

△ 180

OFFALY

KILDARE

△ 181

Ferbane ●

LEIX

WICKLOW

Gort ●

163 △

LISCANNOR

161 △ ● Liscannor

160 △ Lough Derg

CLARE

CARLOW

Ferns
189 △ ●

KILKENNY

158
△

WEXFORD

Kilrush ●
△
162

TIPPERARY

LIMERICK

Carrick-on-Suir ●
187 △

KERRY

WATERFORD

173 △
172 △ Dingle
171 △ ●

CORK

△ 165
Coachford

Ardmore ●
△ 186

Killarney ●

△ 164

174 △

IRELAND

Key to Maps

ENGLAND

Bedfordshire
1. Holy Well at Stevington
2. Nell's Well, Turvey

Berkshire
3. St Anne's Well, Caversham

Buckinghamshire
4. Schorne Well, North Marston

Cambridgeshire
5. Holy well at Holywell

Cheshire
6. Wishing well on Alderley Edge
7. Hampston's Well, Burton
8. St Oswald's Well, Winwick

Cornwall
9. Dupath Well, Callington
10. St Cuby's Well, Duloe
11. St Sampson's Well, Golant
12. Holy well and chapel at Madron
13. Holy well at St Cleer
14. St Clether's holy well and chapel, St Clether
15. St Keyne's Well, St Keyne
16. St Levan's Well, St Levan
17. St Anne's Well, Whitstone

Cumbria
18. St Ninian's Well, Brisco
19. St Helen's Well, Great Asby
20. St Oswald's Well, Kirkoswald
21. St Patrick's Well, Patterdale

Derbyshire
22. St Ann's Well, Buxton
23. Mompesson's Well, Eyam
24. Five wells at Tissington

Devon
25. St Gudula's Well, Ashburton
26. Fitz's Well, Okehampton
27. St Nectan's Well, Stoke
28. St Nectan's Well, Welcombe

Dorset
29. St Augustine's Well, Cerne Abbas
30. Holy well at Holwell
31. Wishing well at Upwey

Essex
32. Running Well, Runwell

Gloucestershire
33. Seven Wells, Bisley
34. St Anthony's Well, Forest of Dean
35. Lady's Well, Hempsted
36. St Bride's Well, St Briavels

Hampshire
37. Springs at Holybourne

Hereford and Worcester
38. St Kenelm's Well, Clent Hills
39. St Ethelbert's Well, Hereford

Surrey

83. Anne Boleyn's Well, Carshalton
84. St Mary the Virgin's Well, Dunsfold
85. St Edward's Well, Sutton Park, Guildford

Warwickshire

86. Holy well at Burton Dassett

West Midlands

87. Berks Well, Berkswell
88. Three wells in Sutton Park, Sutton Coldfield
89. Lady Wulfruna's Well, Wolverhampton

Wiltshire

90. Daniel's Well, Malmesbury
91. Well at Tollard Royal

WALES

Anglesey

92. St Seiriol's Well, Penmon

Brecon

93. Bishop Gower's Well, Llanddew
94. St Ishow's Well, Partrishow

Caernarfon

95. Ffynnon Beuno, Clynnog Fawr
96. Ffynnon Gelynin, Llangelynin
97. Ffynnon Gybi, Llangybi
98. Ffynnon Beris, Nant Peris

Carmarthen

99. St Anthony's Well, Llansteffan

Denbigh

100. Ffynnon Gynhafal, Llangynhafal
101. Ffynnon Ddyfnog, Llanrhaeadr

Flint

102. Ffynnon Beuno, near Tremeirchion
103. St Winefride's Well, Holywell

Glamorgan

104. St David's Well and St John's Well, Newton Nottage
105. Taff's Well, near Tongwynlais

Monmouth

106. St Tewdric's Well, Mathern
107. St Anne's Well, Trellech
108. Wishing well at Wilcrick

Montgomery

109. Ffynnon Fair, Llanfair Caereinion
110. Health wells at Penegoes

Pembroke

111. Llanlawer holy well
112. Ffynnon Fair, Maenclochog
113. St Leonard's Well and St Madoc's Well, Rudbaxton
114. St Non's Well, St David's

SCOTLAND

Aberdeen

115. St Michael's Well, Culsalmond
116. St Drostan's Well, New Aberdour

Angus

117. Silver Well, Arbroath
118. Lady Well, Glamis

Argyll

119. Holy well, Keil, Kintyre

Banff

120. St Colm's Well, Portsoy
121. Red Well, Whitehills

Berwick

122. Nun's Well, Abbey St Bathans
123. Five wells at Ladykirk

Caithness

124. St Mary's Well, Crosskirk Bay

Clackmannan

125. Red Well, Alloa

Dumfries

126. Brow Well, near Clarencefield

East Lothian

127. St Baldred's Well, East Linton
128. Rood Well, Stenton
129. Our Lady's Well, Whitekirk

Fife

130. Well in Dunfermline Abbey
131. St Fillan's Well, Pittenweem
132. Monk's Well, St Andrews

Inverness

133. St Mary's Well, Culloden
134. Well of the Heads, Invergarry

Kincardine

135. St Kieran's Well, Stonehaven

Kinross

136. Well at Scotlandwell

Kirkcudbright

137. Rutherford's Well, Anwoth
138. Lady Well, Terregles

139. St Queran's Well, Troqueer

Lanark

140. St Mungo's Well, Glasgow Cathedral

Midlothian

141. St Anthony's Well, Holyrood Park, Edinburgh
142. St Katherine's Well, Liberton, Edinburgh
143. St Triduana's Well, Restalrig, Edinburgh
144. Our Lady's Well, Stow

Moray

145. Pictish Well, Burghead
146. St Mary's Well, Orton

Peebles

147. Cheese Well, Minch Moor

Perth

148. Iron Well, Fortingall
149. Maiden's Well, Ochil Hills

Renfrew

150. St Fillan's Well, Kilmacolm

Ross & Cromarty

151. Craigie Well/St Bennet's Well, Avoch
152. Fiddler's Well, Cromarty
153. St Boniface's Well, Munlochy

Selkirk

154. Mungo's Well, Selkirk

West Lothian

155. Cross Well, Linlithgow

Wigtown

156. St Medana's Well, Glasserton
157. St Finnan's Well, Mochrum

IRELAND

Carlow

158. St Moling's Well, St Mullins

Cavan

159. St Brigid's Well, Killinagh

Clare

160. Holy well on Inishcaltra
161. St Brigid's Well, Liscannor
162. Holy well on Scattery Island
163. St Cronán's Well and the Eye Well, Temple Cronán

Cork

164. St Gobnet's Well, Ballyvourney
165. St Ólann's Well, Coolineagh

Donegal

166. Doon Well, Rock of Doon, Kilmacrennan

Dublin

167. Holy well at Jamestown, Stepaside
168. Lady's Well, Mulhuddart

Galway

169. St Patrick's Well, Mám Éan
170. St Fechín's Well, Omey Island

Kerry

171. St Molaga's Well, Ballineanig
172. St Manchán's Well, Ballymoreagh
173. St Brendan's Well, Brandon Mountain
174. St Buonia's Well, Killabuonia

Leitrim

175. St Mogue's Well, Rossinver

Mayo

176. St Derivla's Vat, Fallmore
177. St Patrick's Well, Lankill

Meath

178. St Ciarán's Well, Castlekieran

Offaly

179. St Ciarán's Well, Clonmacnoise
180. St Colmcille's Well, Durrow
181. St Manchán's Well, Lemanaghan

Roscommon

182. Bride's Well, Brideswell
183. Lassair Well, Kilronan
184. Tobar Ogulla, near Tulsk

Sligo

185. Tobar an Ailt, Lough Gill

Waterford

186. St Declan's Well, Ardmore
187. Holy well at Ballyquin

Westmeath

188. St Brigid's Well, Cullienmore townland

Wexford

189. St Mogue's Well, Ferns

NORTHERN IRELAND

Antrim

190. St Colman's Well, Churchtown

Derry

191. Wart Well, Dungiven Priory
192. Bishop Aidan's Well, Tamlaghtard

Down

Tyrone

Source Notes

Chapter 1 : The Pre-Christian Evidence for Water Cults
 1. Dr J. Hill Burton, in his book *Book Hunter*.

Chapter 3 : The Healing Powers of Holy Wells
 1. J. Russel Walker, FSA Scot., 'Holy Waters in Scotland', *Proceedings* of the Society of Antiquaries of Scotland, vol. V, New Series, Edinburgh, 1883.
 2. John R. Allan, *The North-East Lowlands of Scotland*.
 3. Dr Robert Trotter, *Proceedings* of the Society of Antiquaries of Scotland, vol. VIII, New Series.
 4. *Notes and Queries*, 1876.
 5. O'Connor, *Ordnance Survey Letters*, p. 368.
 6. Description written in 1836 and quoted in Wood-Martin, p. 99.
 7. MS by Thomas Moore, quoted in 'Manx Calendar Customs:Wells', *Folklore* 52 (1941), p. 191.
 8. Quoted in Lady Gregory, *A Book of Saints and Wonders*, The Coole Edition (Gerrards Cross: Colin Smythe Ltd, 1971), p. 22.
 9. Unknown writer, quoted in Quiller-Couch, pp. 127–9.
 10. Bishop Hall, *The Invisible World*, Book I, Section 8.
 11. *Sunday Express*, 28 March 1982.
 12. A footnote under the entry for Valentine Greatrakes in J. Caulfield, *Remarkable Persons from Edward III to Revolution* (1813).
 13. Report from the *Inverness Courier*, date unknown but presumably shortly after 14 August 1877.

Chapter 4 : Pilgrimages, Rituals and Gifts
 1. A correspondent of Chambers's *Book of Days*.
 2. *Daily Record* (Glasgow), 7 May 1934.
 3. Revd J. E. Vize, MA, FRMS, 'The Parish of Forden' in *Collections Historical & Archaeological Relating to Montgomeryshire*, vol. XVII (Powysland Club, 1884), p. 115.
 4. Revd J. Wilson in the *Penrith Observer*.
 5. J. H. Hutton, Collectanea in *Folklore* vol. 31 (1920), pp. 231–3.
 6. R. M. Fergusson, *Rambles in the Far North*.
 7. Quoted in Wood-Martin, pp. 51–2.
 8. Revd Elias Owen, 'Folk-Lore, Superstitions, or What-Not, in Montgomeryshire', *Collections Historical & Archaeological Relating to Montgomeryshire*, vol. XV (Powysland Club, 1882), pp. 132–3.
 9. Revd Elias Owen, 'The Holy Wells of North Wales', *Collections Historical & Archaeological Relating to Montgomeryshire*, vol. XXVII (Powysland Club, 1893), p.278.

10. Baxter, *World of Spirits*, p.157.
11. Quoted in Wood-Martin, p. 96.

Chapter 5 : Disappearing Wells, Saints' Blood, and Other Water Lore
1. Thompson, vol. XVII, pp. 62–3.
2. Lady Gregory, *Visions and Beliefs in the West of Ireland*, The Coole Edition (Gerrards Cross: Colin Smythe Ltd, 1970), p. 271.
3. *Archaeologia Cambrensis*, 1st Series, iii, p. 264.

Chapter 7 : Water Divinities
1. Lady Gregory, *Visions and Beliefs in the West of Ireland*, The Coole Edition (Gerrards Cross: Colin Smythe Ltd, 1970), p. 158.
2. Charles C. Smith, 'Fairies at Ilkley Wells', *Folk-Lore Record,* vol. I (1878), pp. 229–31.
3. M. Martin, *A Description of the Western Isles*, c. 1695.
4. Revd Elias Owen, *Welsh Folk-Lore* (first published 1888, reissued 1976 by EP Publishing Ltd), p. 141.
5. Otta Swire, *The Highlands and Their Legends* (Oliver & Boyd, 1963), p. 207.

Chapter 8 : Ghosts at Wells, Lakes and Rivers
1. Hugh Miller, *My Schools and Schoolmasters* (1877), I, p. 202.
2. Quoted in Charlotte Sophia Burne, *Shropshire Folk-Lore*, Part 1 (first published 1883, reissued 1973 by EP Publishing Ltd), p. 76.
3. *Swanage Times*, 12 July 1967.
4. Both witnesses quoted in Andrew Green, *Phantom Ladies* (Bailey Brothers & Swinfen Ltd, 1977), pp. 120–1.
5. Letter from Miss Godley, quoted in Sir Ernest Bennett, *Apparitions and Haunted Houses* (Faber and Faber, 1939), pp. 37–8.
6. Letter from Mrs Cummins, 16 January 1937, quoted in Bennett, op.cit., pp. 291–2.
7. Letter from F. L. Luck, 26 June 1936, quoted in Bennett, op.cit., pp. 288–9.

Chapter 9 : The Past – and the Future
1. Letter to the authors.

Bibliography

Denbigh, Kathleen, *A Hundred British Spas*, London: Spa Publications, 19 Sheridan Road, London SW19 3HW, 1981

Elliott, J. Steele, *Bygone Water Supplies*, Survey of Ancient Buildings, vol. II, The Bedfordshire Historical Record Society, 1933

Gregor, W., 'Guardian Spirits of Wells and Lochs', *Folk-Lore*, vol. 3 (1892), pp. 67–73

Hardy, P. D., *The Holy Wells of Ireland*, Dublin, 1836

Hartland, E. Sidney, 'Pin-Wells and Rag-Bushes', *Folk-Lore*, vol. 4 (1893), pp. 451–70

Hartley, Dorothy, *Water in England*, London: Macdonald and Jane's, second edition, 1978

Hope, Robert Charles, *The Legendary Lore of the Holy Wells of England*, London: Elliot Stock, 1893; reissued 1968 by Singing Tree Press, Detroit, MI, USA

Horne, Dom. Ethelbert, *Somerset Holy Wells*, The Somerset Folk Series No. 12, London: Somerset Folk Press, 1923

Jones, Francis, *The Holy Wells of Wales*, Cardiff: University of Wales Press, 1954

Lane-Parker, Revd A., *Holy Wells of Cornwall*, Federation of Old Cornwall Societies, 1970

Logan, Patrick, *The Holy Wells of Ireland*, Gerrards Cross: Colin Smythe Ltd, 1980

M'Kenzie, Dan, 'Children and Wells', *Folklore*, vol. 18 (1907), pp. 253–82

Mackinlay, James M., *Folklore of Scottish Lochs and Springs*, Glasgow: William Hodge & Co., 1893

Masani, R. P., *Folklore of Wells, Being a Study of Water-Worship in East and West*, Bombay: D. B. Taraporevala Sons & Co., 1918

Meyrick, J., *Holy Wells of Cornwall*, published by the author in Falmouth, Cornwall, 1982

Moore, A. W., 'Water and Well-Worship in Man', *Folk-Lore*, vol. 5 (1894), pp. 212–29

Morris, Ruth and Frank, *Scottish Healing Wells*, Sandy: The Alethea Press, Everton, Sandy, Beds, 1981

Morris, T. E., 'Sacred Wells in Wales', *Folk-Lore*, vol. 4 (1893), pp. 55–79

North, F. J., *Sunken Cities*, Cardiff: University of Wales Press, 1957

Owen, Revd Elias, 'The Holy Wells of North Wales', *Collections Historical & Archaeological Relating to Montgomeryshire*, vol. 27, London: Powysland Club, 1893

Parsons, Coleman A., 'Association of the White Lady with Wells', *Folklore*, vol. 44 (1933), pp. 295–305

Quiller-Couch, M. and L., *Ancient and Holy Wells of Cornwall*, London: Chas. J. Clark, 1894

Ross, Anne, *Pagan Celtic Britain*, London: Routledge & Kegan Paul, 1967

Smith, Revd W., *The Ancient Springs and Streams of the East Riding of Yorkshire*, London: A. Brown & Son Ltd, 1923

Thompson, Beeby, 'Peculiarities of Waters and Wells', a series of articles published in the *Journal* of the Northamptonshire Natural History Society, vol. XVI, Dec. 1911 – vol. XVII, Dec. 1914

Valentine, Mark, *The Holy Wells of Northamptonshire* (booklet), Northampton: The Hundreds Press (35 Grafton Way, New Duston, Northampton, NN5 6NG), 1984. From the same address can also be obtained details of the Holy Wells Research and Preservation Group, and a holy wells newsletter

Walters, R. C. Skyring, *The Ancient Wells, Springs, and Holy Wells of Gloucestershire*, Bristol: The St Stephen's Press, 1928

Wood-Martin, W. G., *Traces of the Elder Faiths of Ireland*, London: Longmans, Green, and Co., 1902 – Chapter III, 'Well Worship and its Concomitants'

Index

DATE DUE

MAY	5 '89		

HIGHSMITH   #LO-45220